Margaret Hibbert.

PORTRAIT OF
GLENCOE, BEN NEVIS & FORT WILLIAM

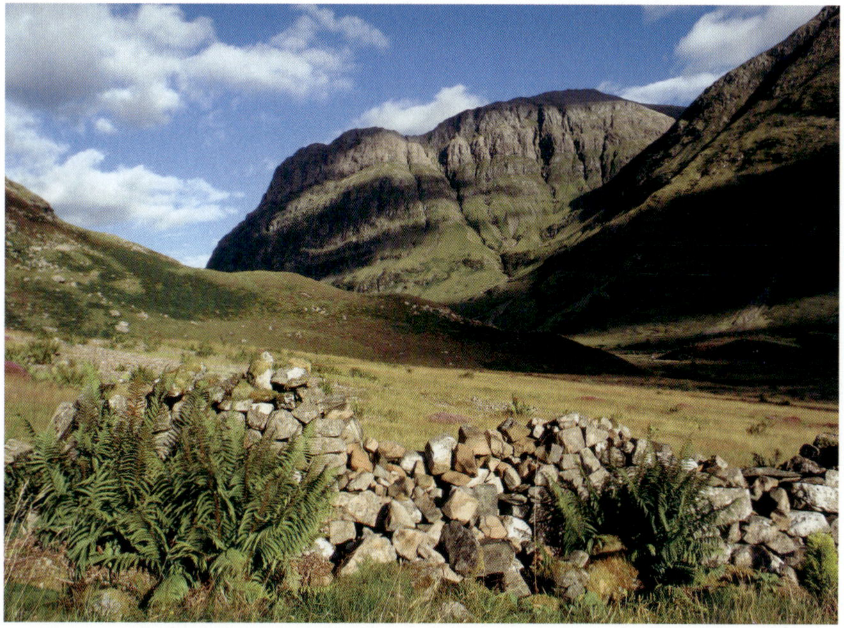

JERRY RAWSON

HALSGROVE

First published in Great Britain in 2008

Title page photograph: *The craggy west face of Aonach Dubh, Glencoe, seen from near the Clachaig Inn.*

British Library Cataloguing-in-Publication Data
A CIP record for this title is available from the British Library

ISBN 978 1 84114 728 4

HALSGROVE
Halsgrove House
Ryelands Industrial Estate
Bagley Road, Wellington, Somerset TA21 9PZ
Tel: 01823 653777 Fax: 01823 216796
email: sales@halsgrove.com
website: www.halsgrove.com

Printed and bound by
D'Auria Industrie Grafiche, Italy

INTRODUCTION

However many times I travel along the A82 road across the vast expanse of Rannoch Moor towards Glencoe (or Glen Coe), and I've done it many times, I never tire of the journey. The lochan-dappled moor overlooked by the Black Mount hills is a prelude to the scene that suddenly bursts into view round one particular bend. That first sight of the cone-shaped Buachaille Etive Mor sweeping up above a carpet of heather and bog, and standing as a sentinel at the junction between Glencoe and Glen Etive, is one of Britain's iconic mountain images.

The road then plunges through the deep trough of Glencoe where you feel dwarfed by the craggy buttresses, ridges and side valleys of the Bidean nam Bian massif on the left and the high barrier of Aonach Eagach, a serrated ridge set against the sky, on the right. This is an uncompromisingly wild and austere place, second to none in the Central Highlands, so it is no surprise that it is popular with film makers. Much of Glencoe is owned by the National Trust for Scotland.

The glen levels out at Loch Achtriochtan where the old road branches off right to Glencoe village. Apart from the obvious attractions of the area for walkers and climbers, the glen is probably best known for its infamous Glencoe Massacre. This occurred on 13 February, 1692, which resulted in the slaughter of 38 MacDonalds by a regular regiment of the British Army raised from the Clan Campbell, many of them billeted with the local MacDonalds. There were worse atrocities committed during those troubled times but the Glencoe event apparently gained notoriety mainly because of the violation of the ethic of Highland hospitality.

Beyond Loch Achtriochtan the main road continues through gentle pastures to the sea at Loch Leven. The road now heads through Ballachulish, across the bridge over Loch Linnhe and on to Fort William. However, a road around Loch Leven provides a more scenic route via Kinlochleven, entrance to the Mamores. The Mamores, along with Glencoe, Grey Corries and the Ben Nevis range, all fall within the Lochaber Area of the Highland Council. Such is the geological importance of the area that Lochaber gained European Geopark status in 2007.

Fort William, overlooked by the huge, round-shouldered bulk of Ben Nevis, Britain's highest mountain, lies at the heart of Lochaber and is the area's capital. Nearby Glen Nevis, the starting point for the 'easy' walker's route up Ben Nevis is a beautiful valley surrounded by stunning mountains. The town is also the gateway to the Great Glen and the Road to the Isles.

The choice of photographs for the book is purely personal and takes you on a photographic odyssey starting at Rannoch Moor and exploring Glencoe, Ben Nevis and the surrounding areas. The images capture the character of the area throughout all the seasons, although snow can fall anytime from September to May. I can even remember one year being in a snow storm at the summit of Ben Nevis in August. Hopefully the selection of photographs has captured the beauty and majesty of this precious landscape, and maybe will encourage readers to go and discover this area for themselves.

Jerry Rawson

LOCATION MAP – Glencoe

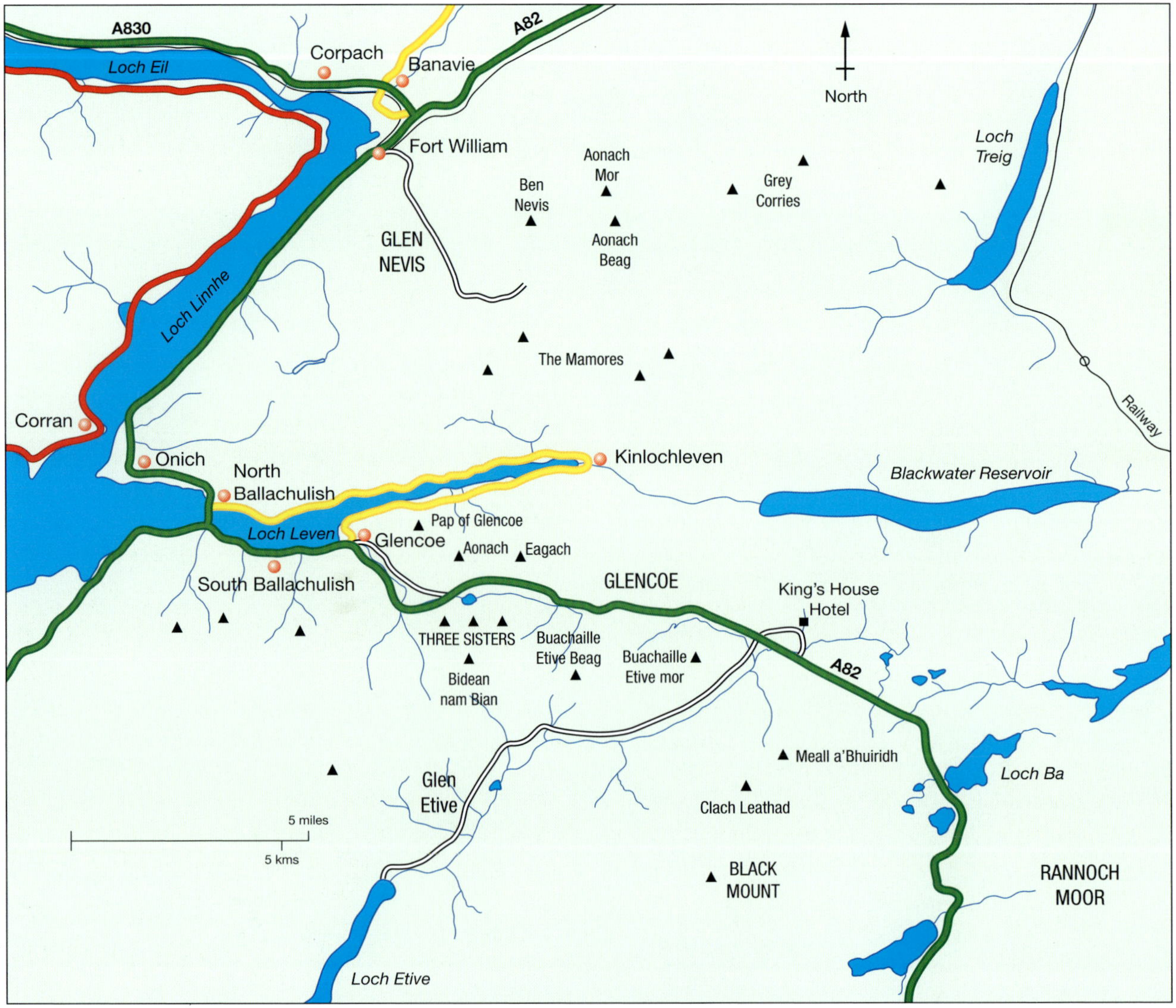

AUTHOR'S ACKNOWLEDGEMENTS

I would like to acknowledge the help and support from my wife Katy with proof reading, artwork and map.

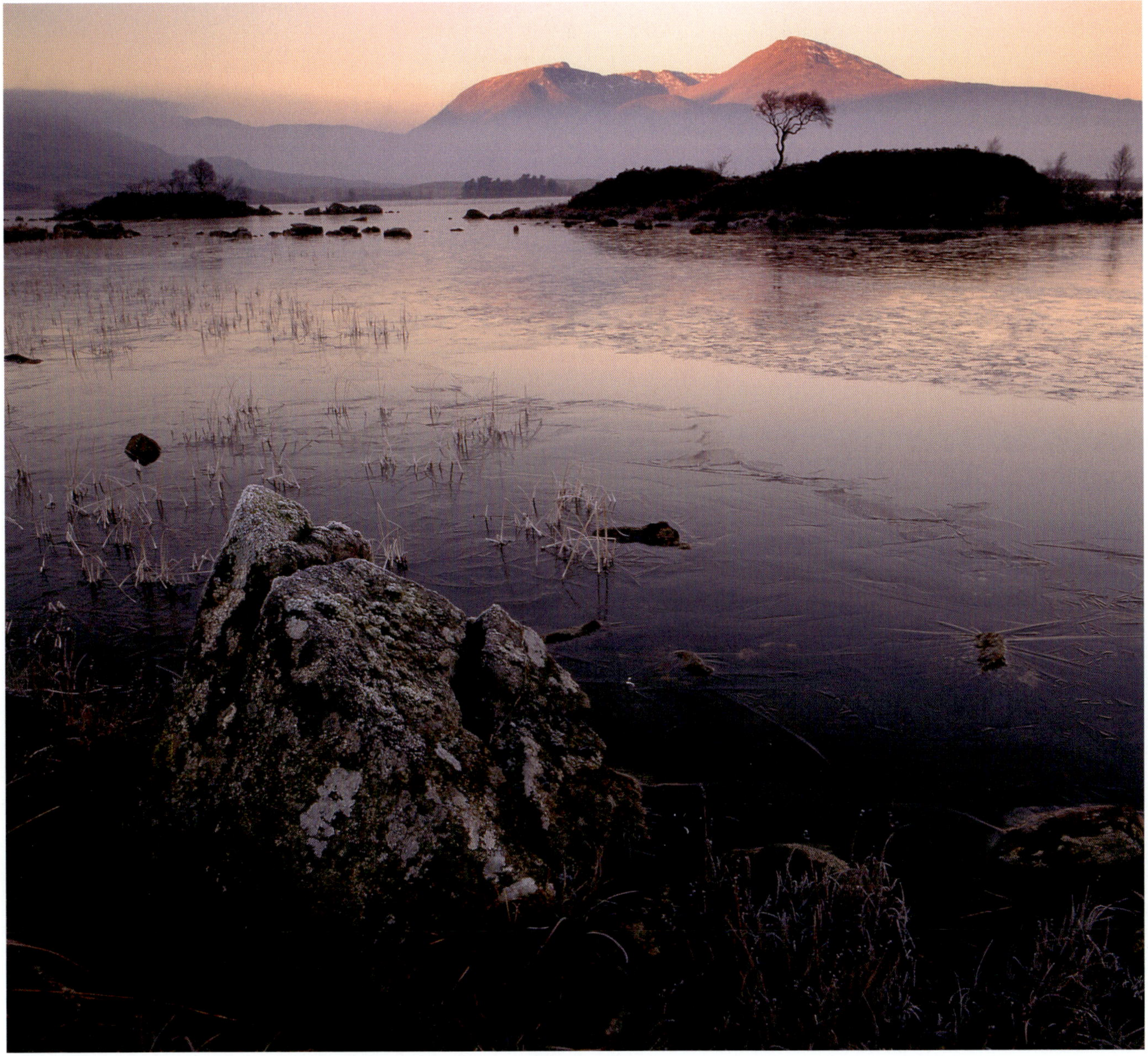

Dawn glow.

Low winter sunshine slants across Lochan na h'Achlaise to the Black Mount hills on the fringe of the wild and desolate Rannoch Moor.

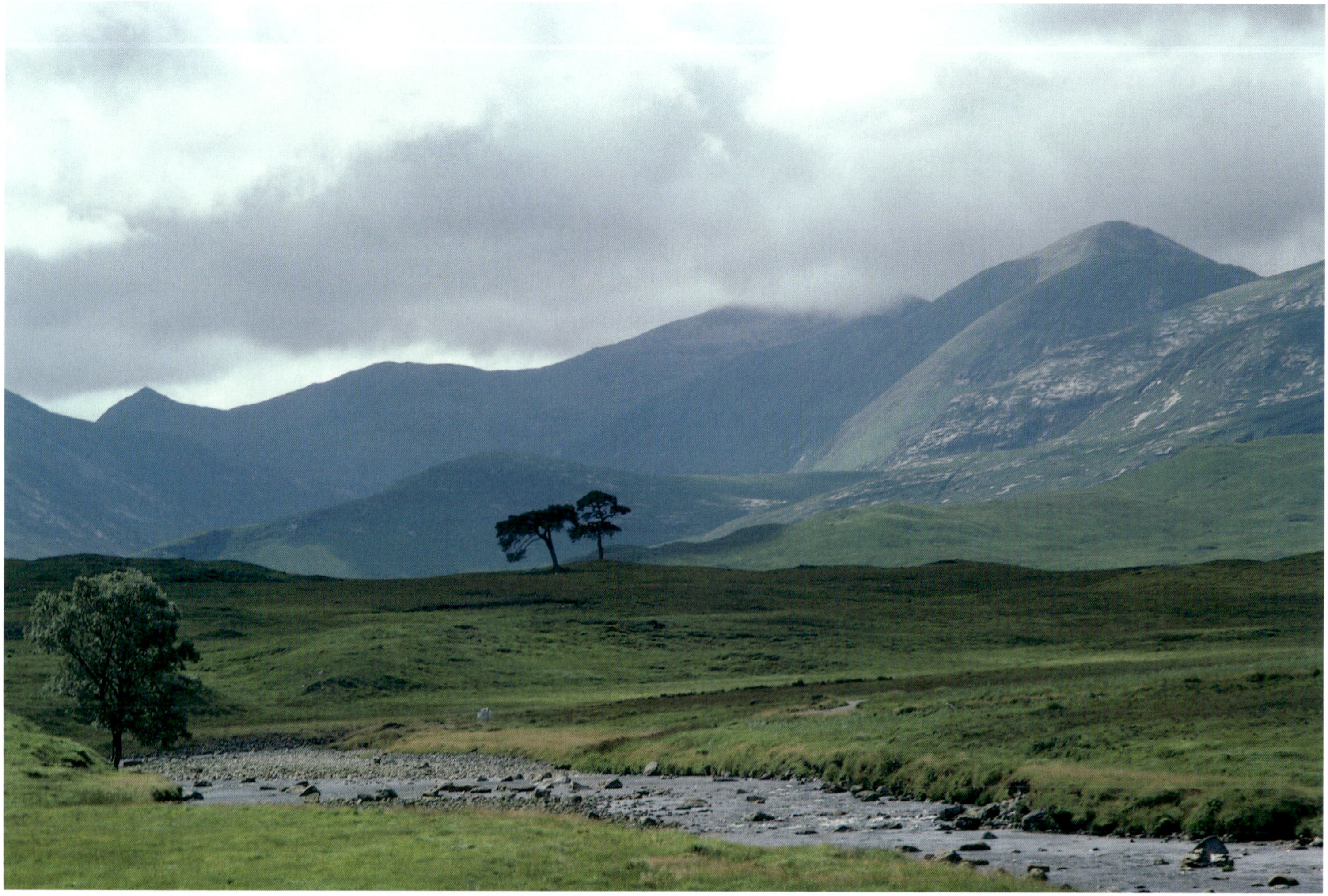

Approaching storm.
Dark clouds sweep across the Black Mount range of hills which dominate the southern skyline on the journey across Rannoch Moor to Glencoe.

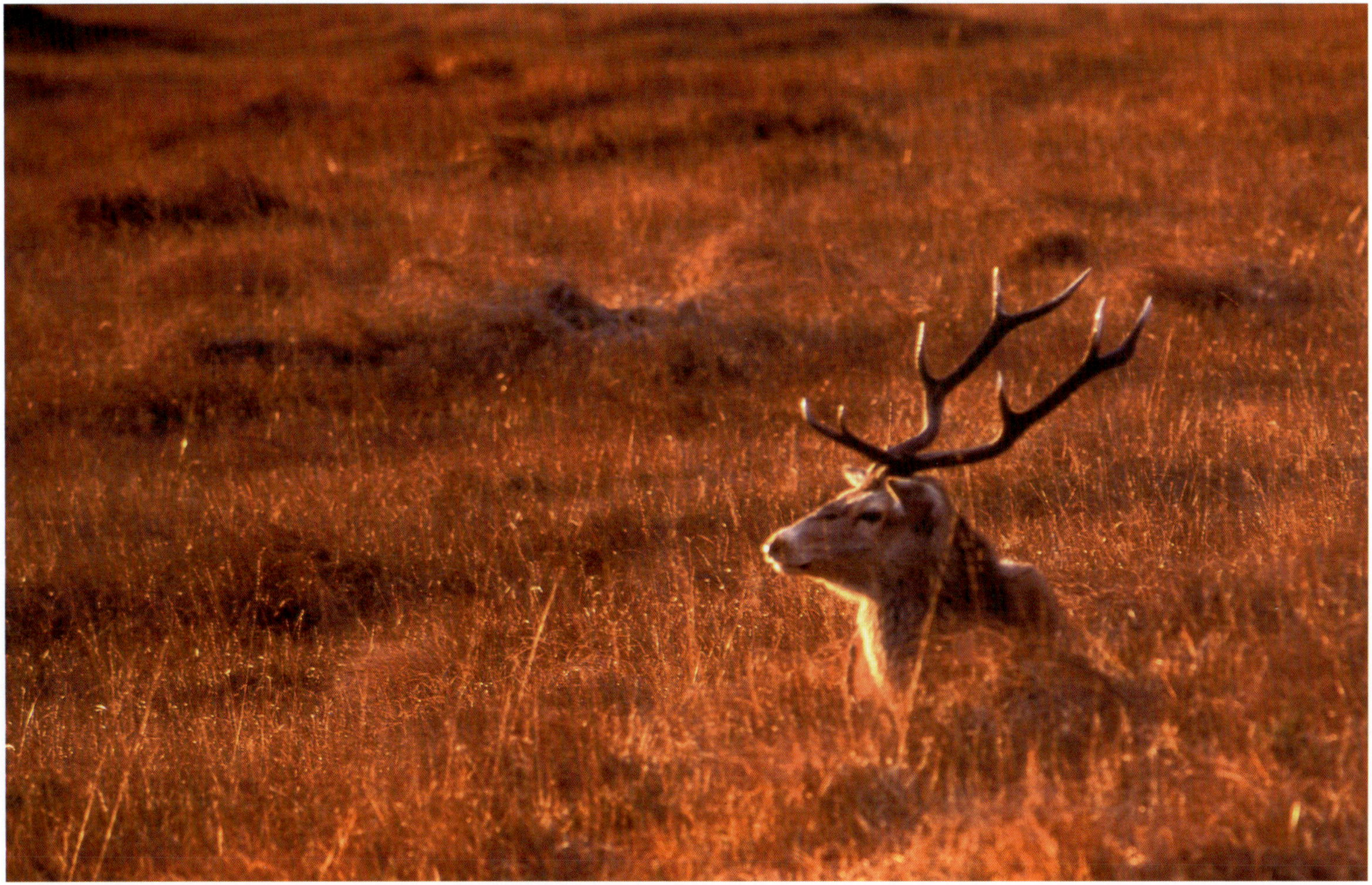

Welcome rest.
A stag at dusk on Rannoch Moor soaks up the weak autumn sunshine.

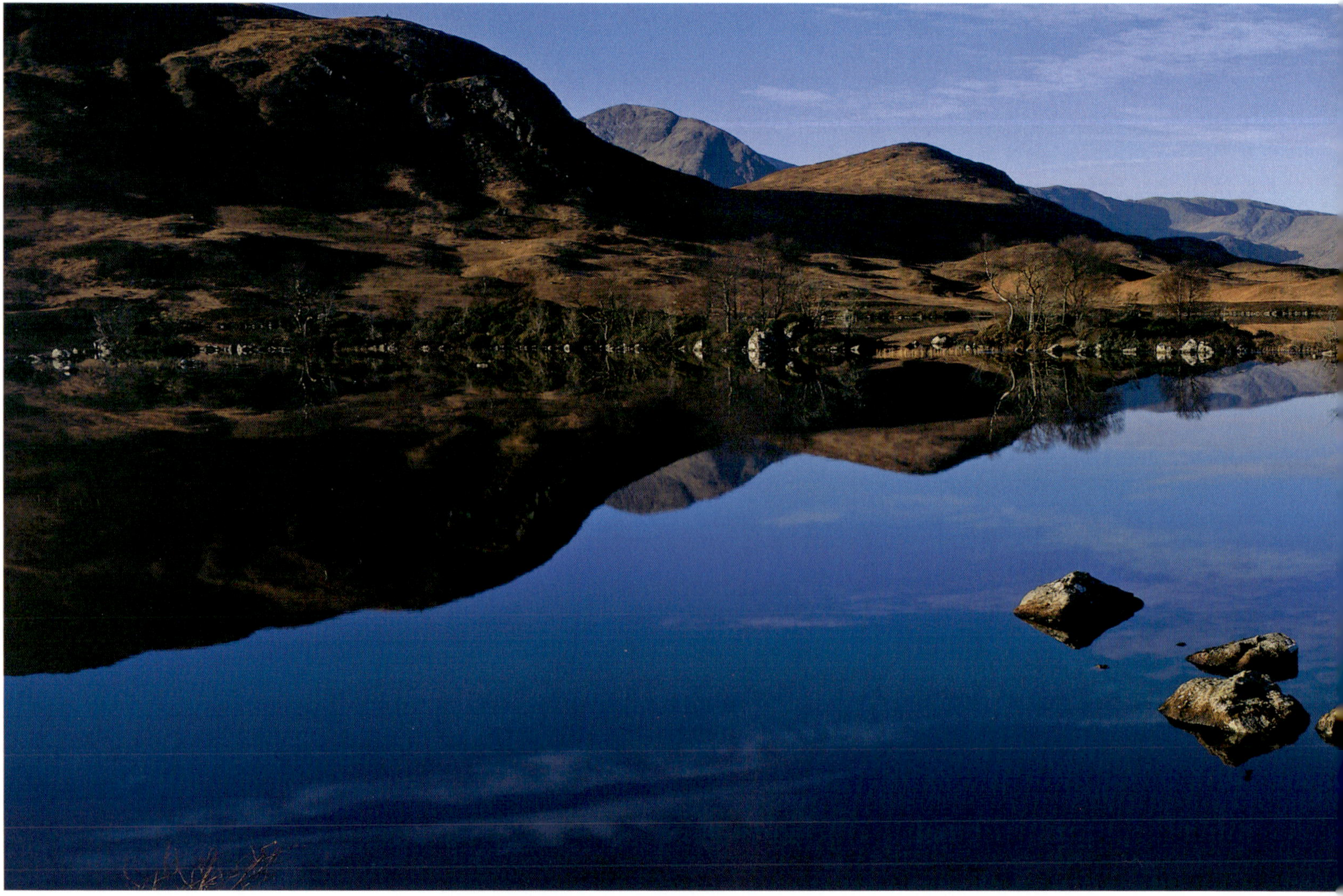

Autumn reflections.
The peaks of Clach Leathad and Meall a'Bhuiridh (*hill of the bellowing*) on the northern end of Black Mount are perfectly reflected in Lochan na h'Achlaise.

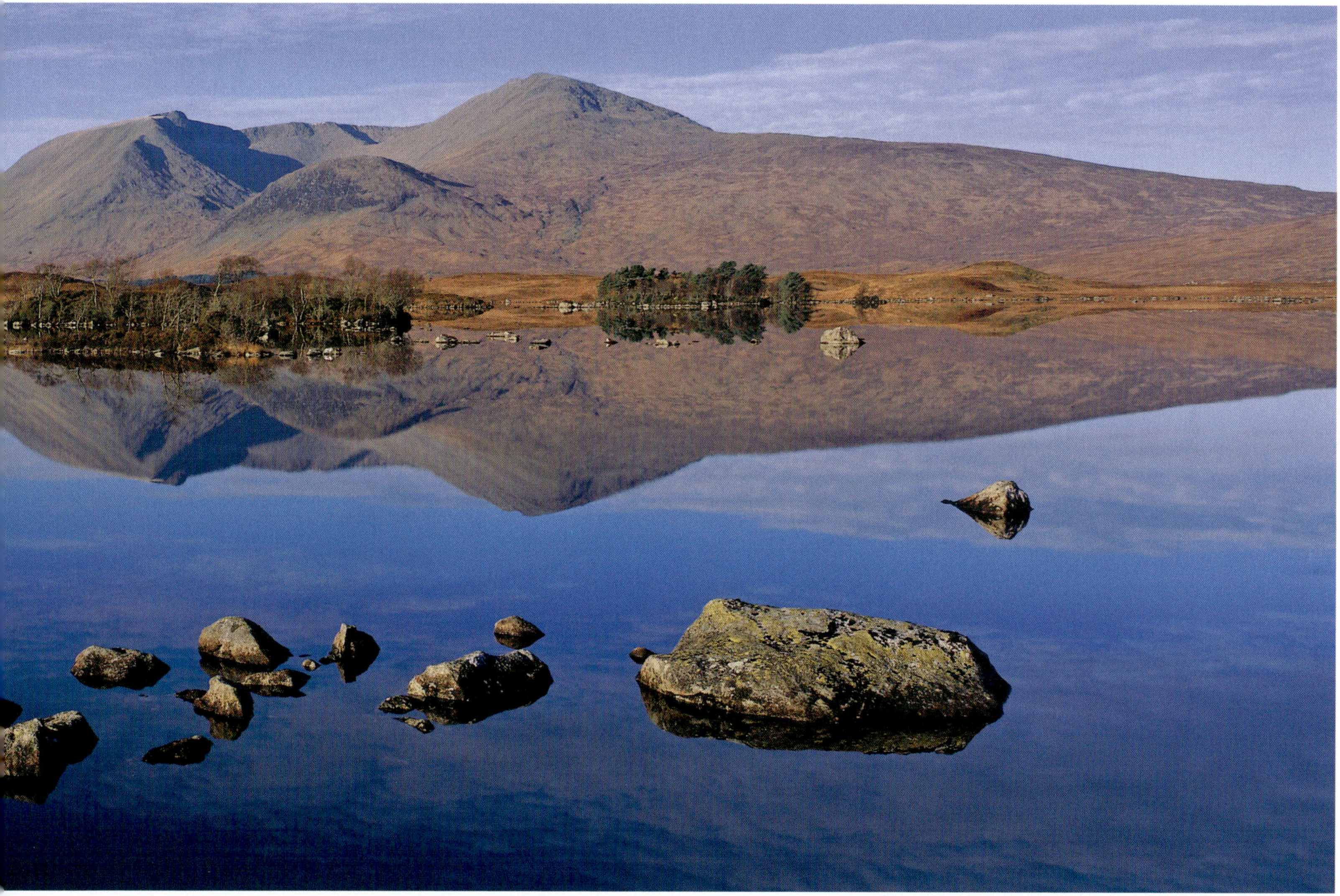

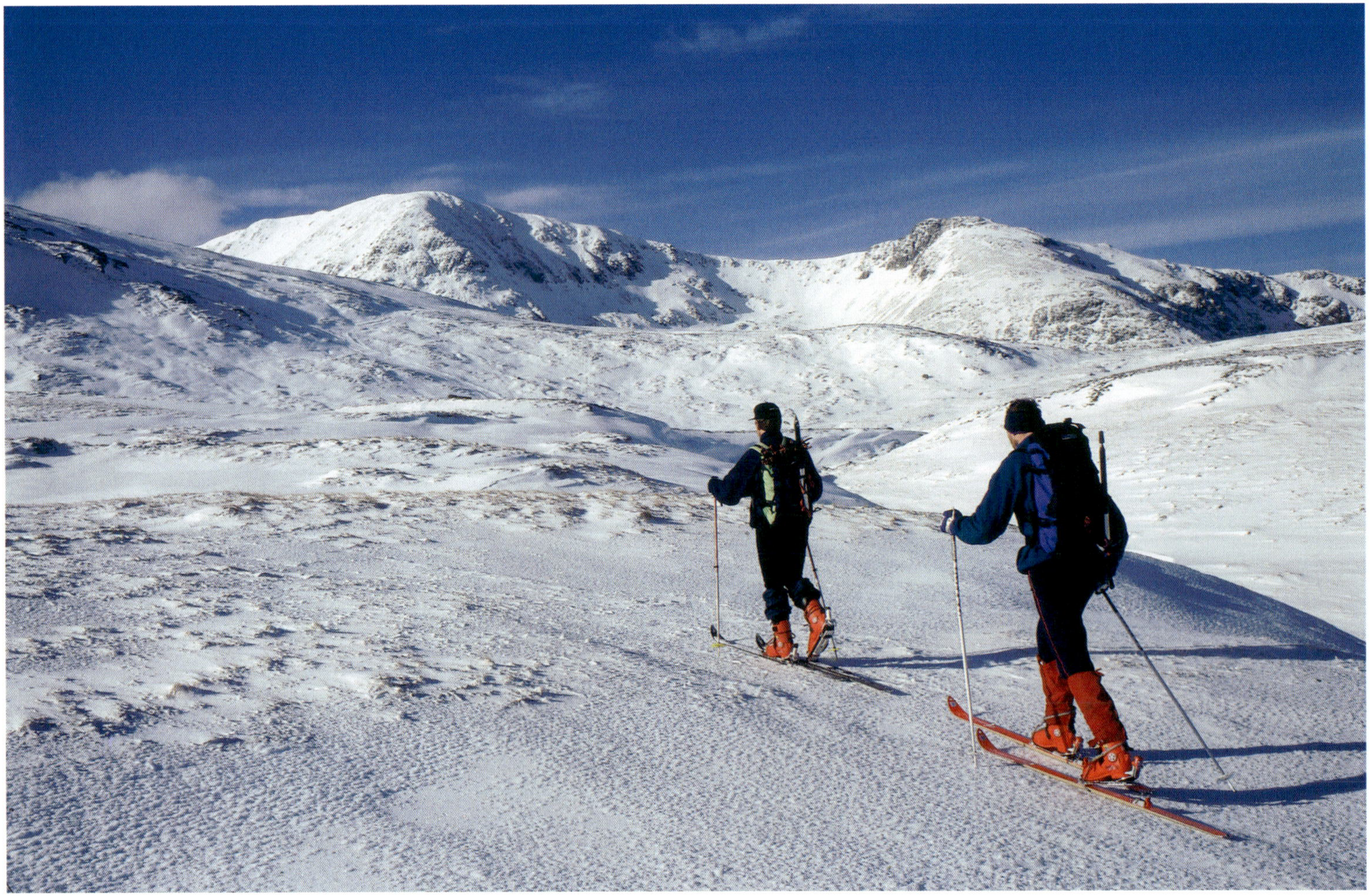

A grand tour.
Ski mountaineers crossing the icy slopes of Meall a'Bhuiridh at the start of a tour over the Black Mount hills.

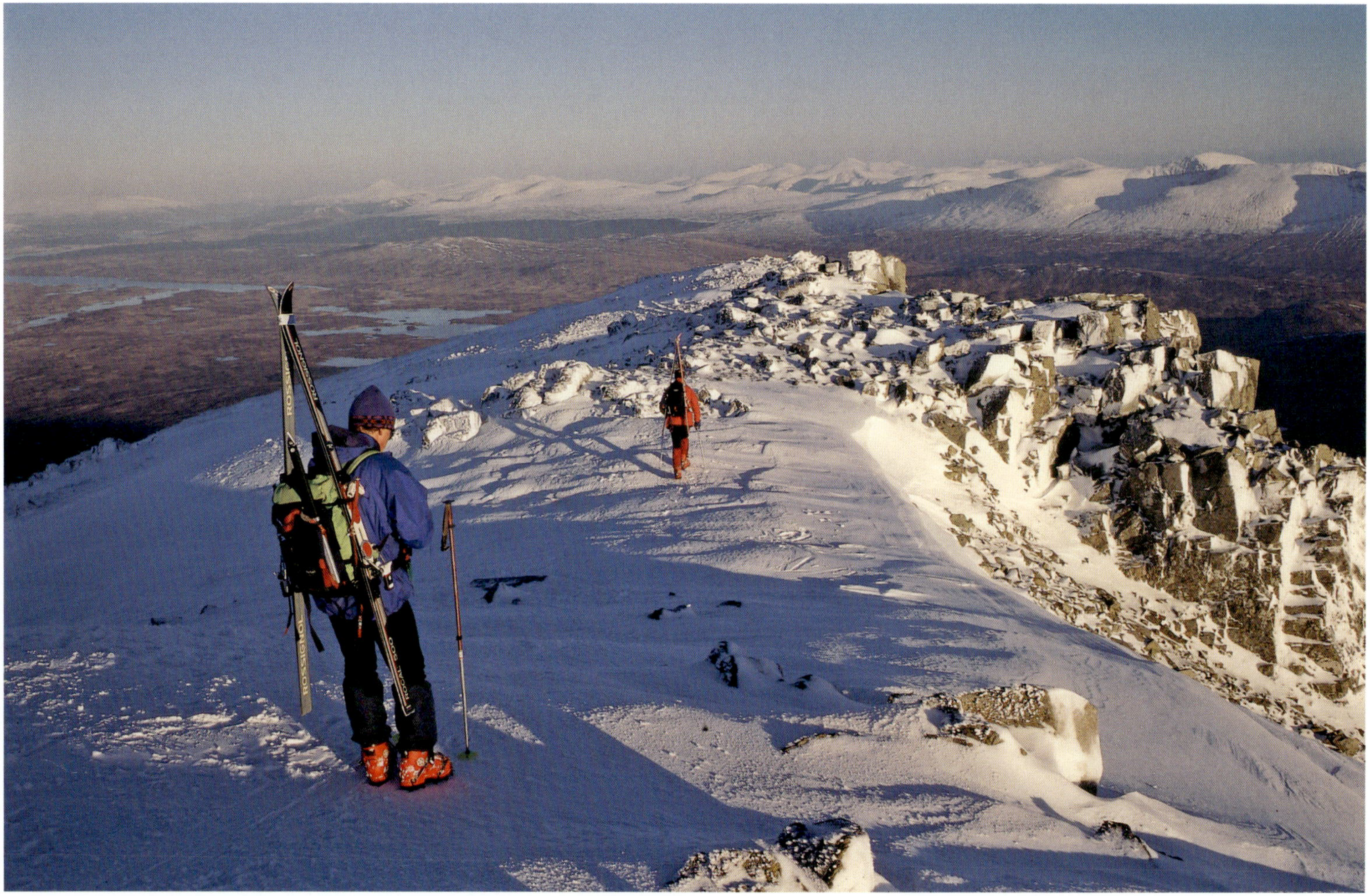

End of a perfect day.
Approaching the rocky top of Meall a'Bhuiridh at dusk and the start of a steep ski descent to the valley.

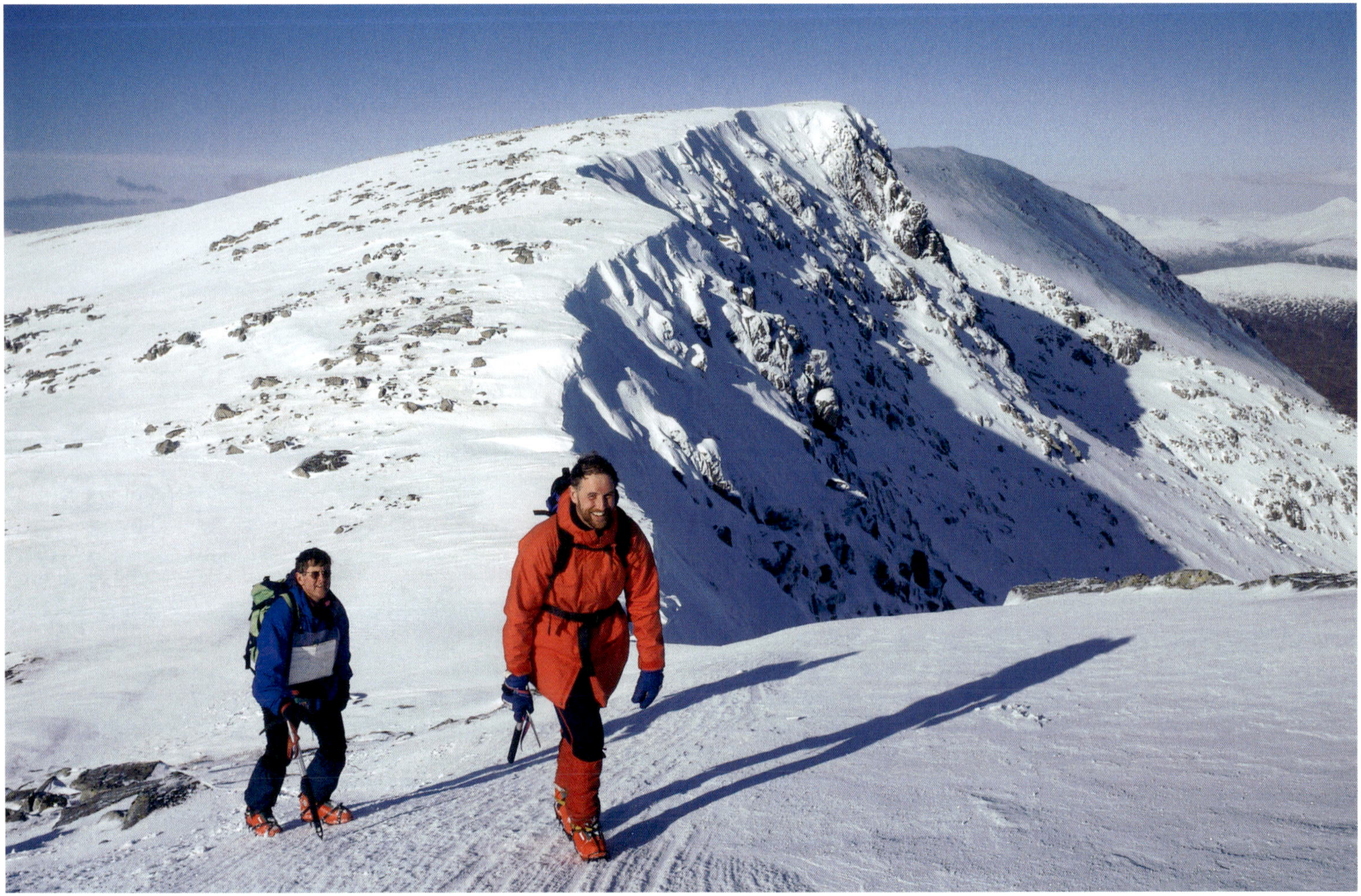

A superb winter's day.

Walkers cross the corniced ridge linking Creise and Clach Leathad on the northern end of Black Mount on a splendid winter's day.

Among mountains.
The slopes of Creise offer a great view of the shapely snow-covered Meall a'Bhuiridh in whose north-east corrie are the chair lifts and tows of one of Scotland's main ski mountains.

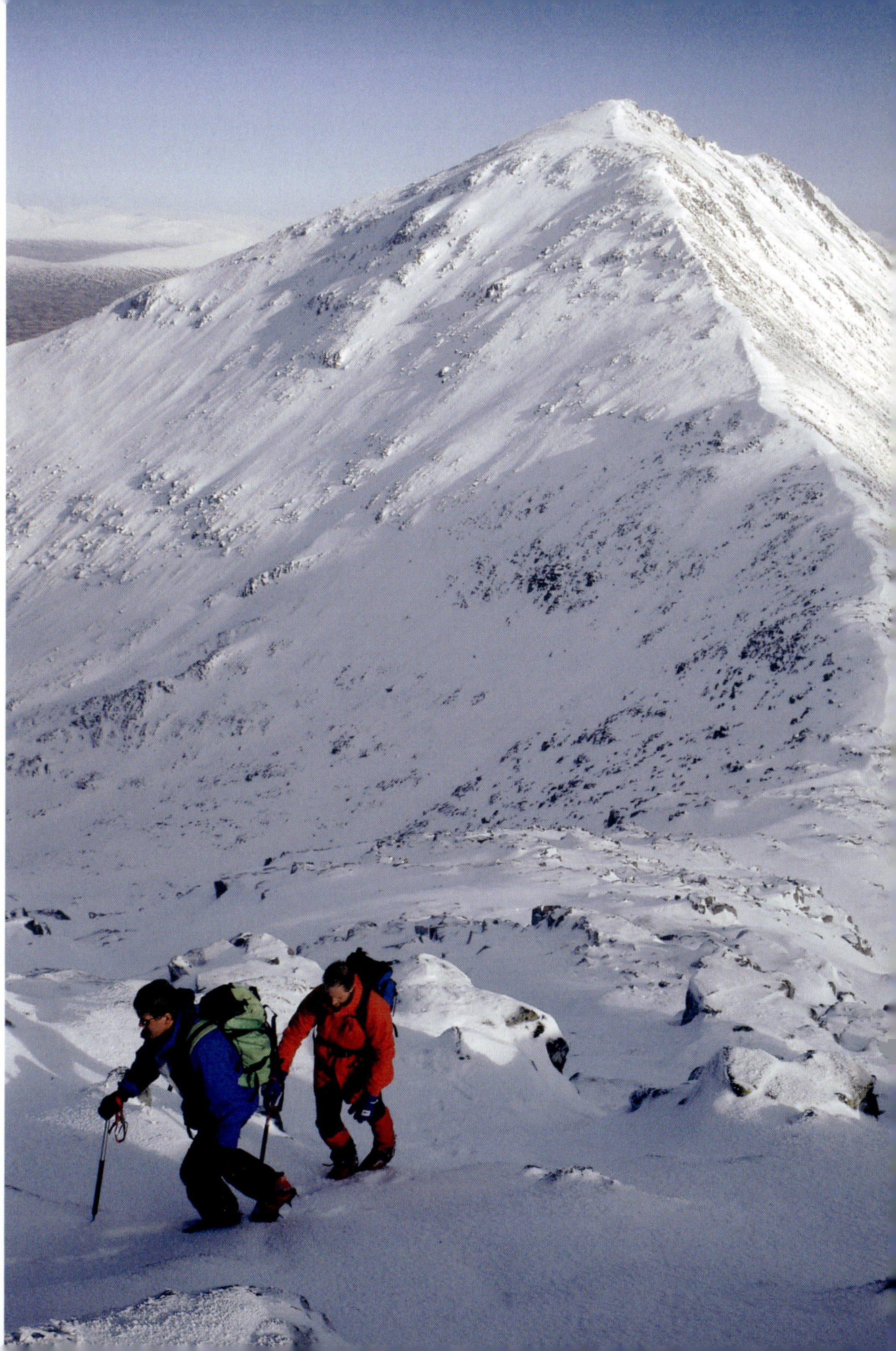

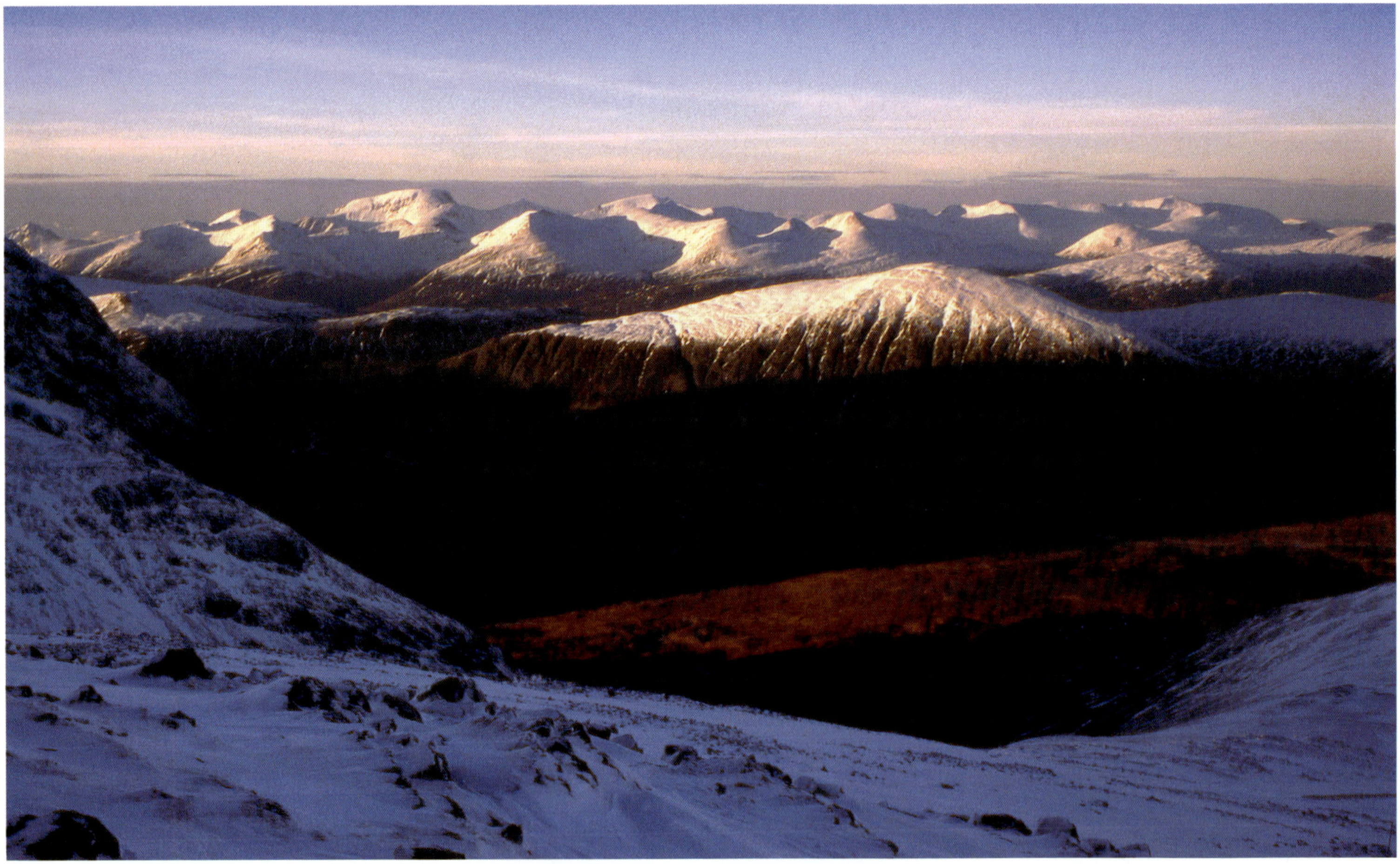

Beyond the mountain shadows.
The setting sun casts a pink glow over the distant Lochaber hills of Ben Nevis, the Mamores and Grey Corries seen from Meall a'Bhuiridh.

Opposite: Sunlit stones.
Early morning summer sunshine illuminates boulders in the River Coupal which acts as a foreground for a view of Stob a Ghlais Choire, the most northerly peak of the Black Mount range.

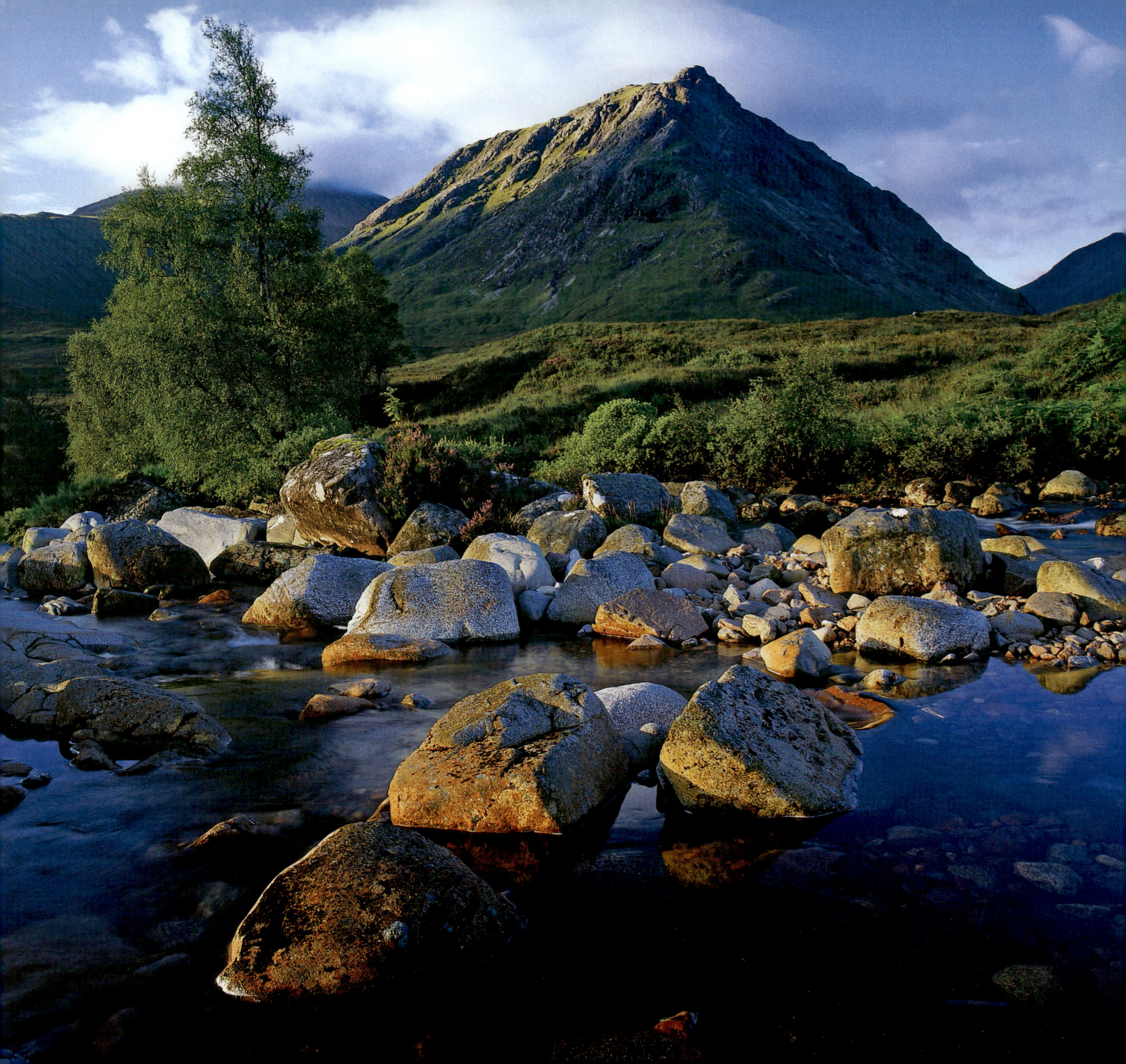

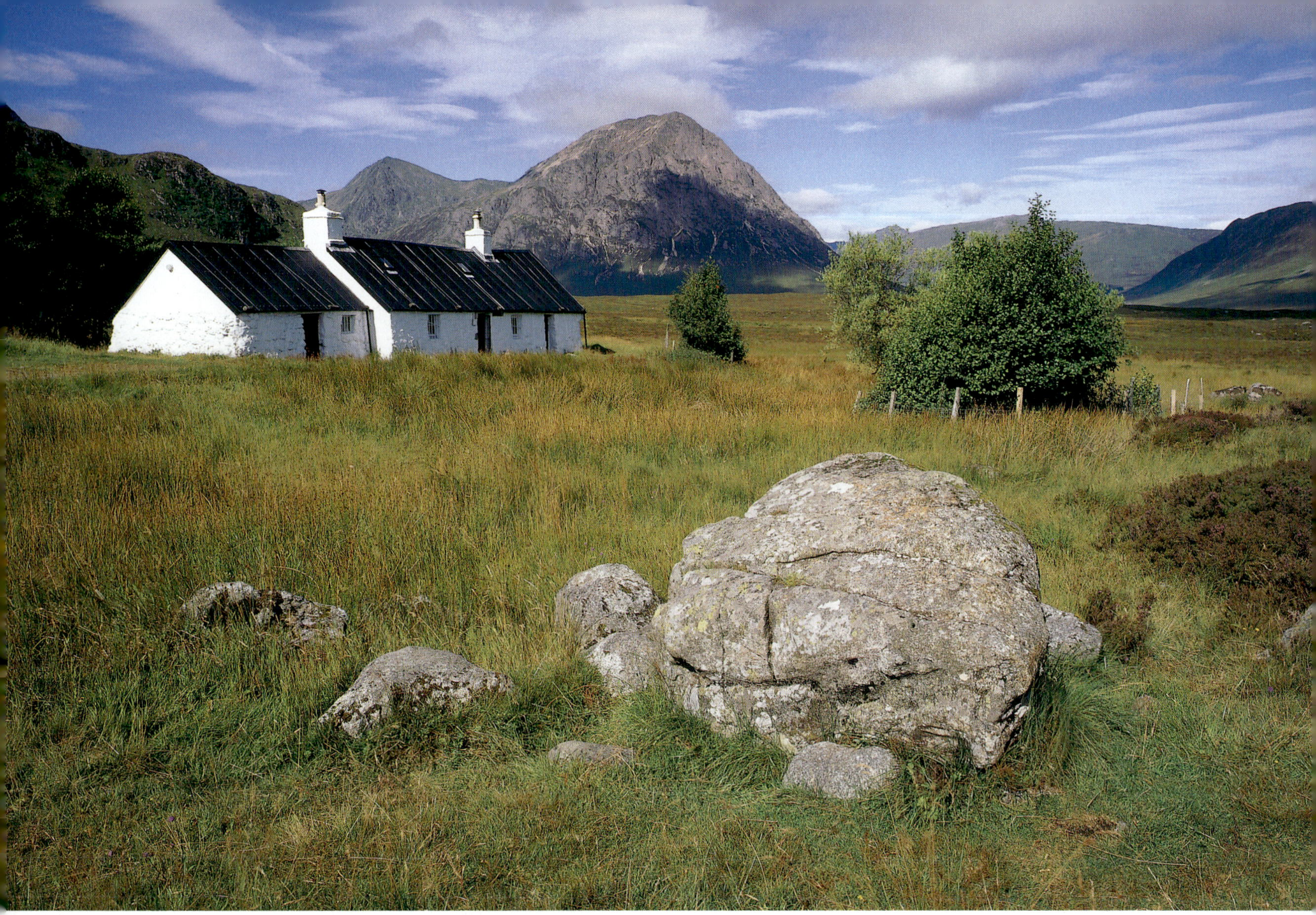

Black Rock Cottage.

Owned by the Ladies Scottish Mountaineering Club, the building lies on the old military road from Bridge of Orchy to Kingshouse, now part of the West Highland Way trail. The pyramid-shaped Buachaille Etive Mor in the background is echoed by the boulder.

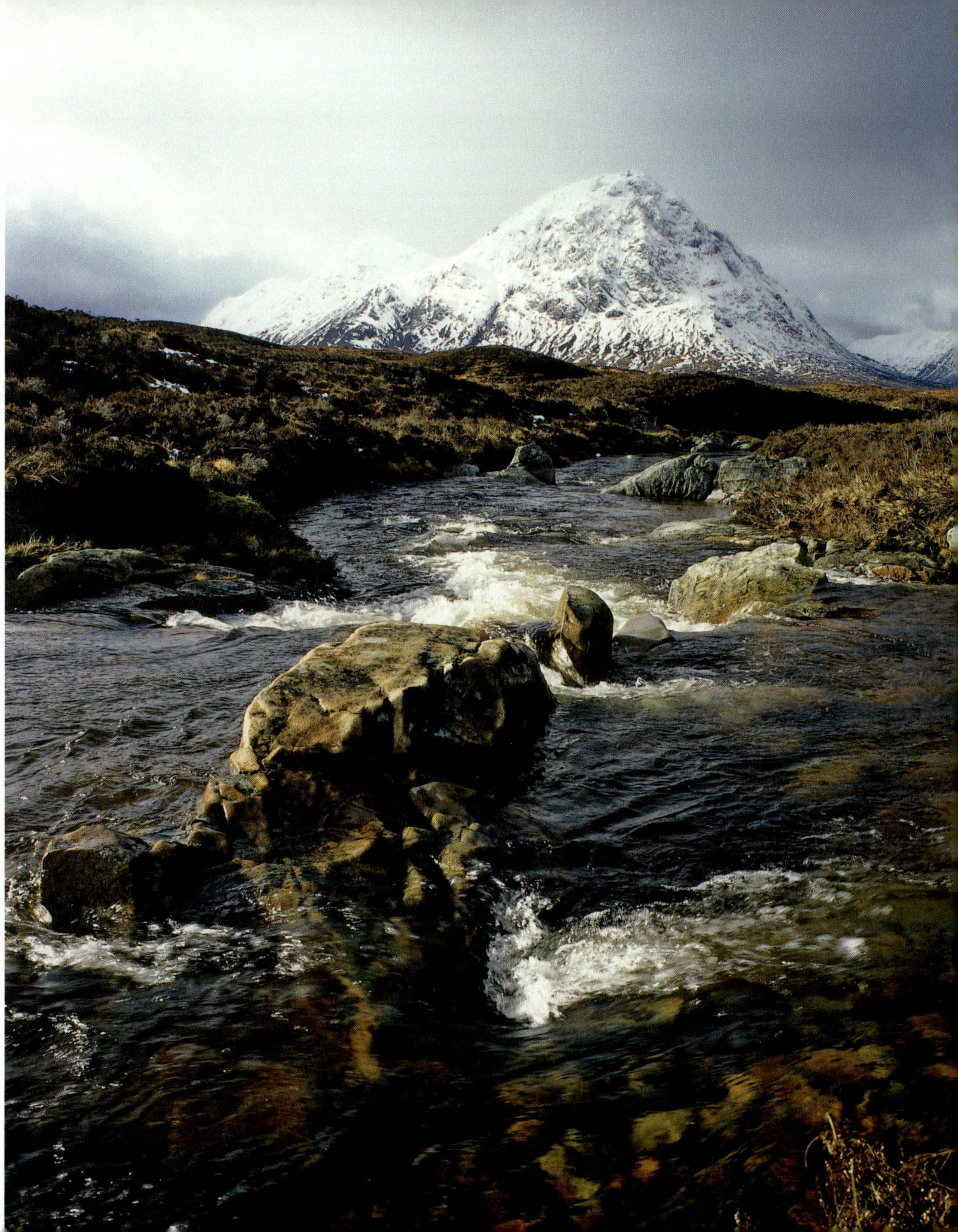

Winter snows.
The Allt nan Guibhas rushes from Rannoch Moor towards the great edifice of a snow-capped Buachaille Etive Mor, standing guard at the junction of Glencoe and Glen Etive.

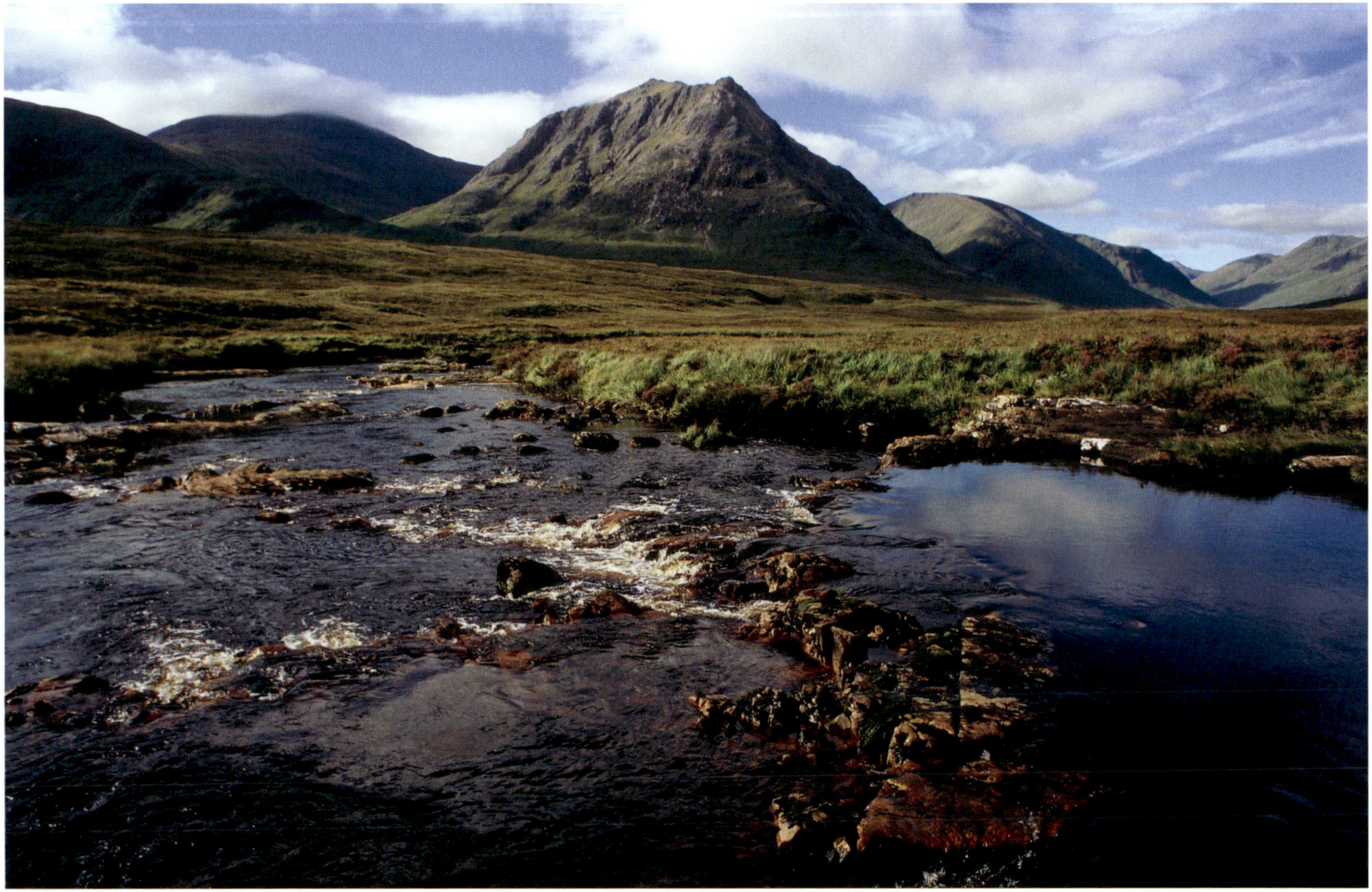

Entrance to the glen.

The River Etive, whose tributaries drain the vast moorland plateau of Rannoch Moor, meanders slowly towards Glen Etive on its journey to the sea. This long and remote glen forms the south-east boundary of the Glencoe hills.

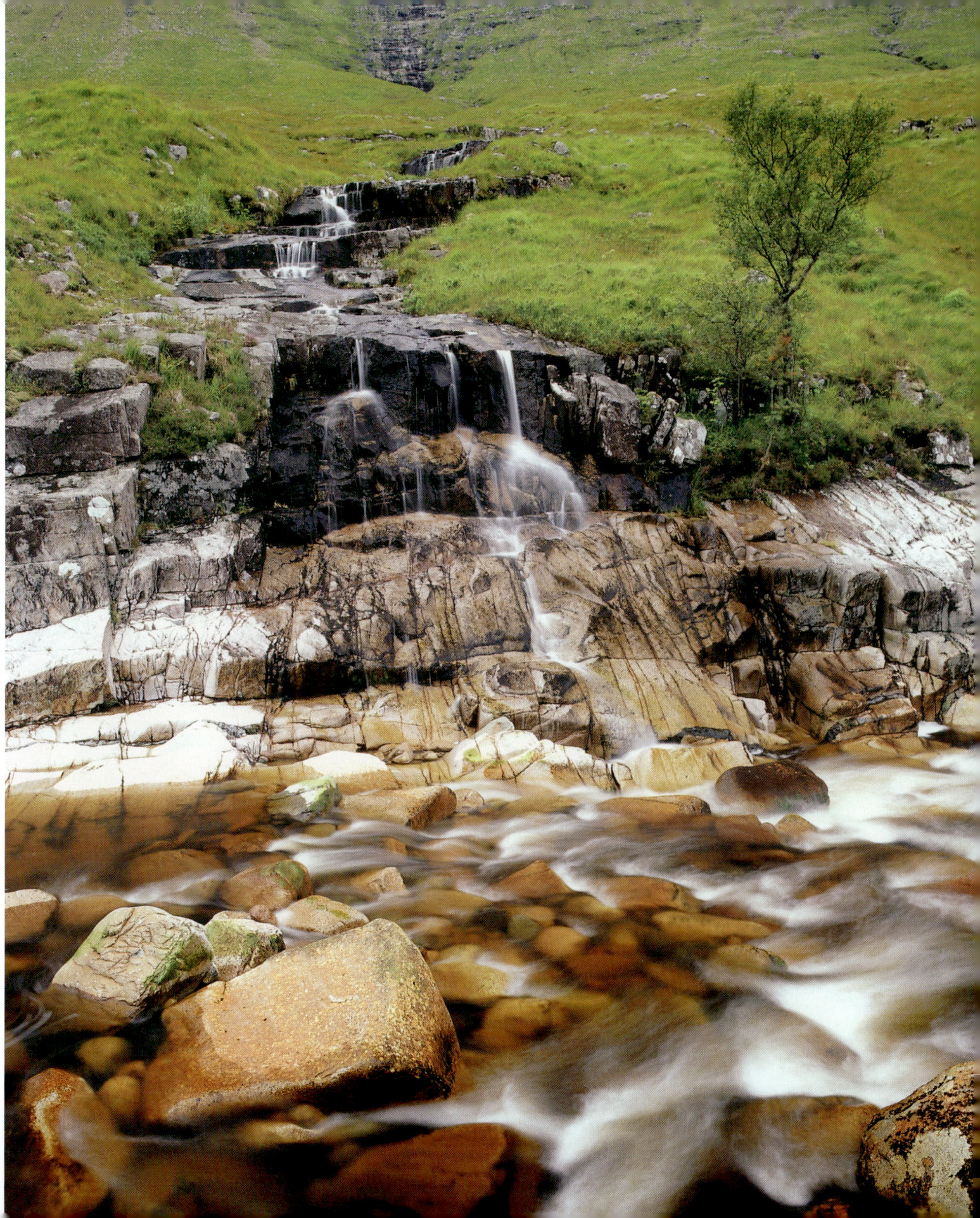

Cascades.
Water cascades down the northern flank of Glen Etive to confluence with the River Etive.

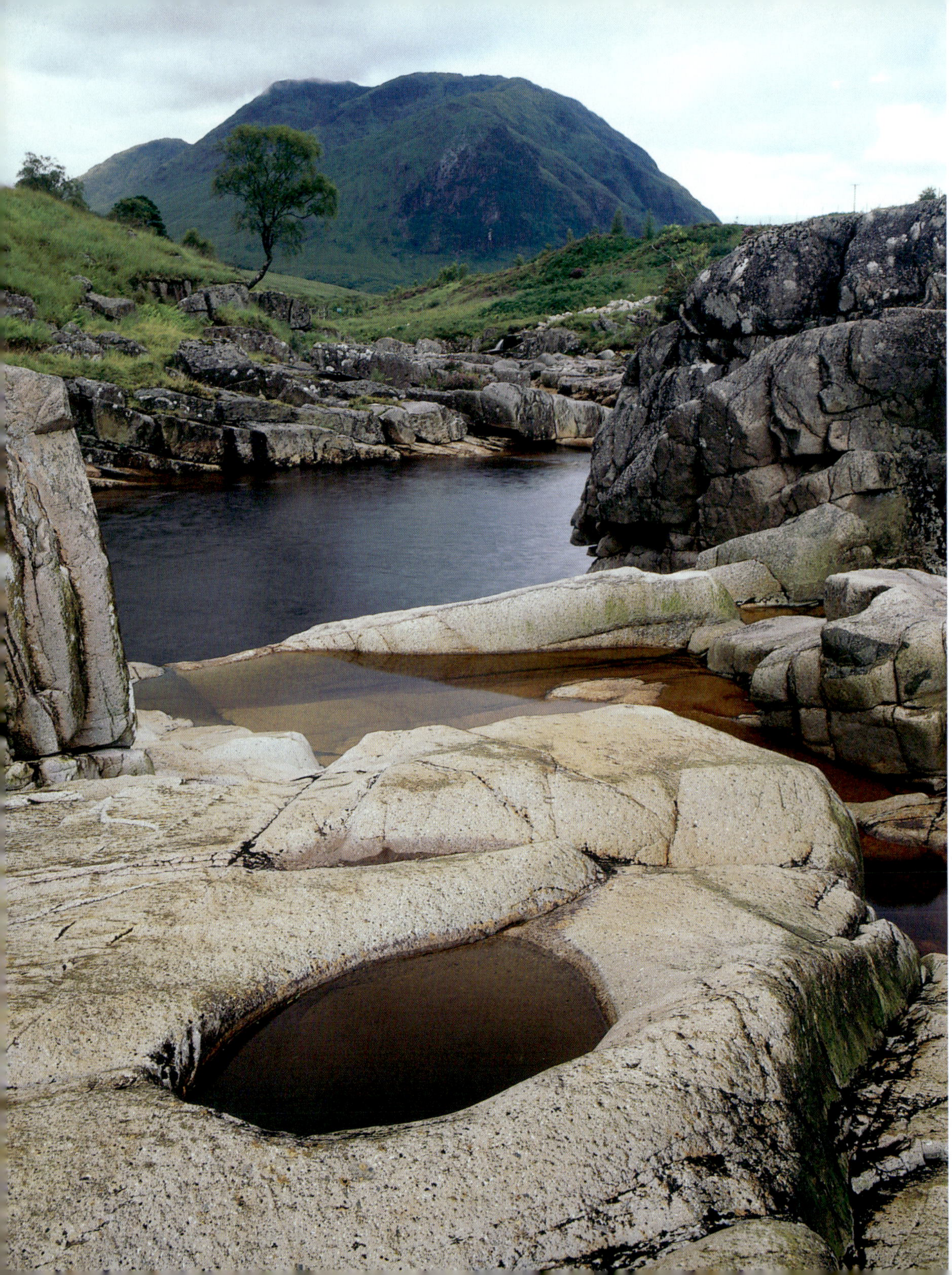

Meandering river.
The River Etive follows a meandering line along the valley between rock banks and rowans before rushing through rocky gorges and over steep falls with numerous deep pools.

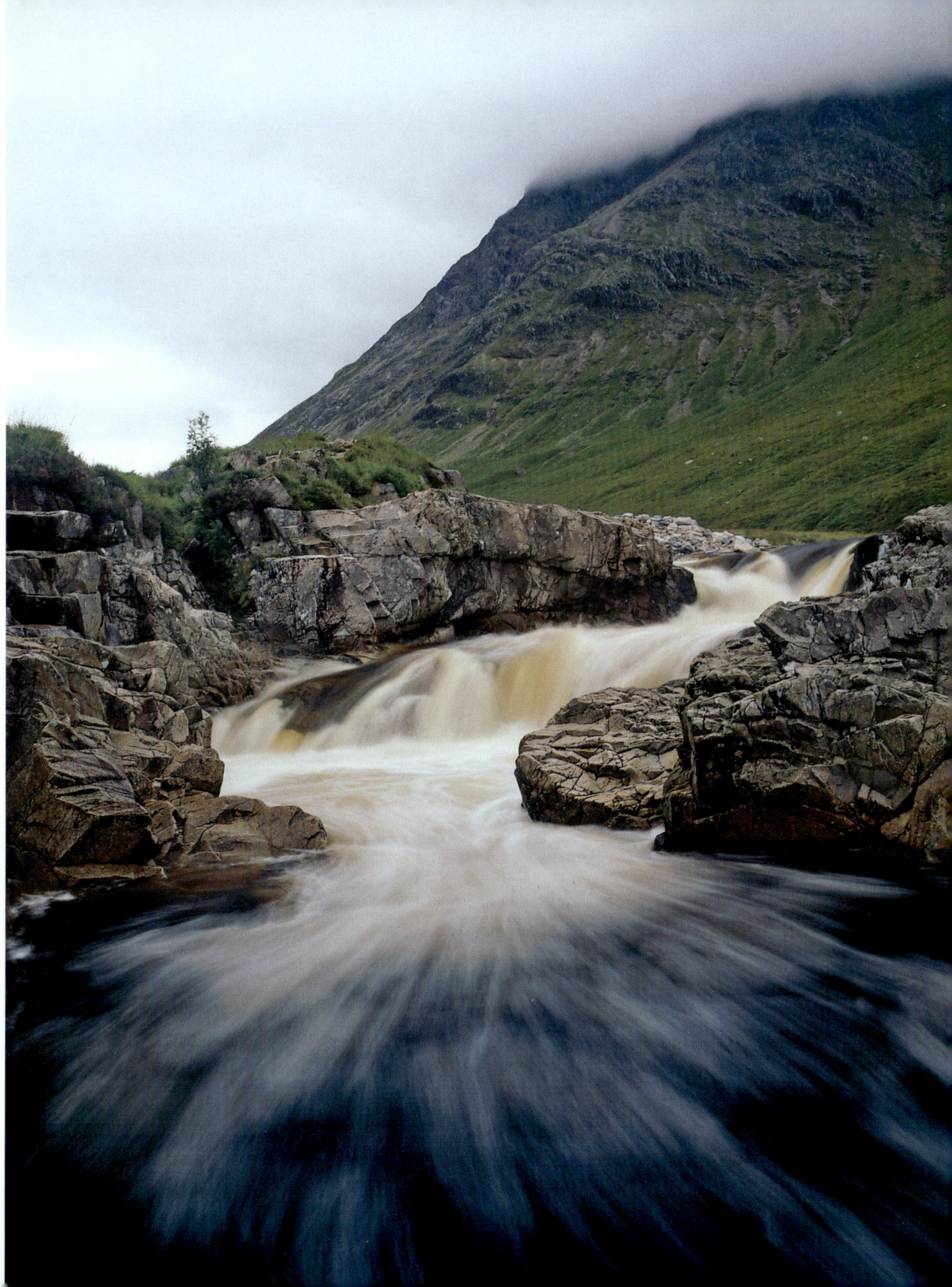

River in spate.
The River Etive dashes below the craggy profile of Sron na Creise.

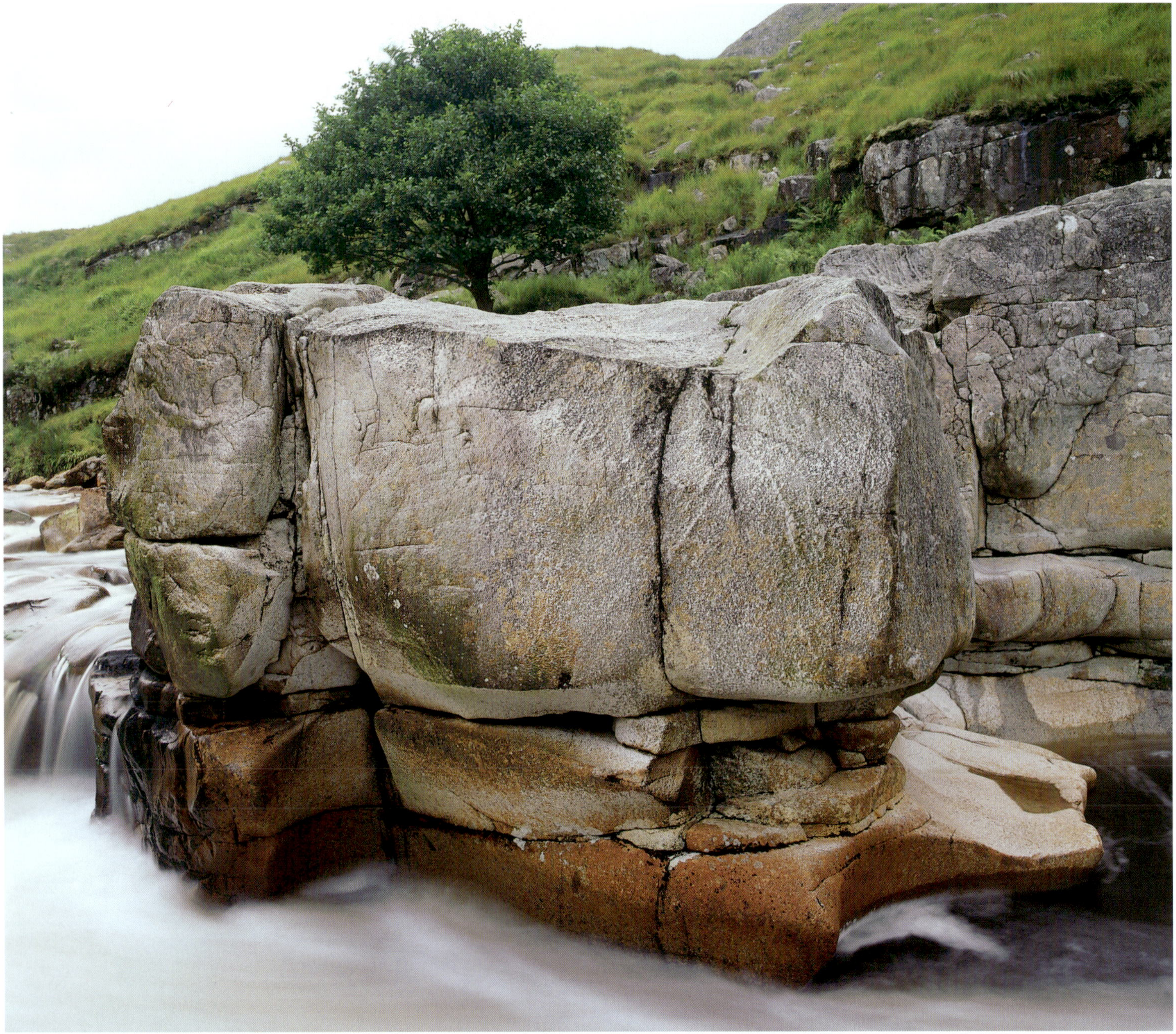

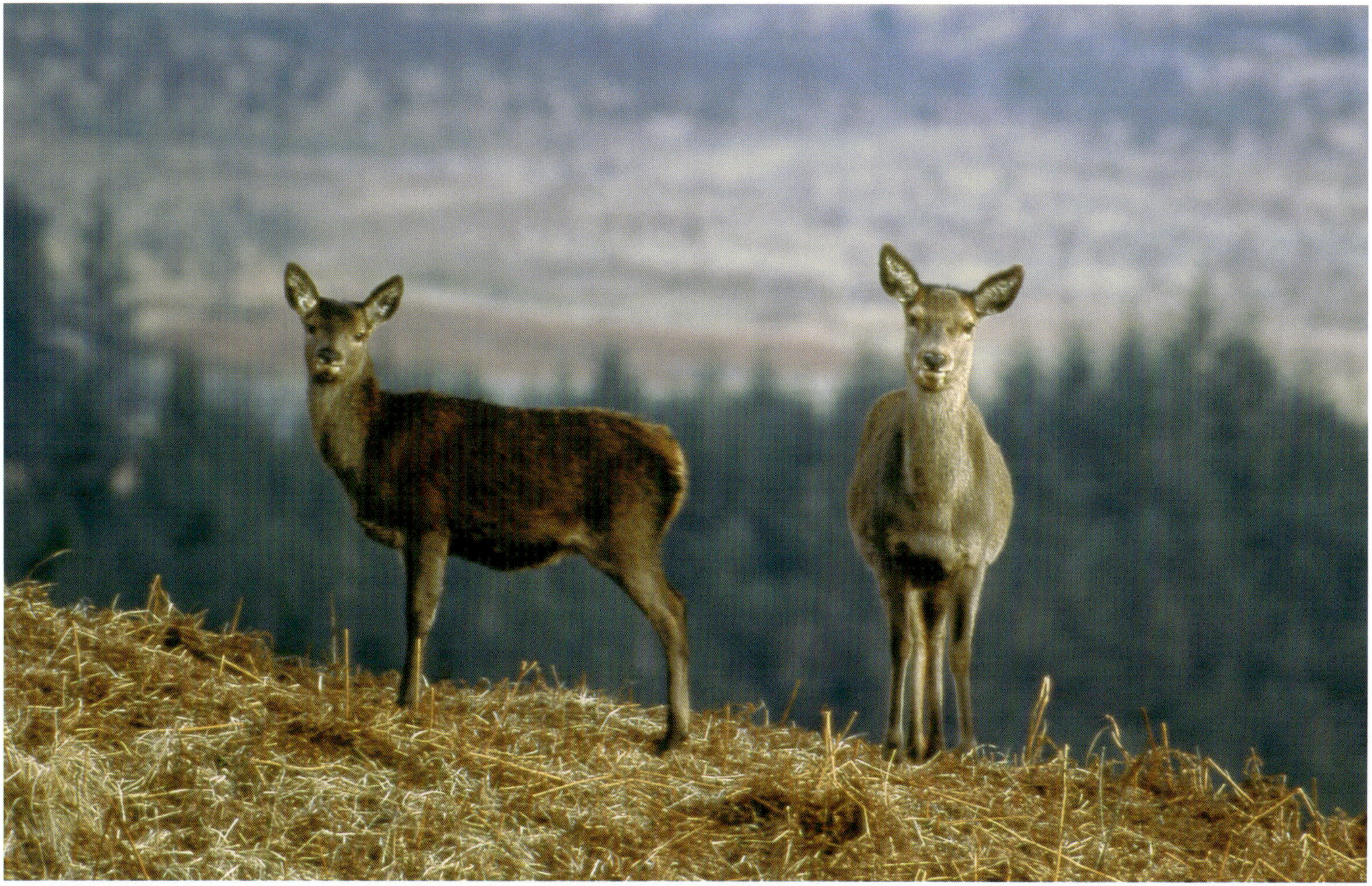

Inquisitive hinds.
During the winter months, red deer can often be seen wandering along the valley floor of Glen Etive.

Opposite: Erosion.
Glen Etive rocks worn smooth and polished by the passage of time.

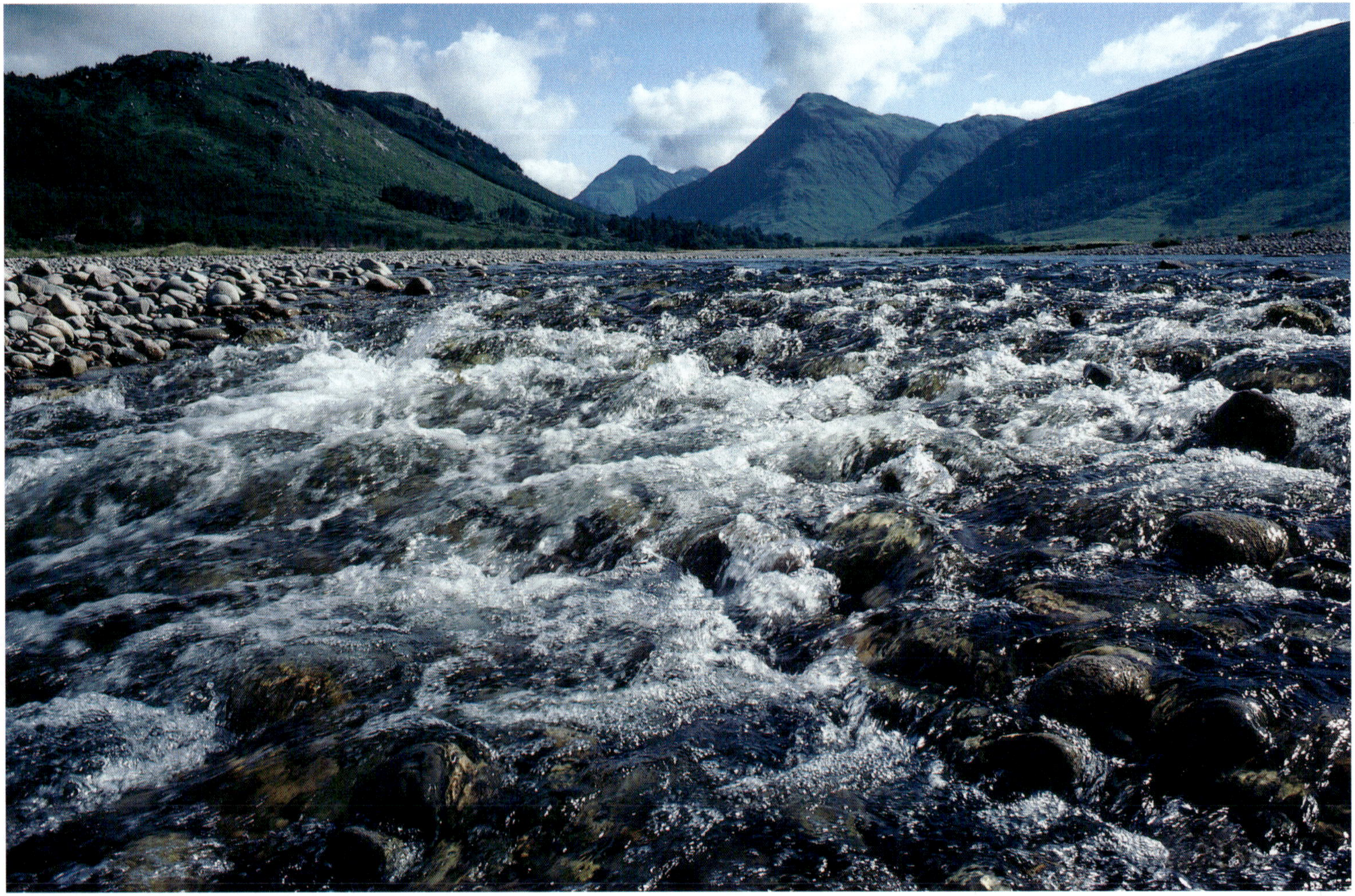

Bubbling river.
A wide River Etive enters Loch Etive near Gualachulain. Back up the glen Buachaille Etive Mor is visible.

Opposite: Break in the clouds.
Late afternoon sunshine breaks through the clouds over Ben Starav which rises dramatically from a partly frozen Loch Etive.

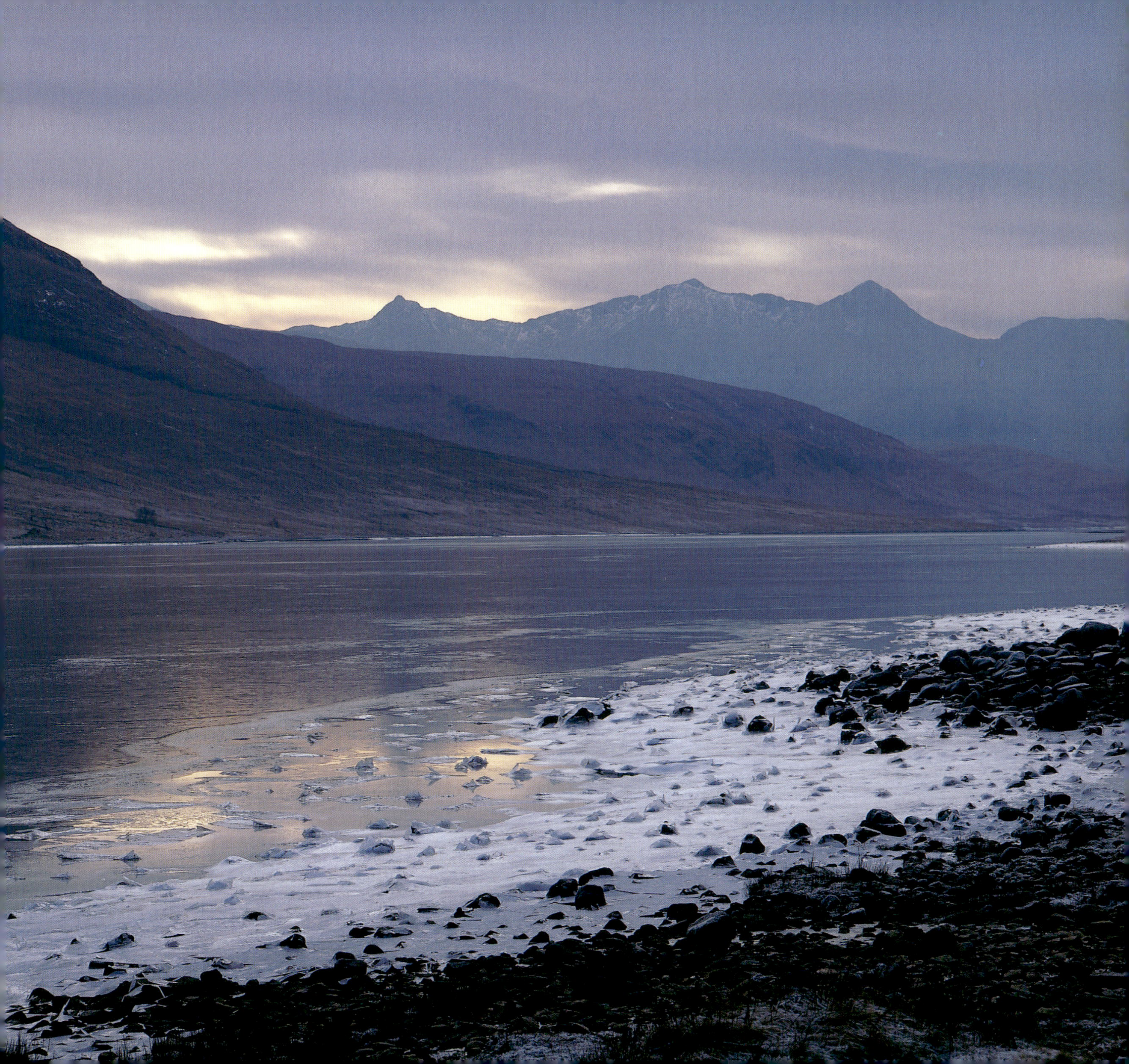

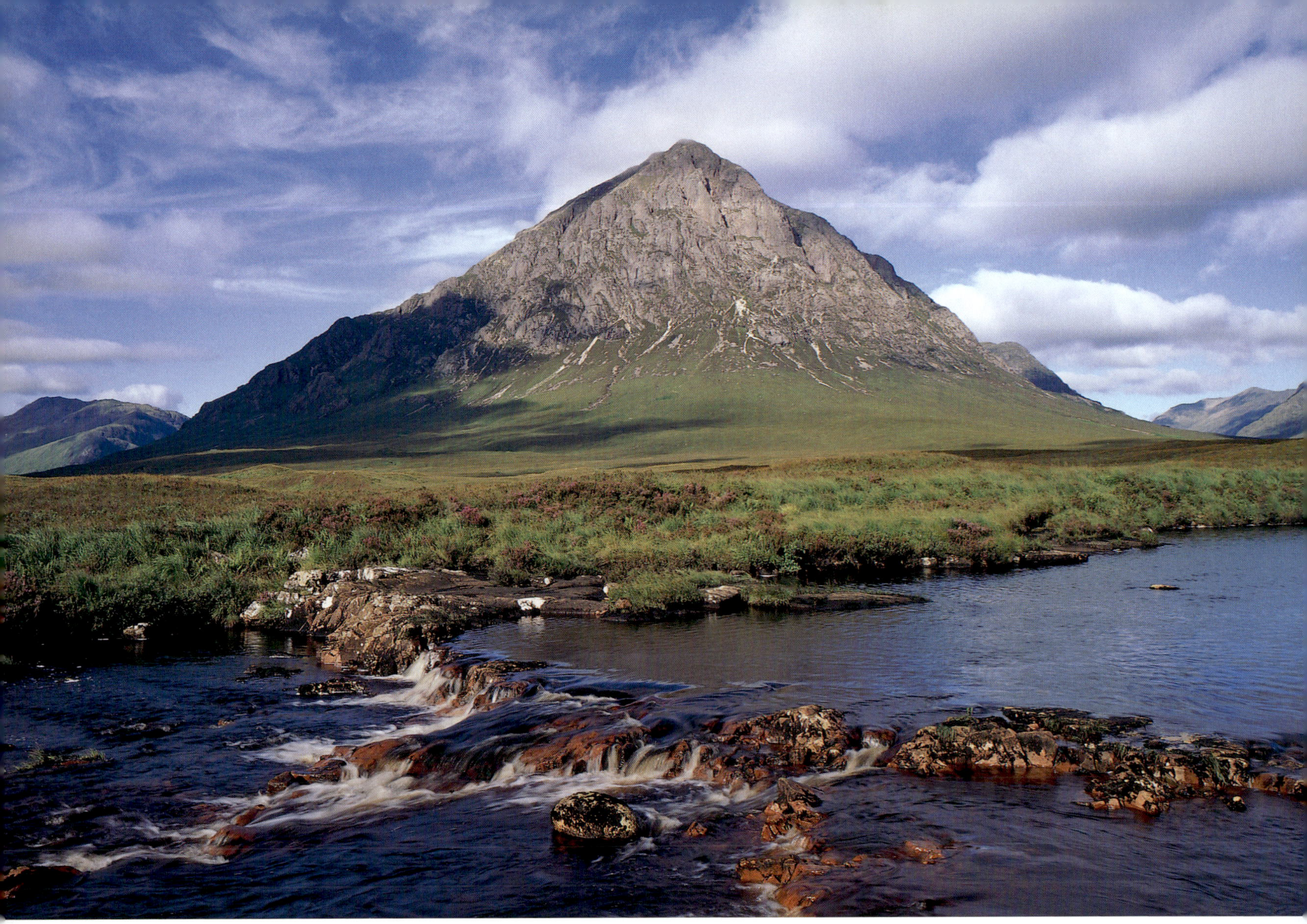

Iconic peak.

The mighty Buachaille Etive Mor (*the big herdsman of Etive*) is a long ridge rising steeply from Glen Etive with its highest point being Stob Dearg (*red peak*) – a name derived from the reddish rhyolite of the upper slopes – sweeping up from Rannoch Moor. Stob Dearg is usually referred to as Buachaille Etive Mor or, more affectionately, The Buachaille. In this summer image the River Etive forms a foreground for this classic view

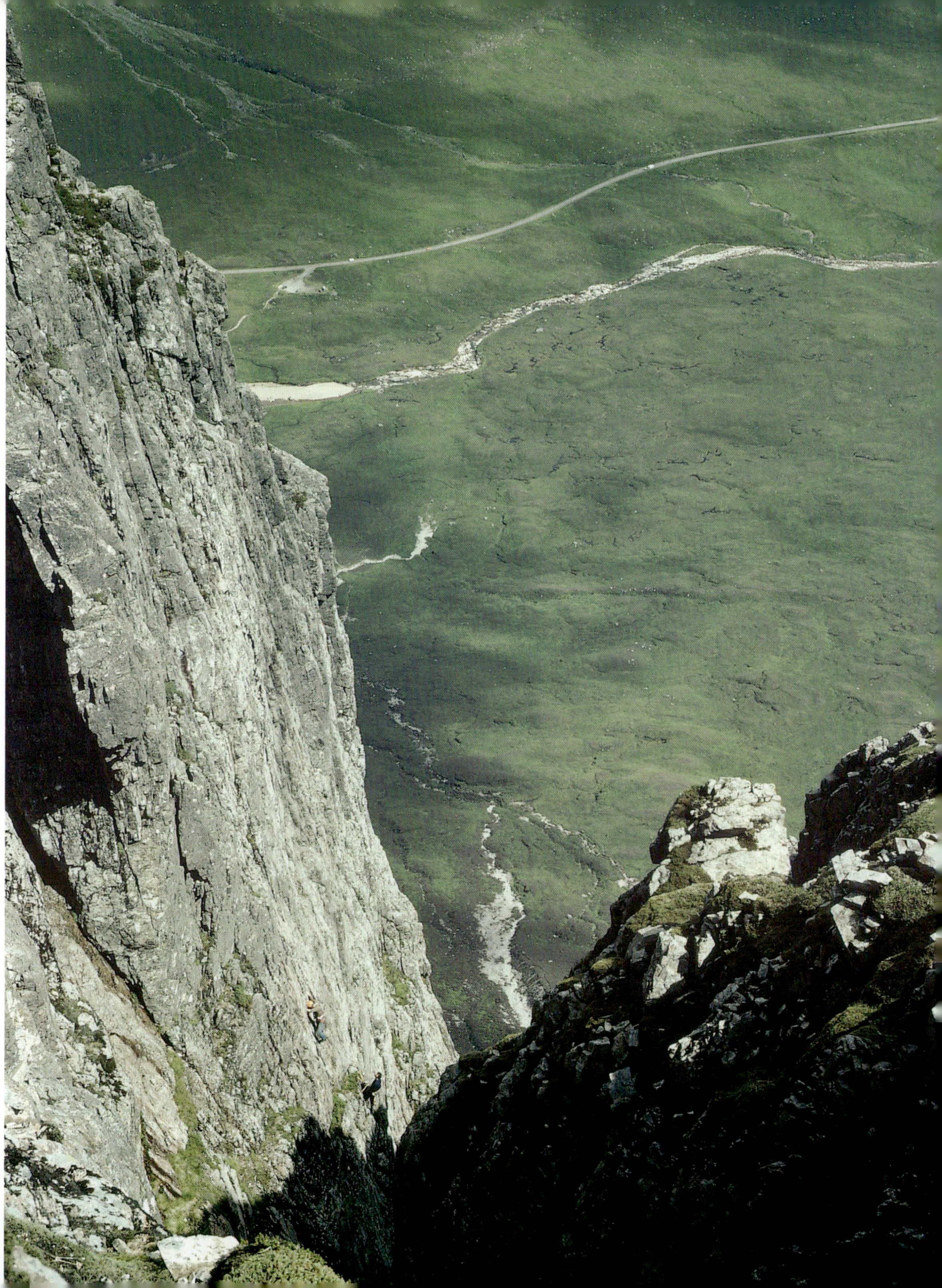

A bird's-eye-view.
From high on Buachaille Etive Mor's craggy slopes you can gaze down on the A82 as it sweeps into Glencoe.

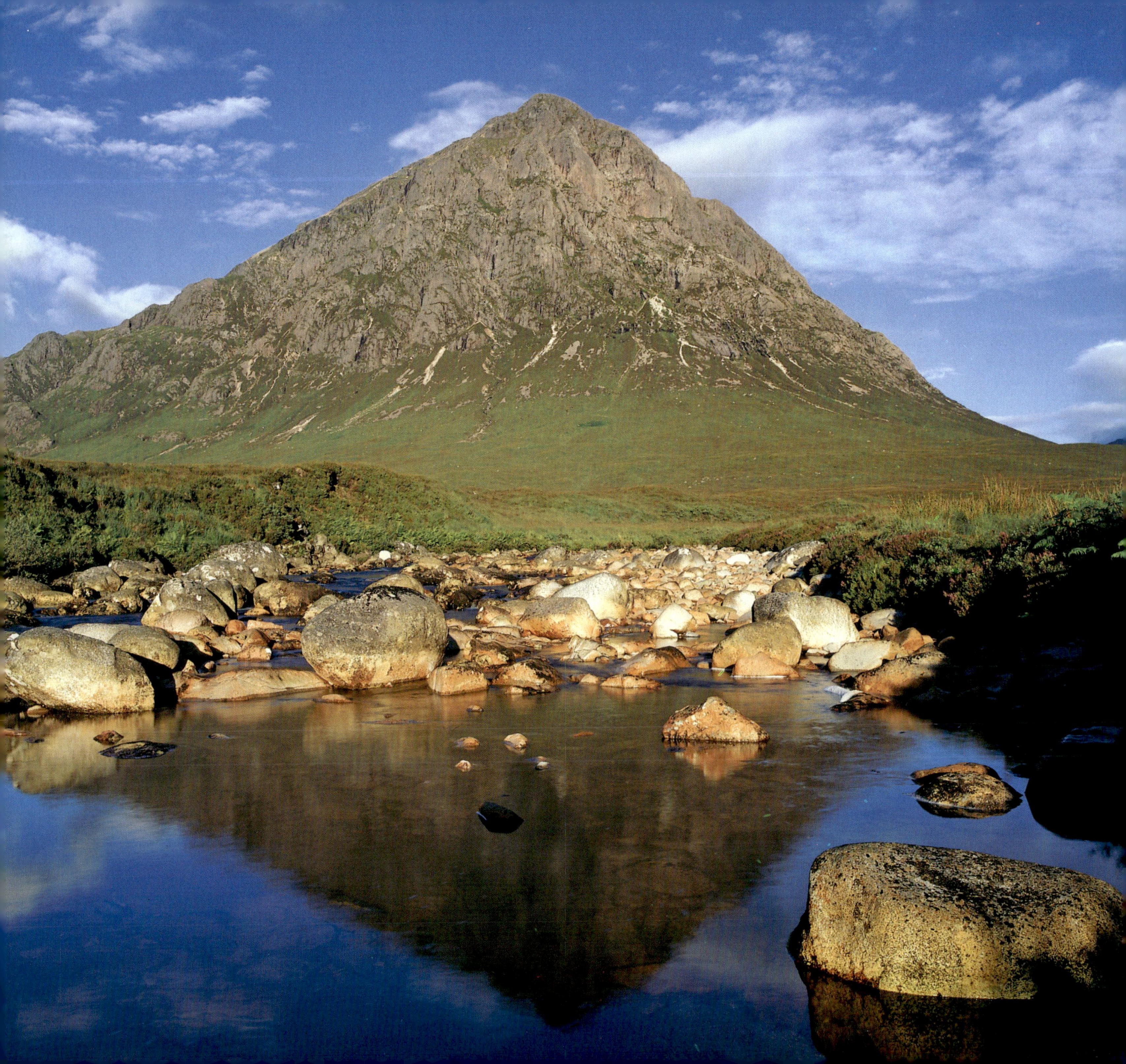

Rocky domain.
The magnificent buttresses and gullies of Buachaille Etive Mor, featuring Rannoch Wall and Crowberry Gully, are a playground for rock climbers and winter mountaineers. The buttresses give the peak an air of impregnability.

Opposite:
Summer reflections at dawn.
The soft play of morning light picks out the unmistakable Buachaille Etive Mor reflected in the River Coupall.

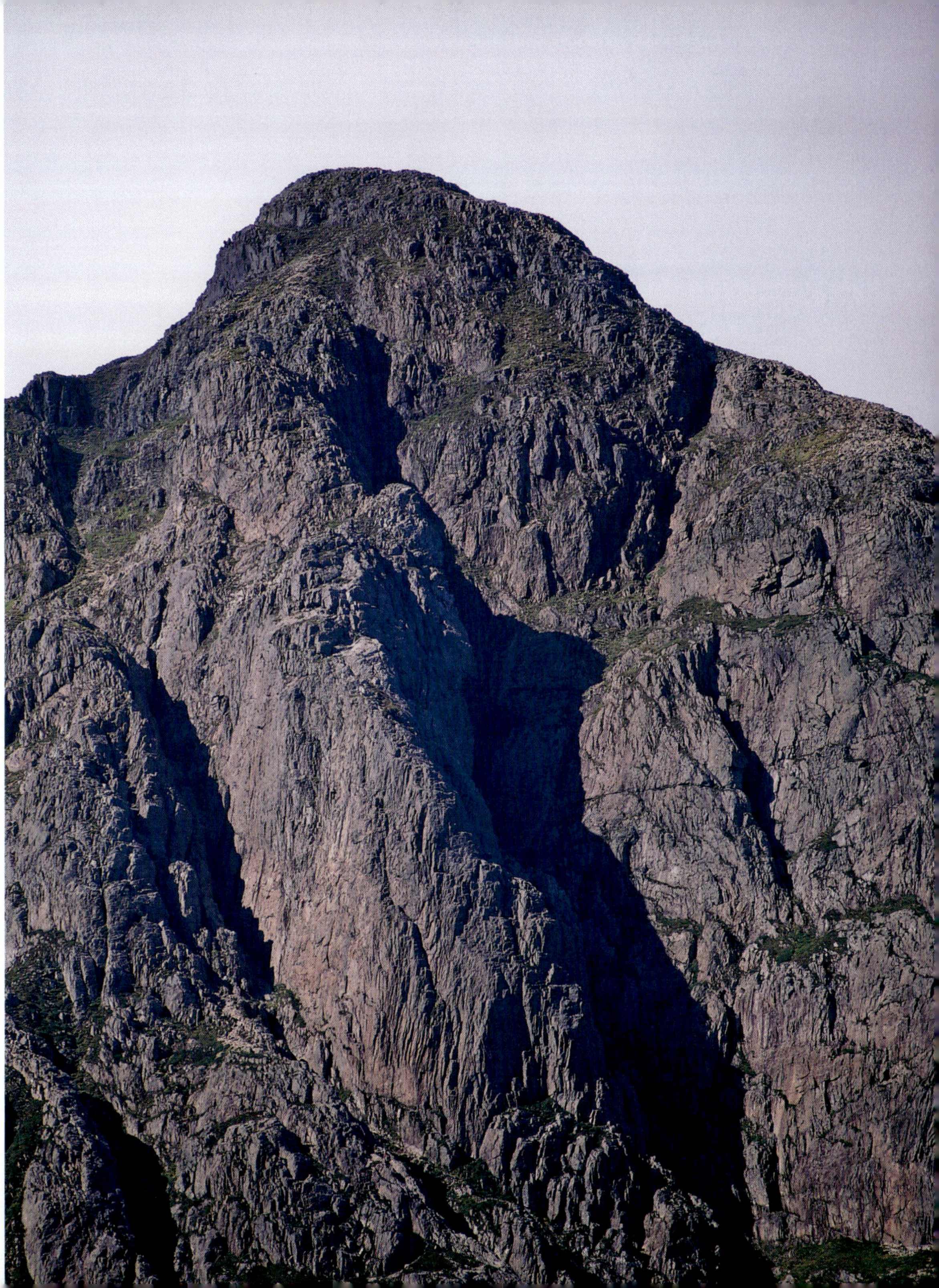

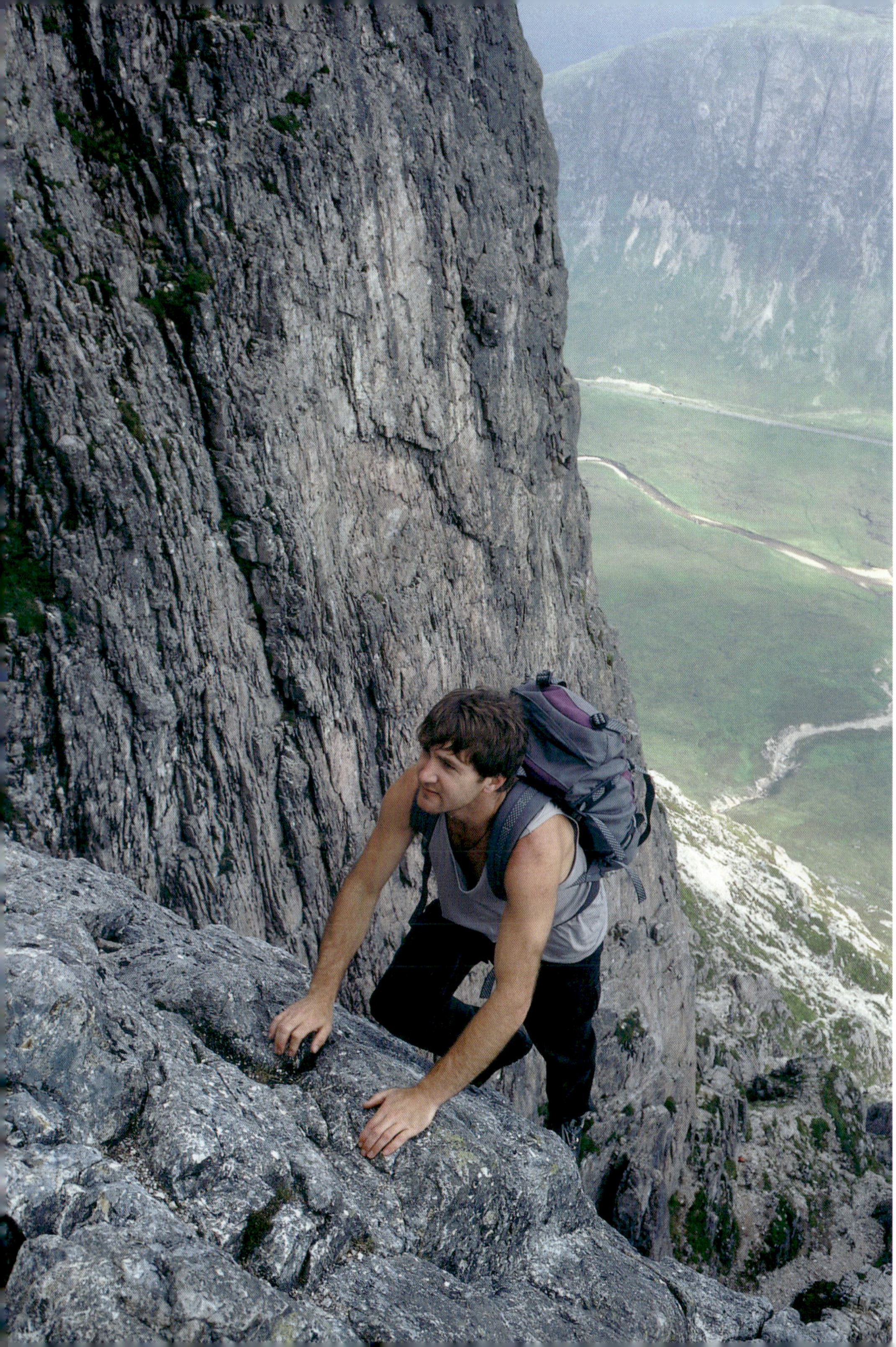

A scrambler's approach.
Ascending Glencoe's most popular scramble, Curved Ridge overlooked by the impressive Rannoch Wall, on Buachaille Etive Mor.

Exposed outlook.
Rannoch Wall's steep pale red porphyry has played an important role in the development of Scottish rock climbing. Here a climber balances his way up the classic 1936 route of Agag's Groove, one of the most popular climbs in Scotland.

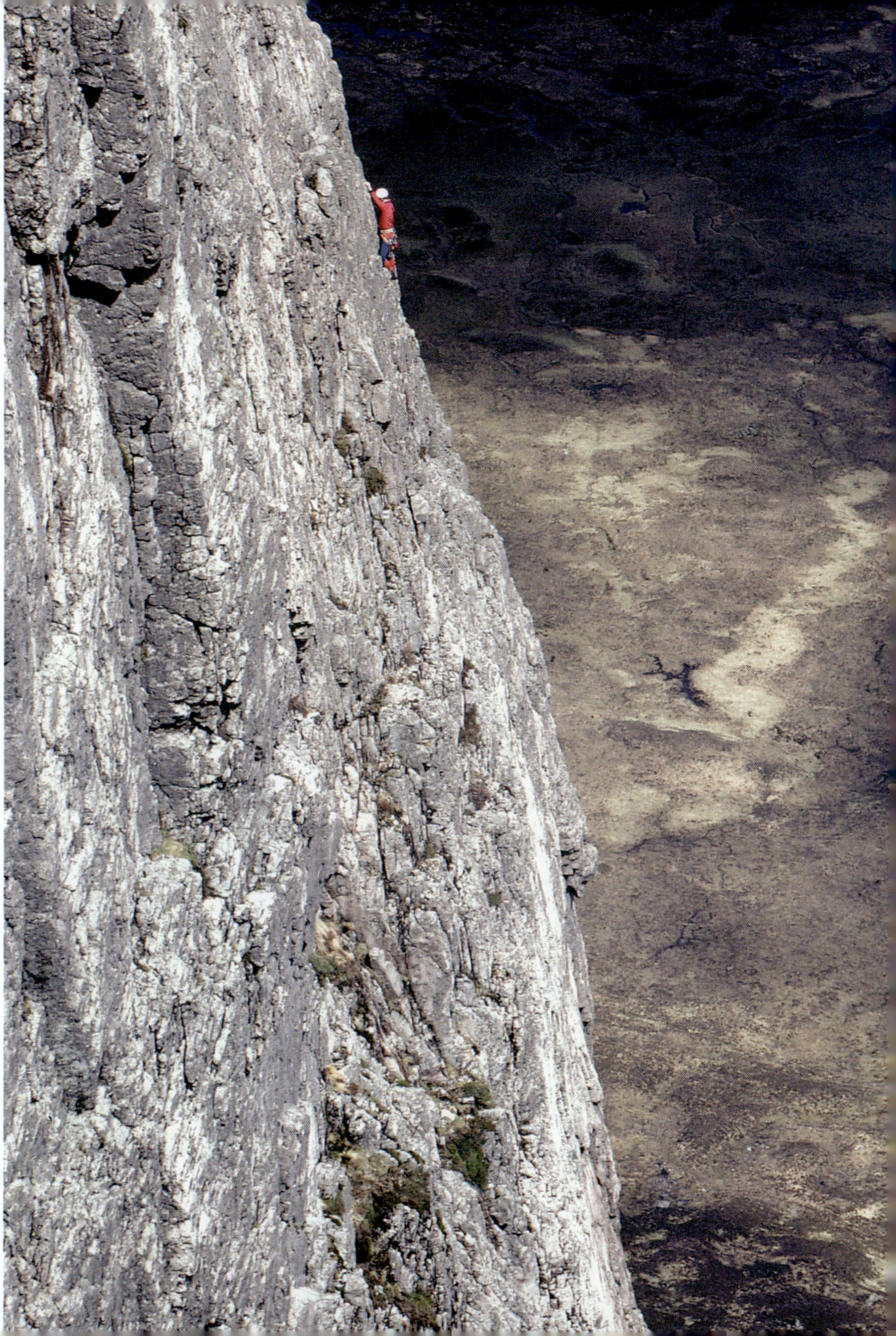

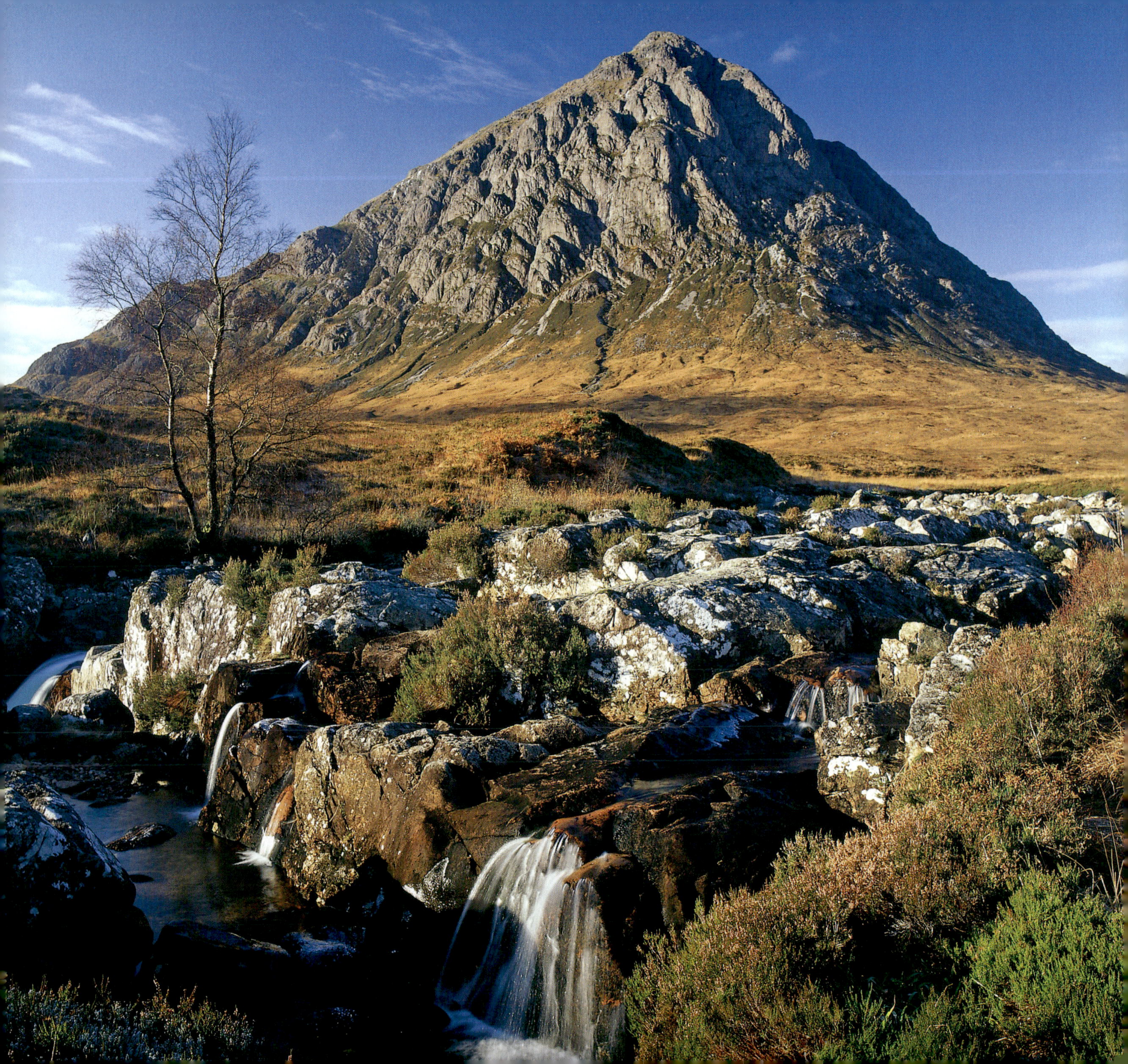

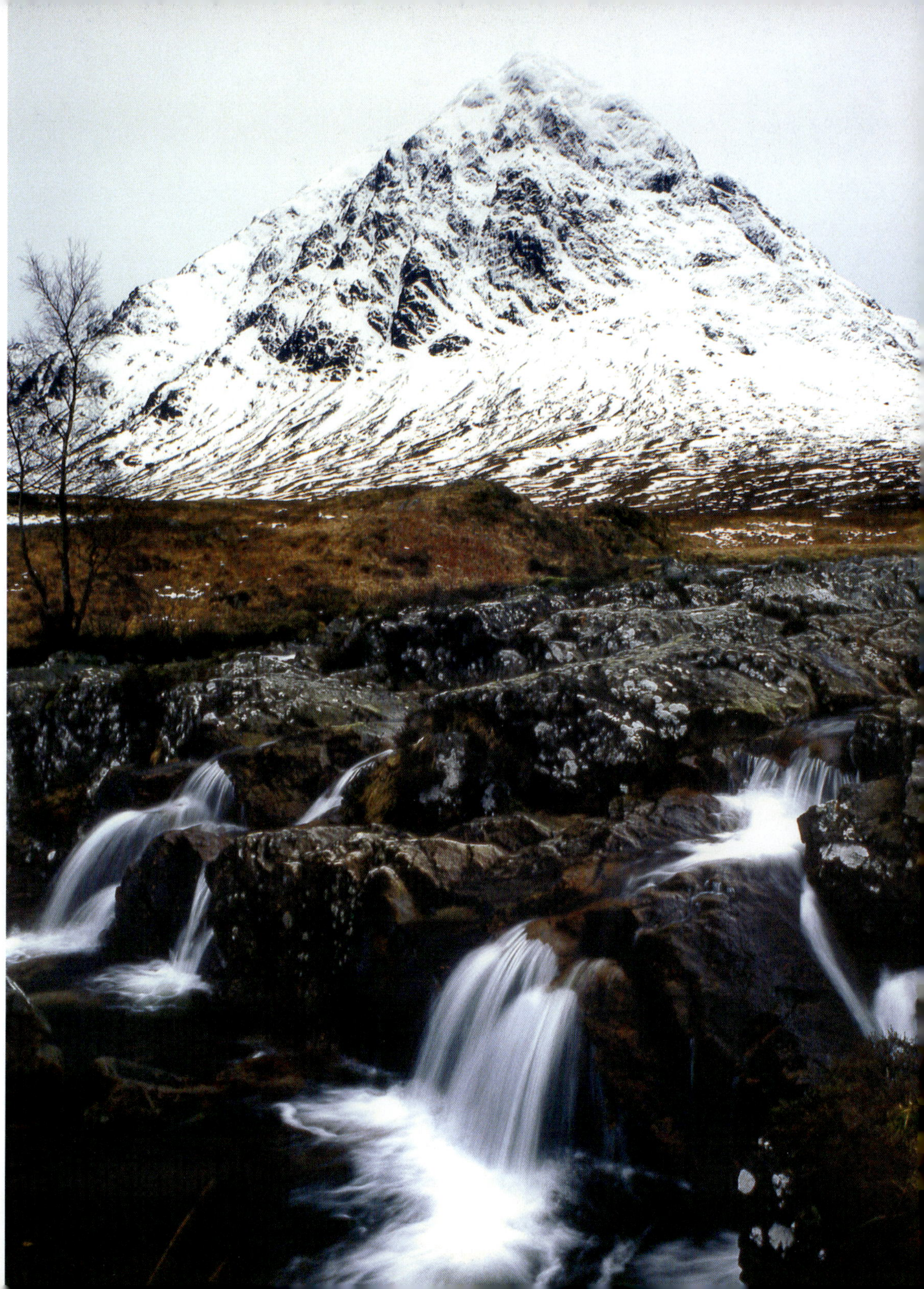

Seasonal changes.
The cascades on the River Coupall provide a foreground for this popular and defining view of Buachaille Etive Mor (Stob Dearg) one of the most familiar peaks of the Scottish Highlands. These two images are taken from the same viewpoint in autumn and winter.

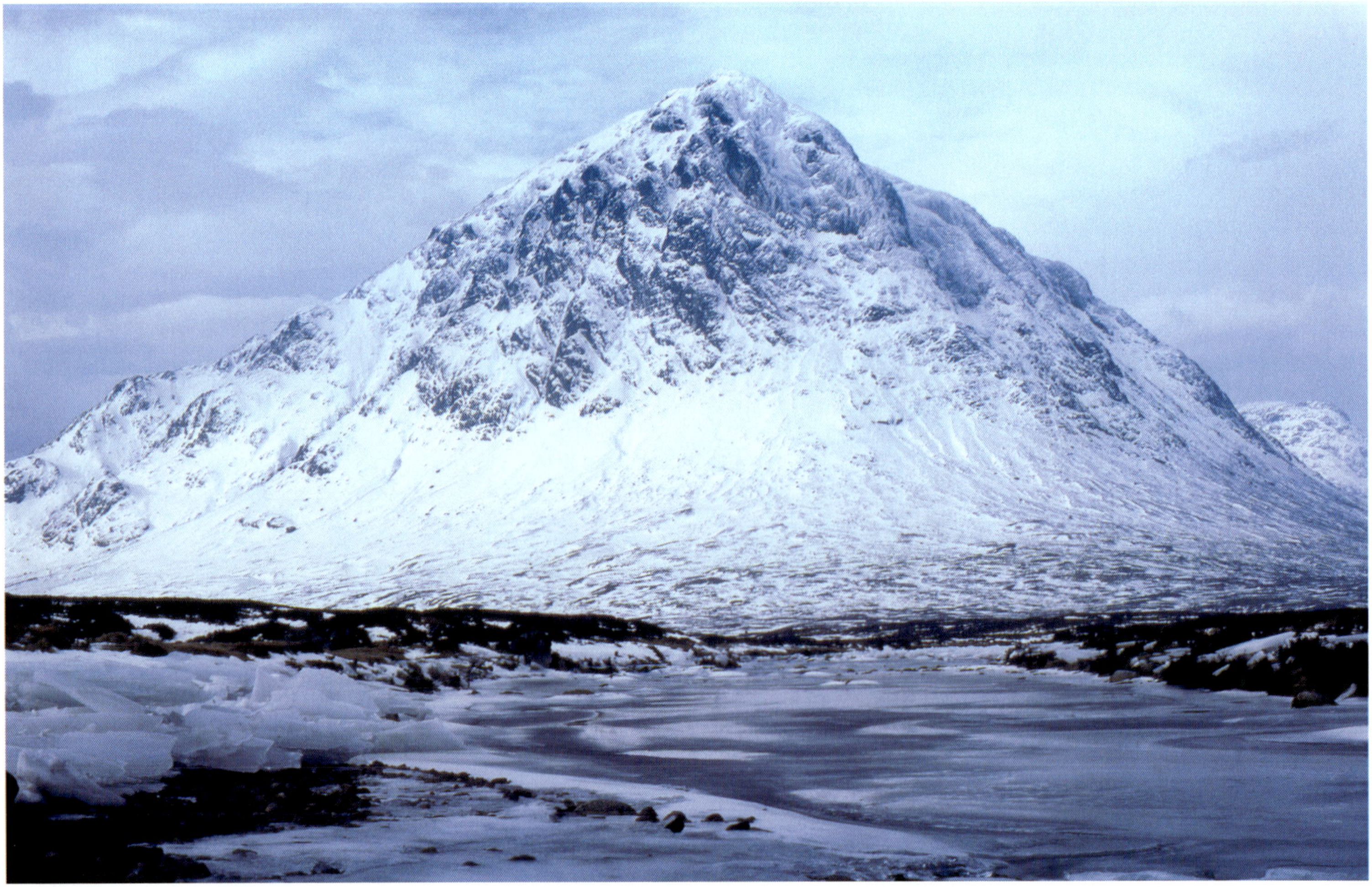

Frozen stillness.
A frozen River Etive leads the eye to Buachaille Etive Mor in its winter mantle.

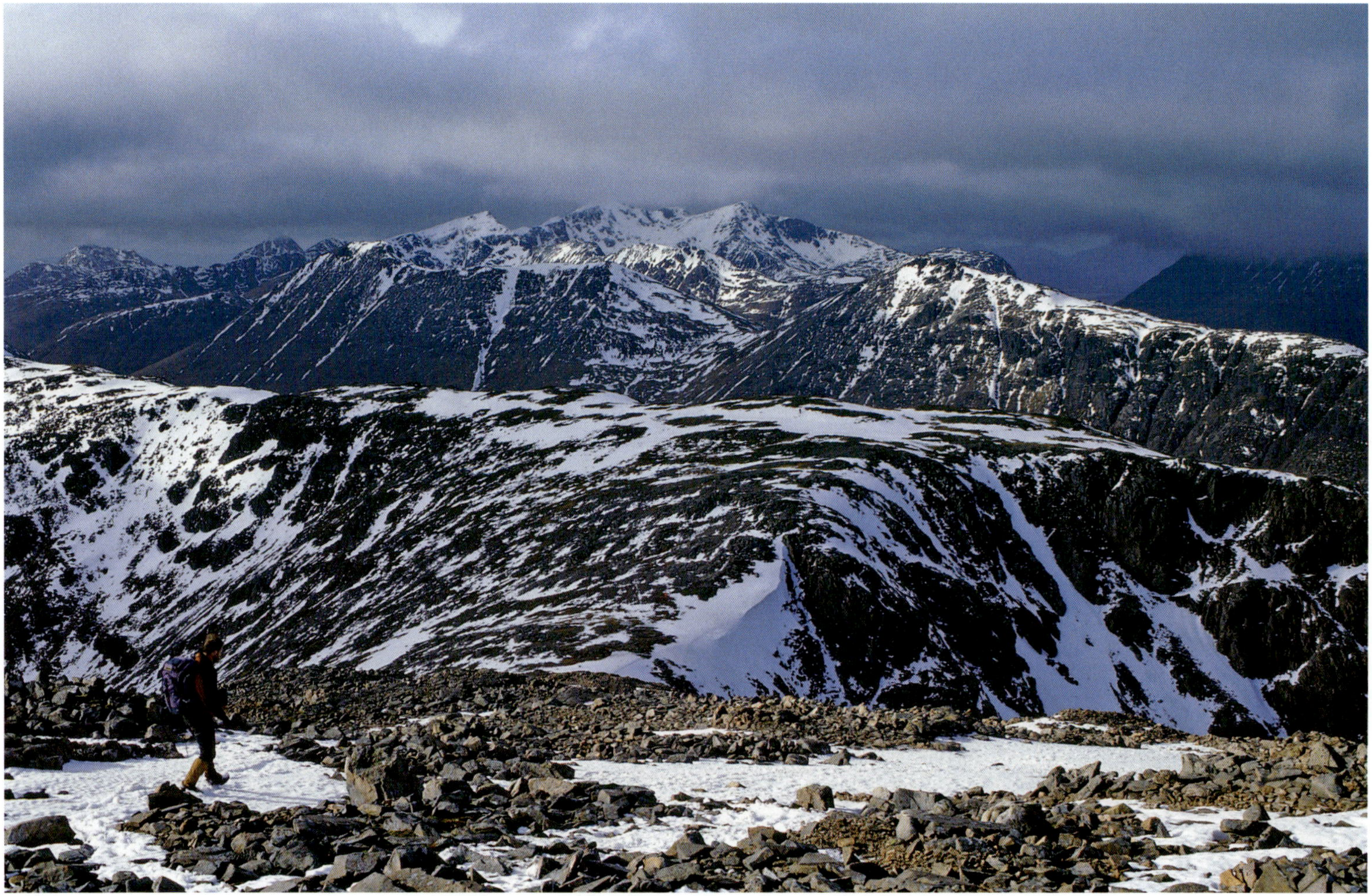

Transient light.
Dappled patches of sunlight on the Bidean nam Bian hills seen from Stob Dearg (Buachaille Etive Mor).

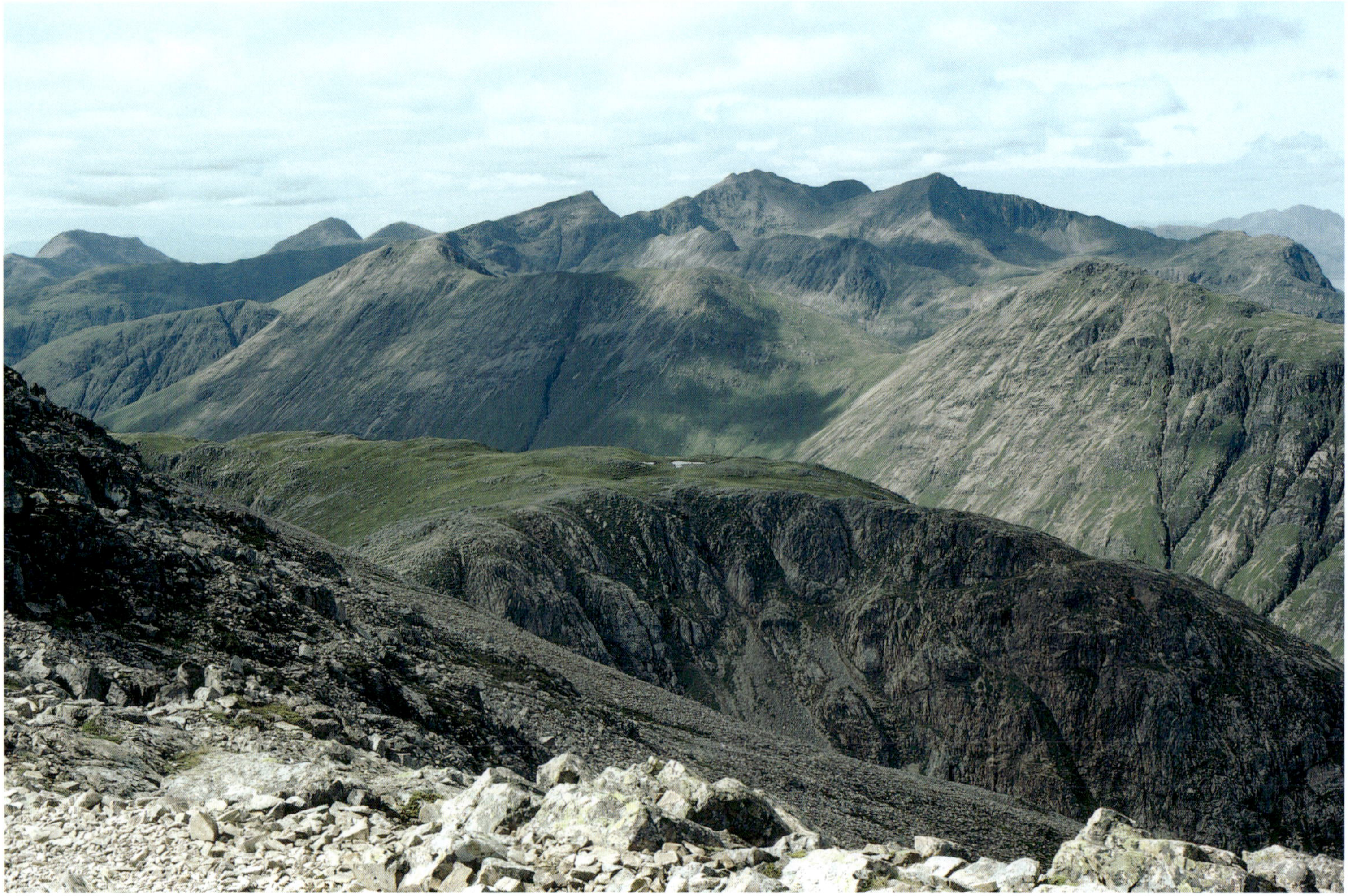

A summit view.
The Glencoe peaks fill the western skyline in this summer view from Stob Dearg (Buachaille Etive Mor) across the head of Coire na Tulaich.

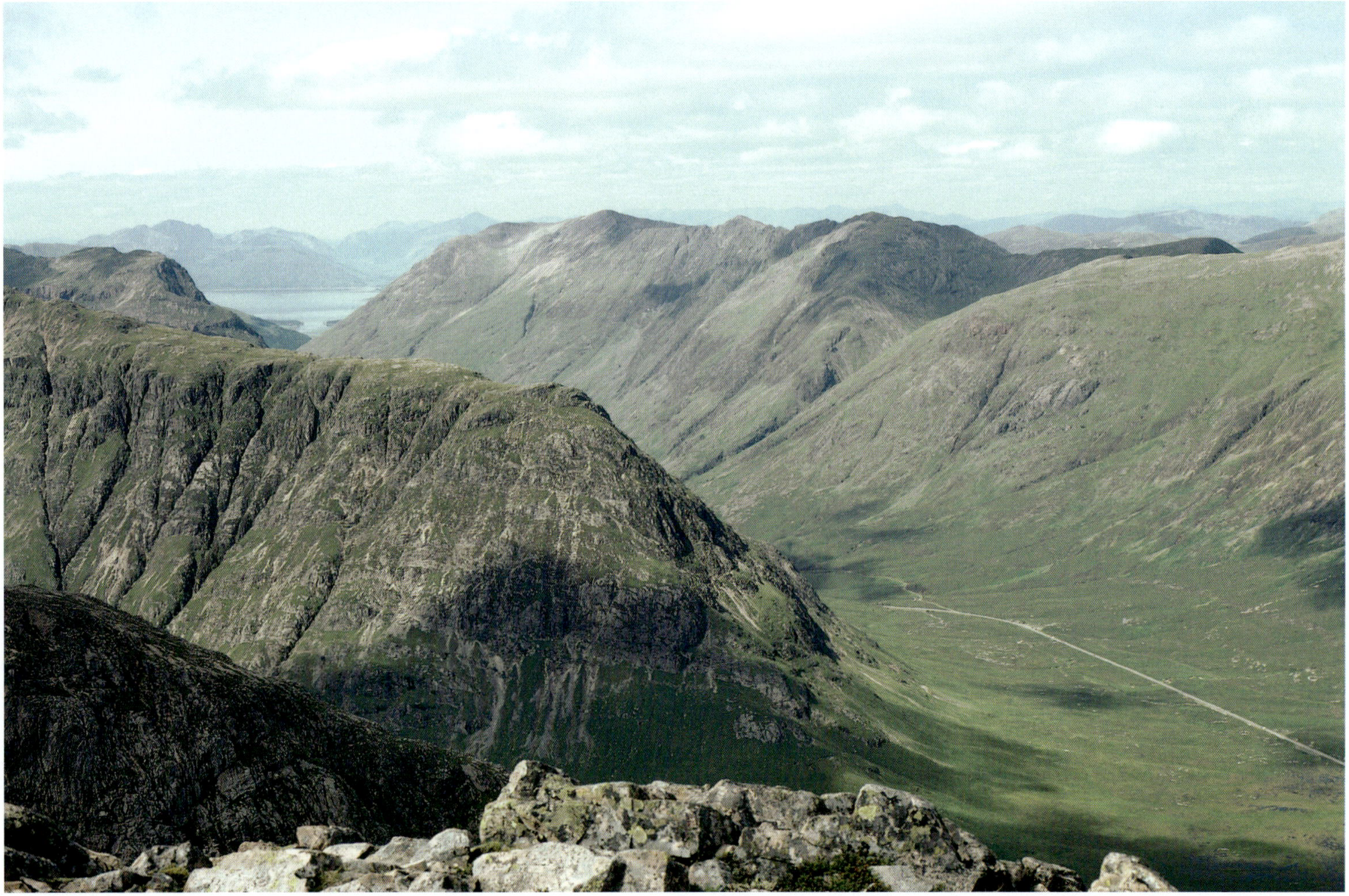

Pass of Glencoe.
The summit of Stob Dearg (Buachaille Etive Mor) offers a bird's-eye-view of the unmistakable V of the Pass of Glencoe and a distant Loch Linnhe.

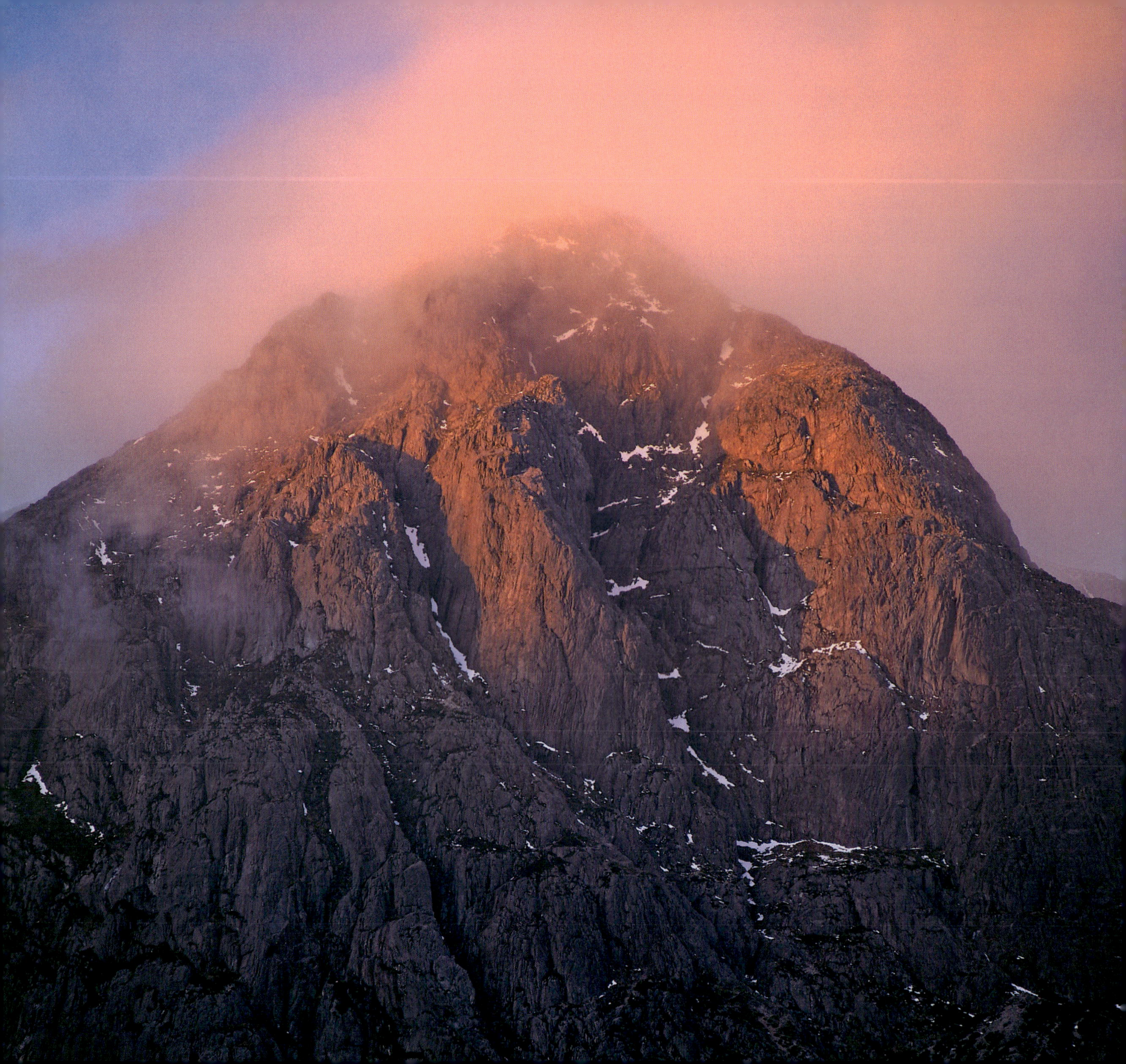

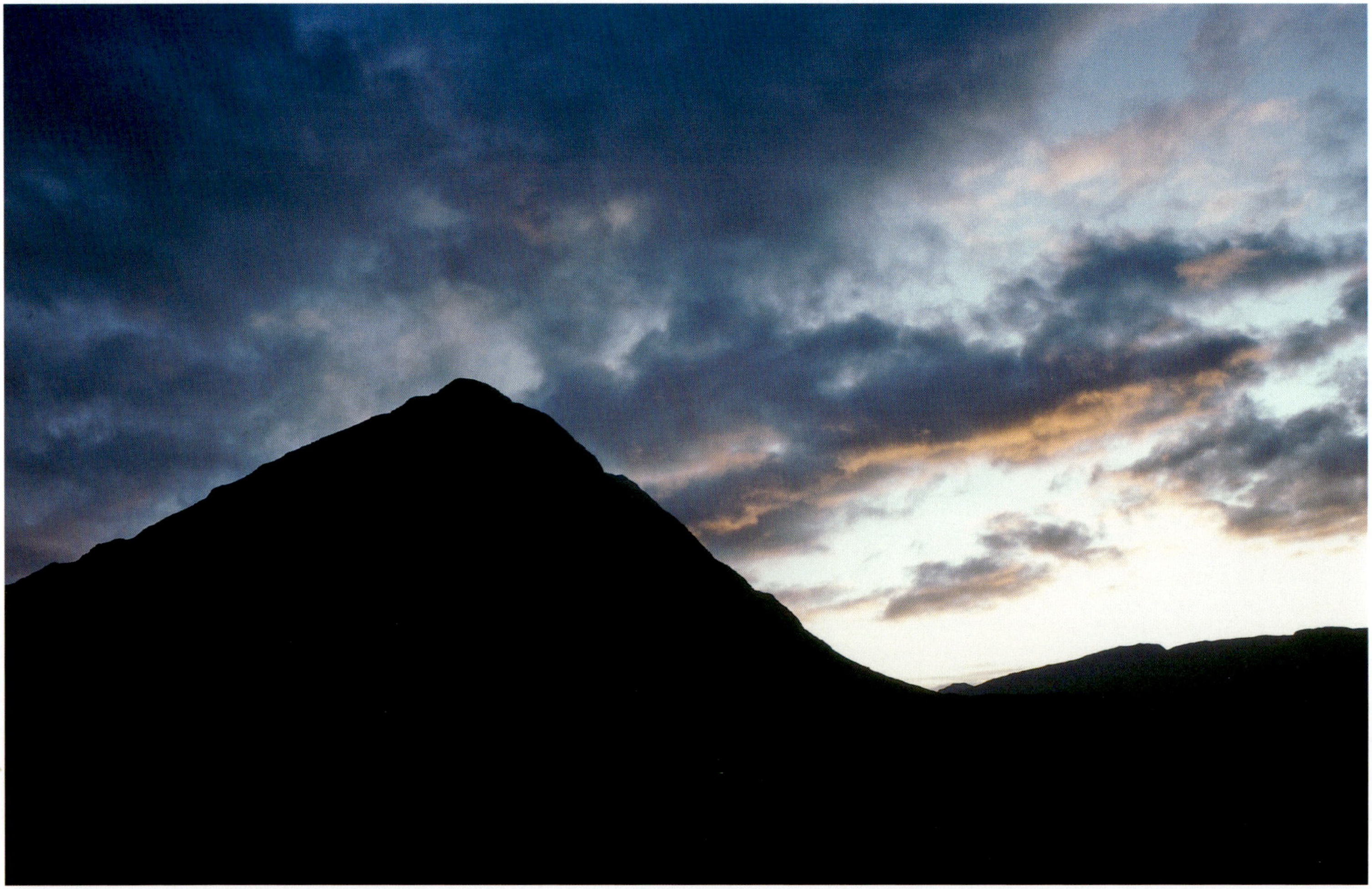

Silhouette.
The familiar profile of Stob Dearg silhouetted against the setting sun.

Opposite: First light.
The rising sun adds a red glow to a mist-crowned Buachaille Etive Mor.

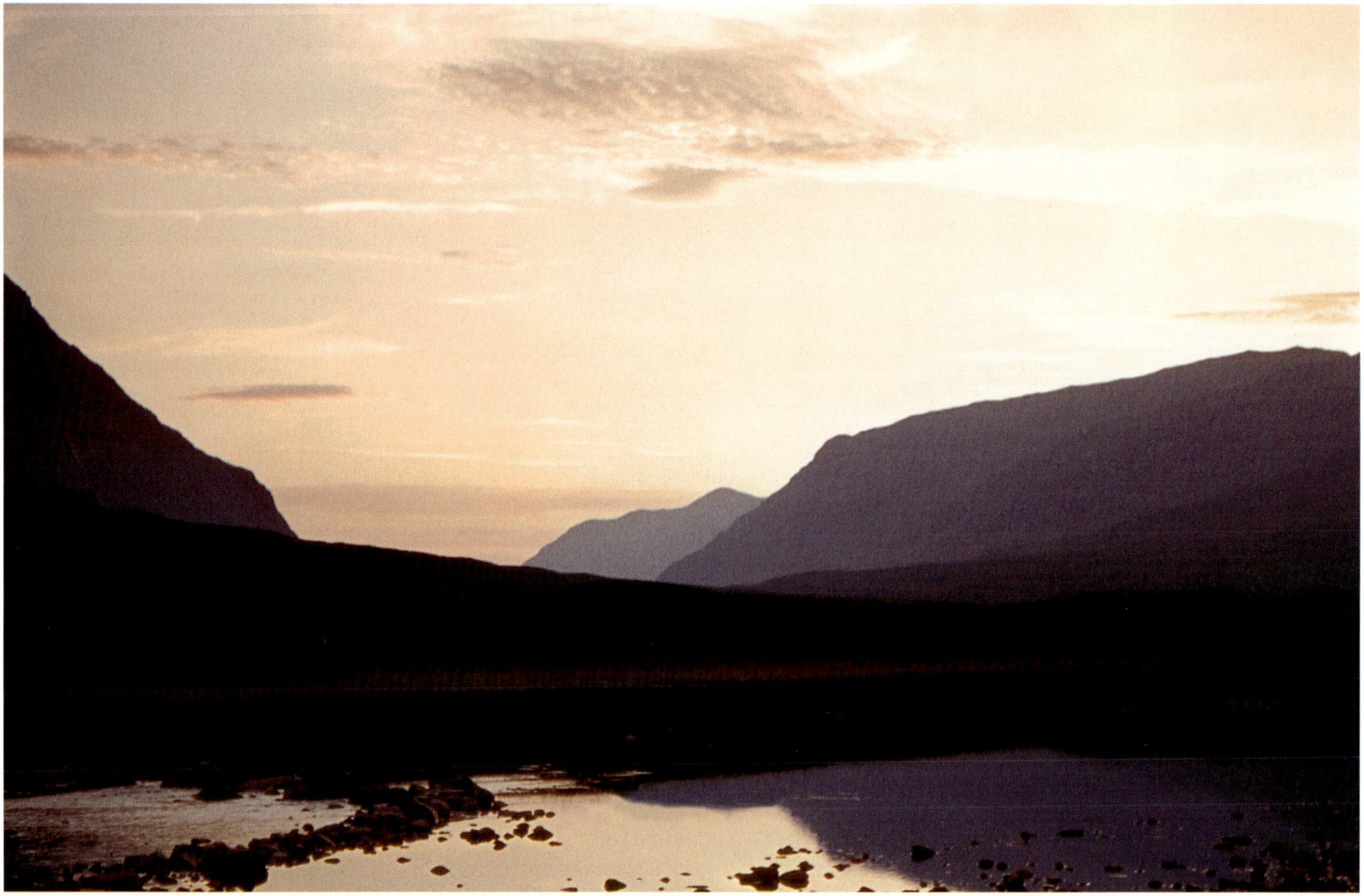

Twilight.
Evening falls in Glencoe framed by the shoulder of Buachaille Etive Mor and Aonach Eagach.

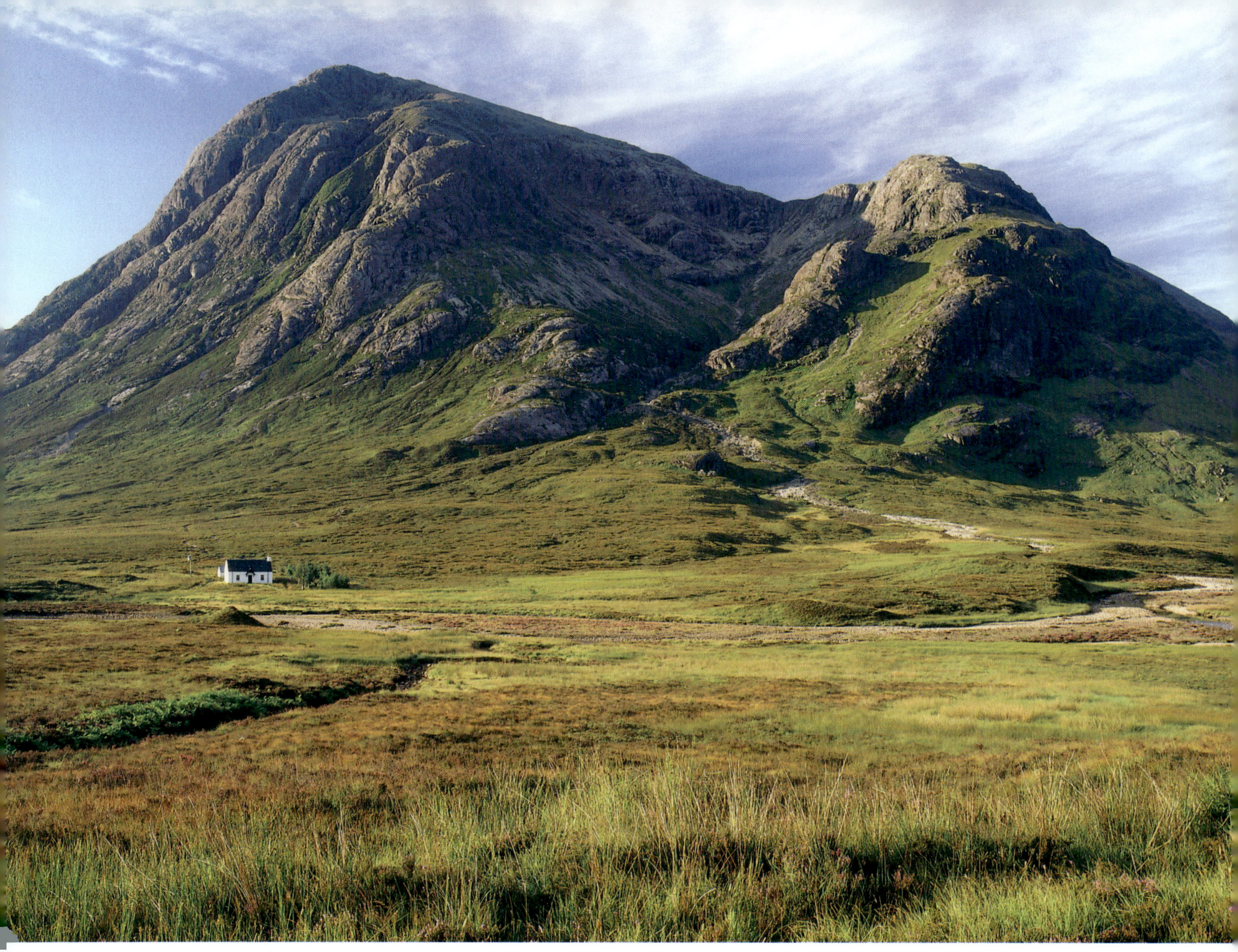

A rough hollow.

Lagangarbh (*the rough hollow*) and the Scottish Mountaineering Club hut overlooked by Coire na Tulaich, the relatively easy way up Buachaille Etive Mor. From Lagangarbh, in the opposite direction, the old military road built by General Caulfield in 1750, and now part of the West Highland Way trail, zigzags north over the Devil's Staircase to Kinlochleven.

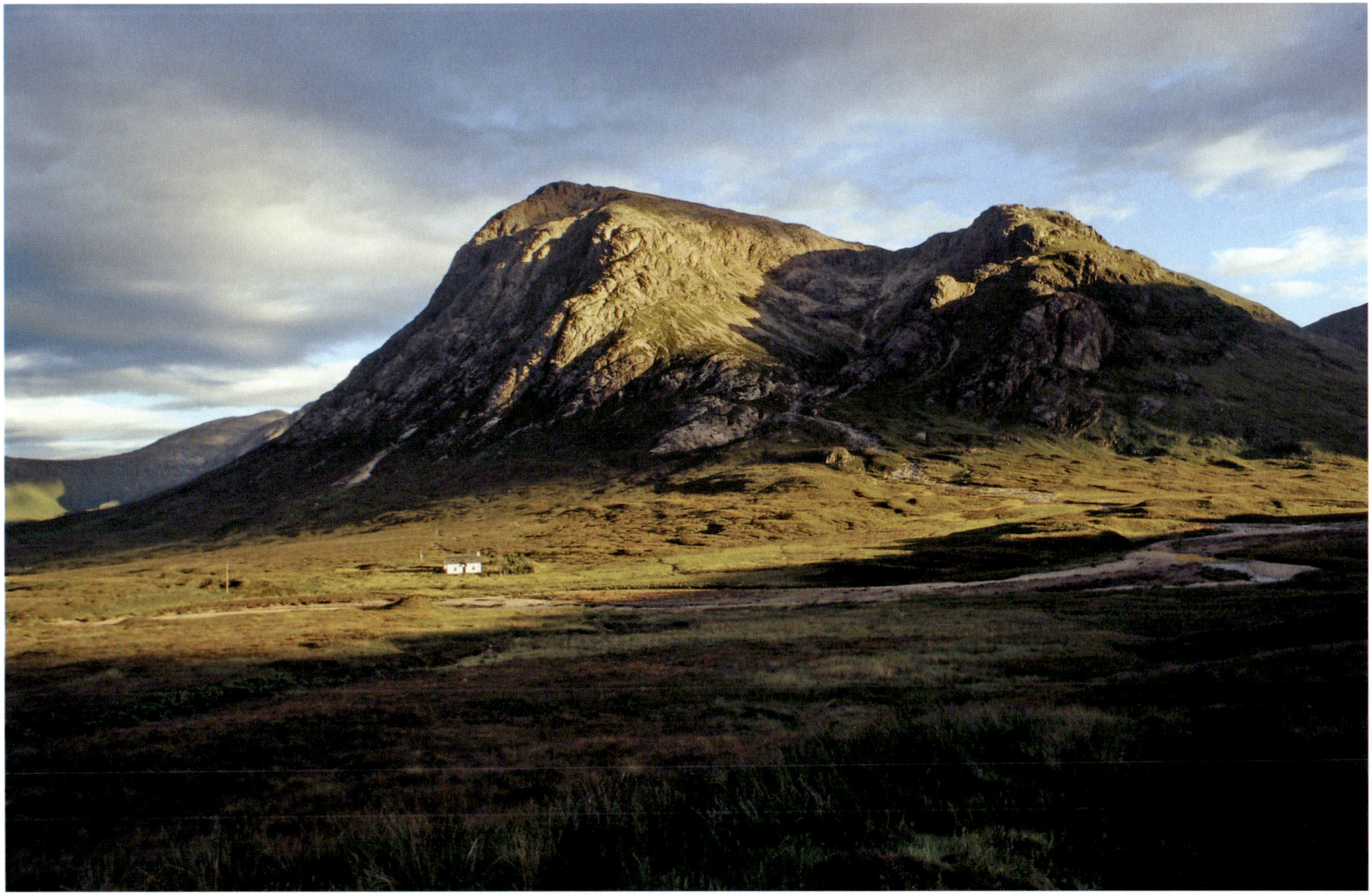

Lingering light.
The lingering light of a summer's evening picks out Lagangarbh and Buachaille Etive Mor.

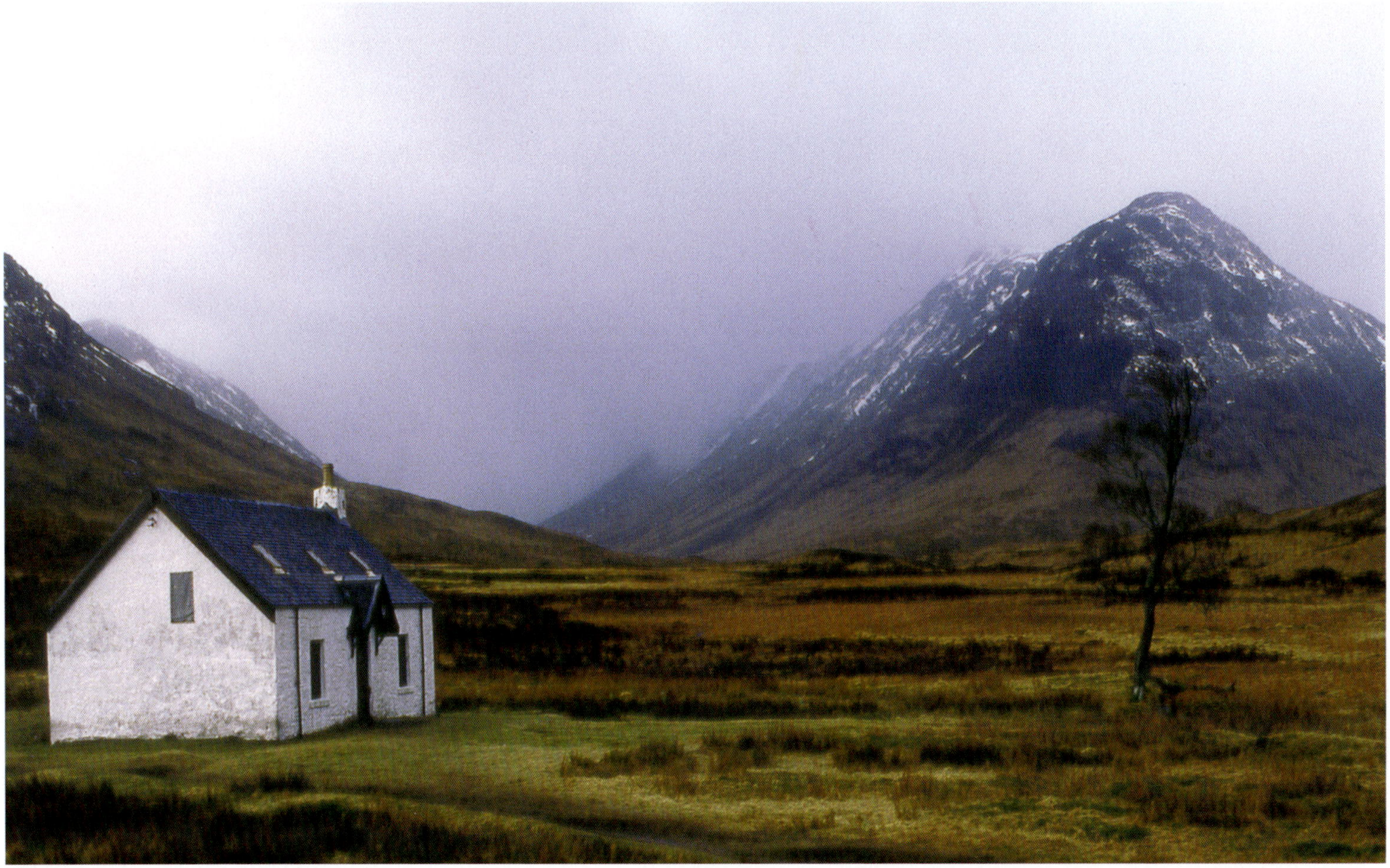

Des res.

Lagangarbh and the Scottish Mountaineering Club hut at the entrance to Larig Gartain which separates Buachaille Etive Mor and Buachaille Etive Beag (*the small herdsman of Etive*).

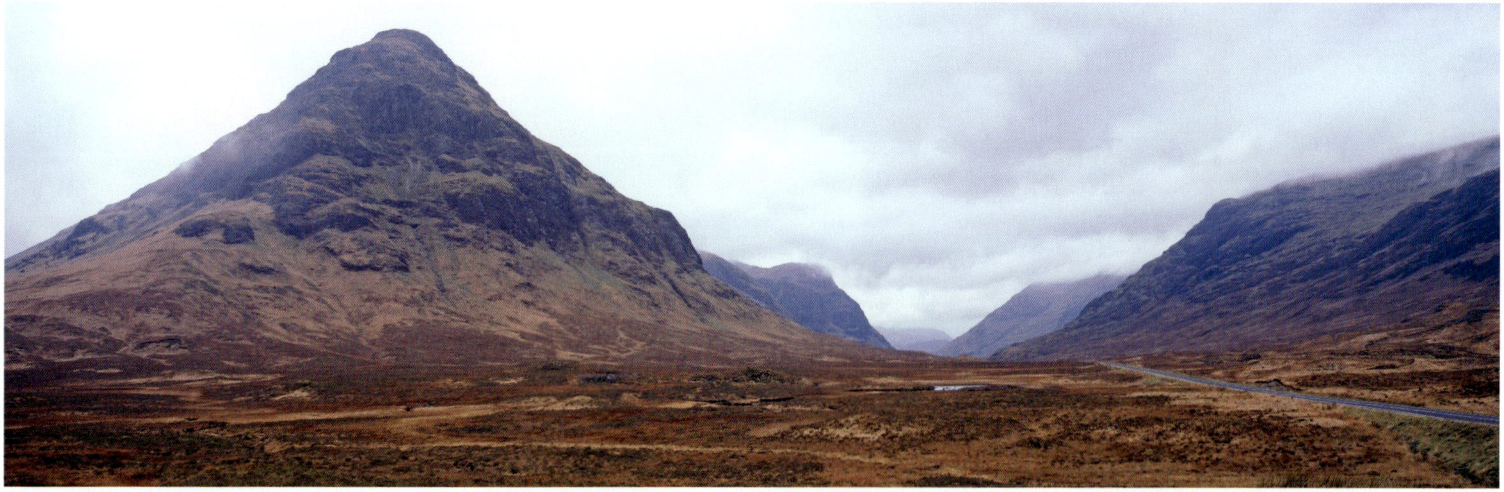

A cloudy morning.
A typical cloudy morning in Glencoe. The A82 road passes below Buachaille Etive Beag before plunging into the depths of Glencoe.

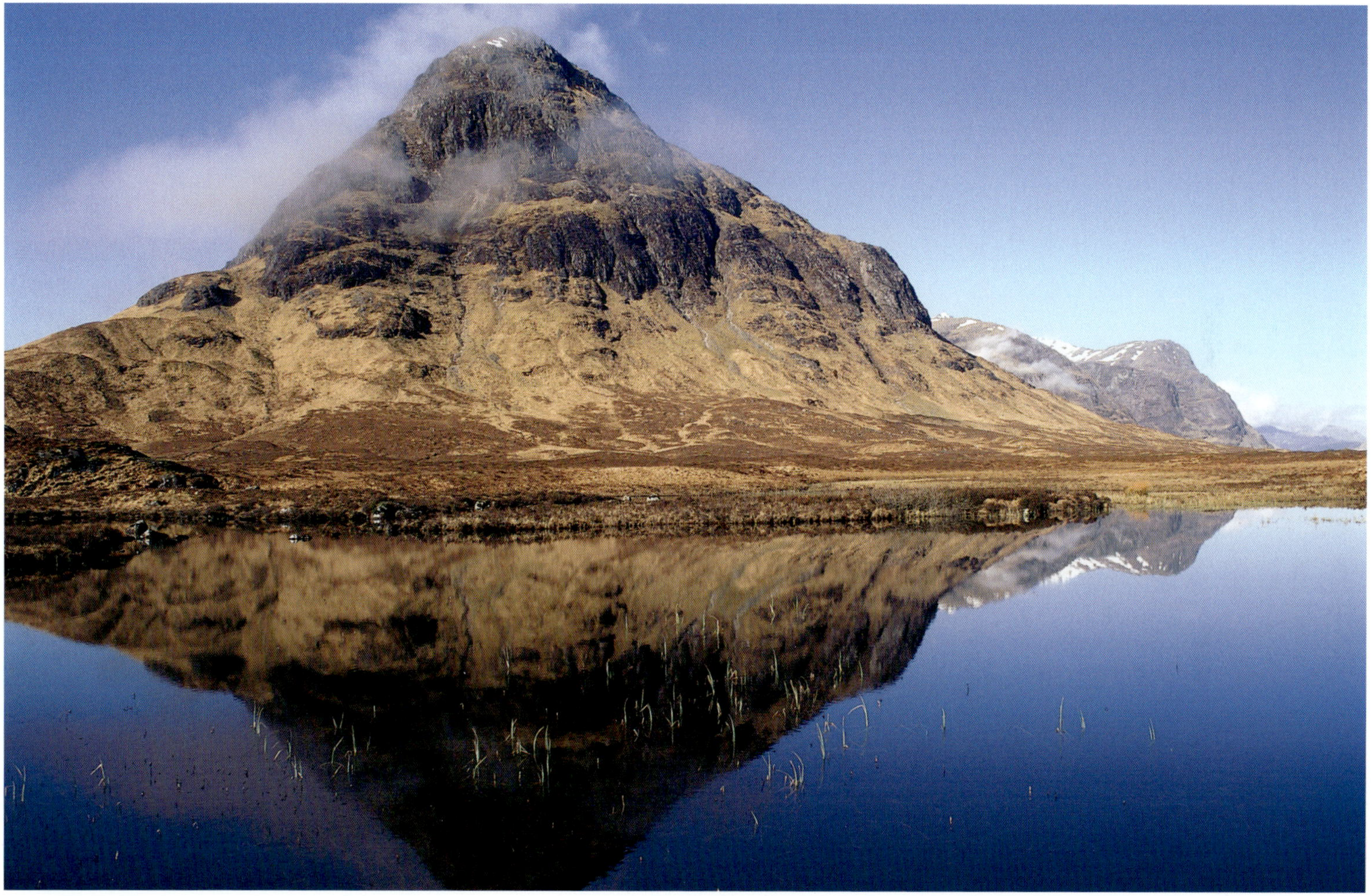

Winter reflections.
Buachaille Etive Beag is beautifully reflected in the still waters of Lochan na Fola (*the little loch of blood*) on a stunning winter's morning.

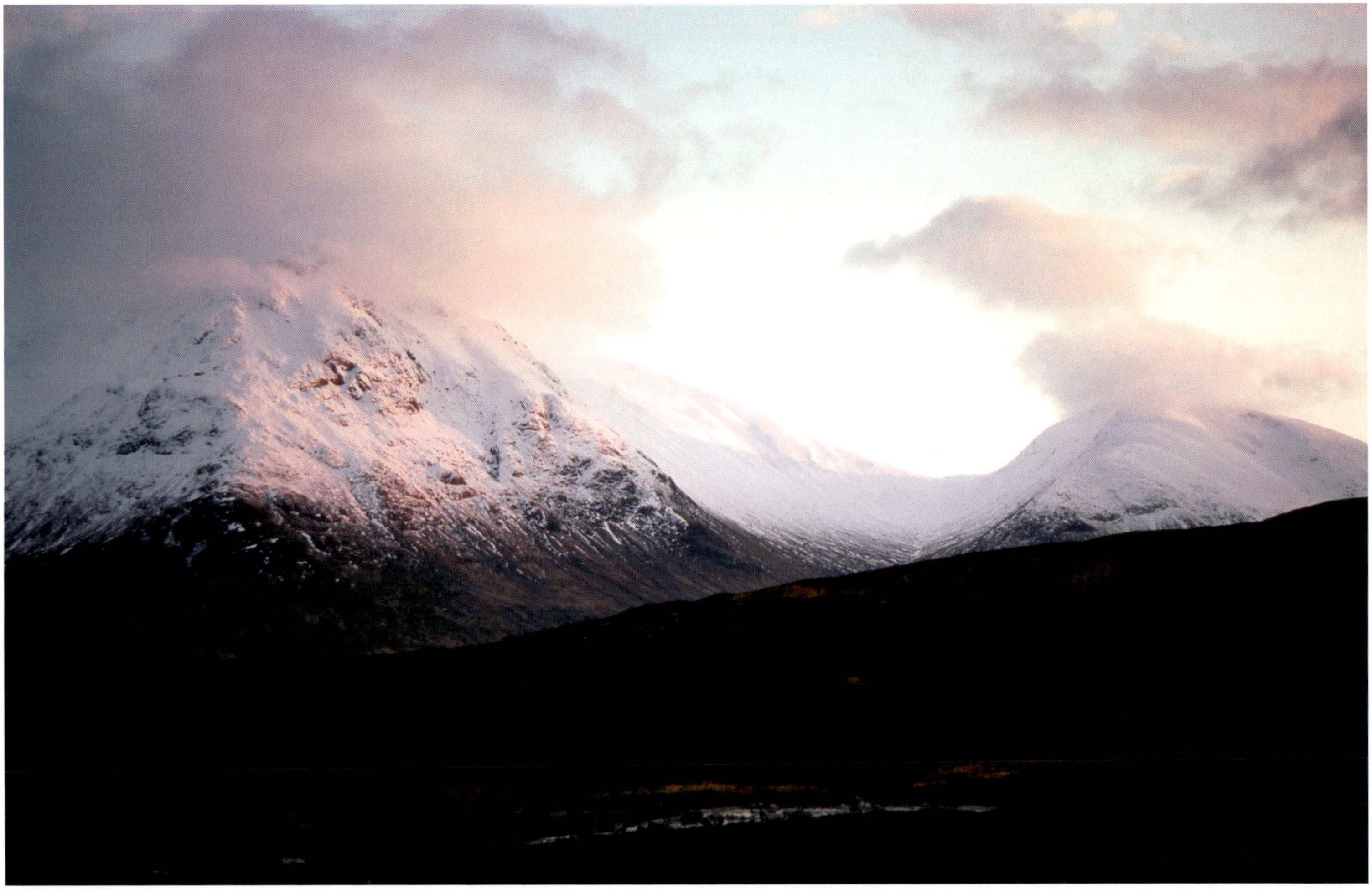

End of the day.
The warm light of a winter sunset illuminates Buachaille Etive Beag.

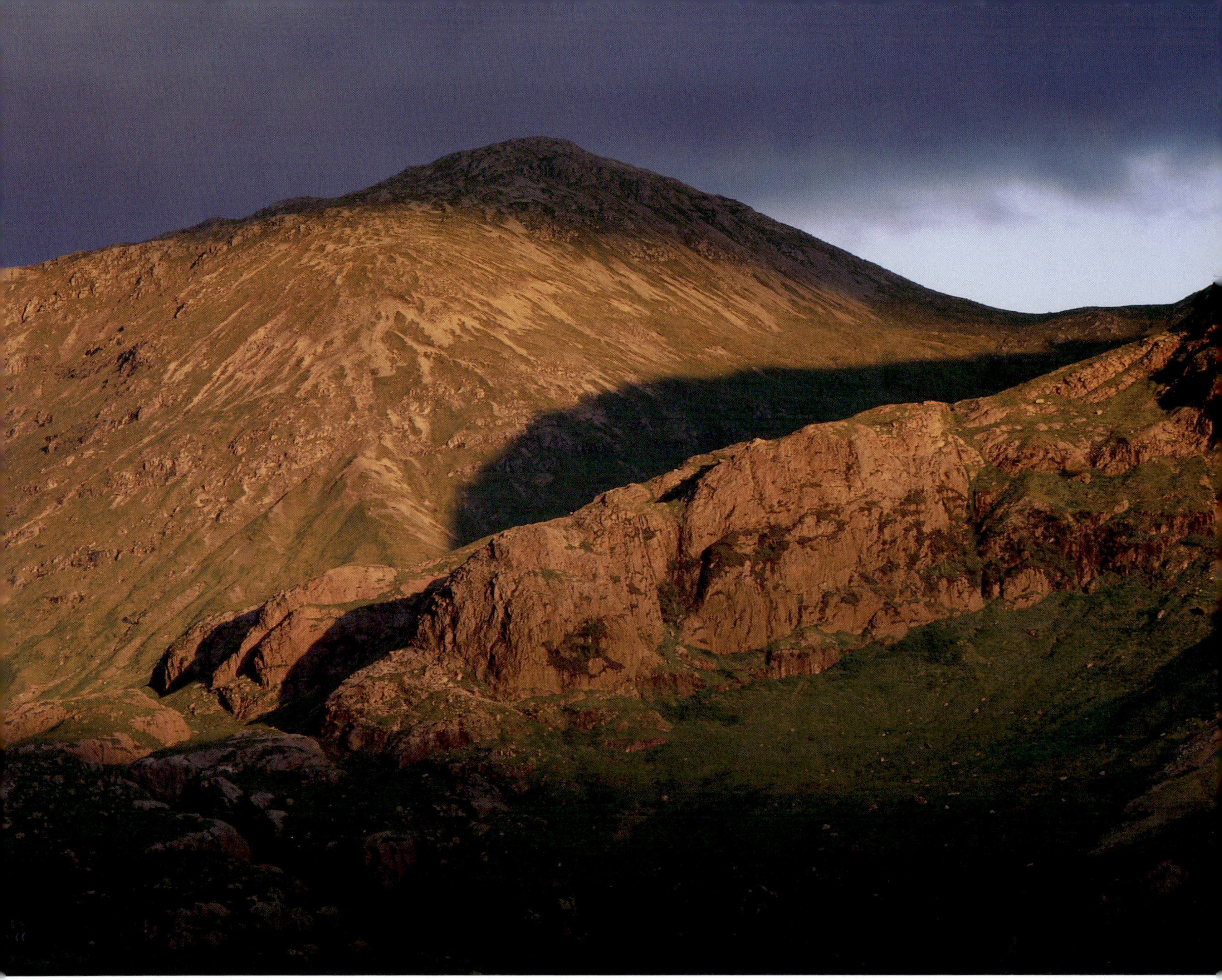

Summer evening.
Buachaille Etive Beag at dusk seen across Larig Gartain

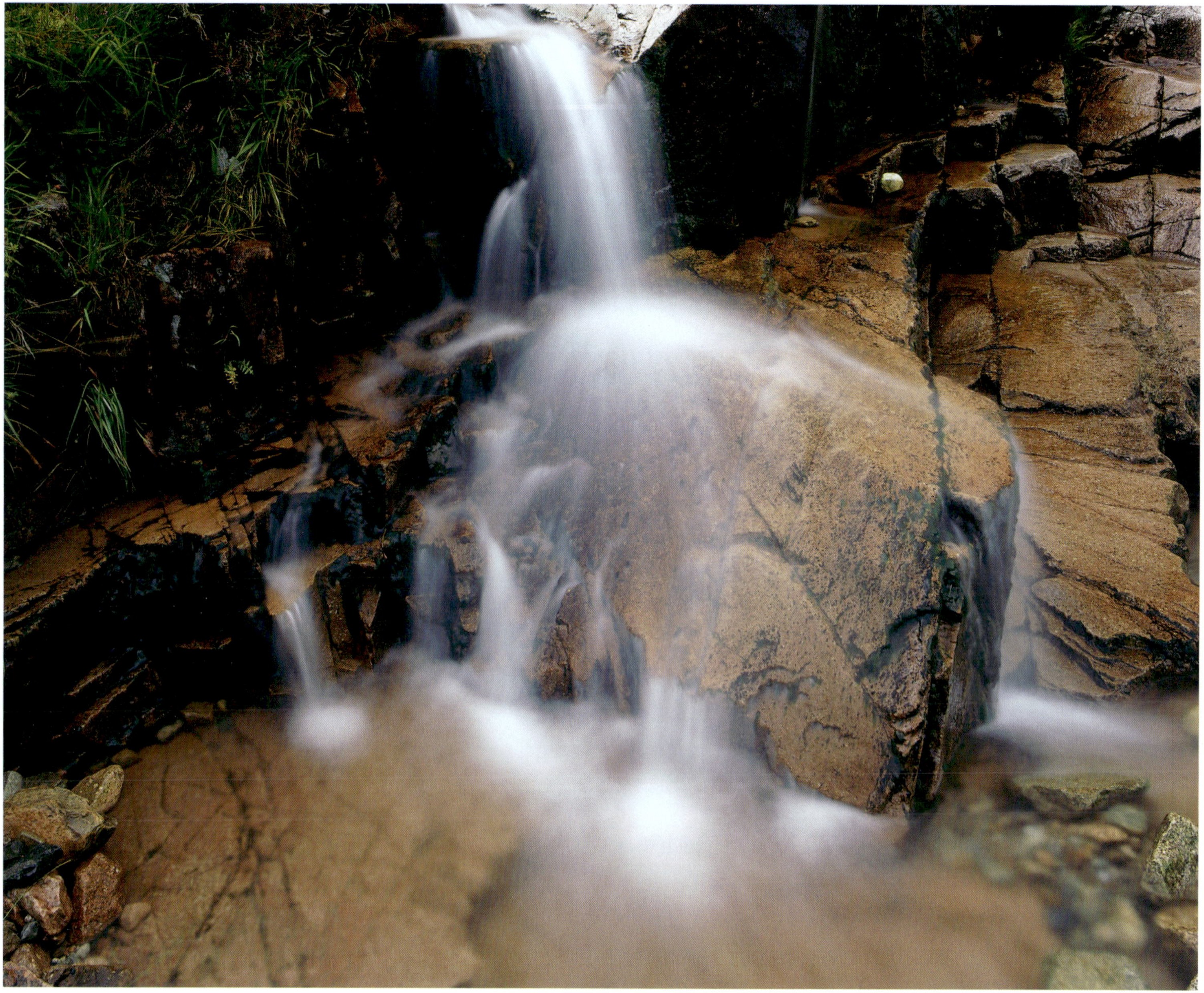

Silky flow.
Water flows silkily over a boulder beside the River Coe.

A framed view.
A tree and the River Coe act as a frame in this popular roadside view from the River Coe close to the watershed.

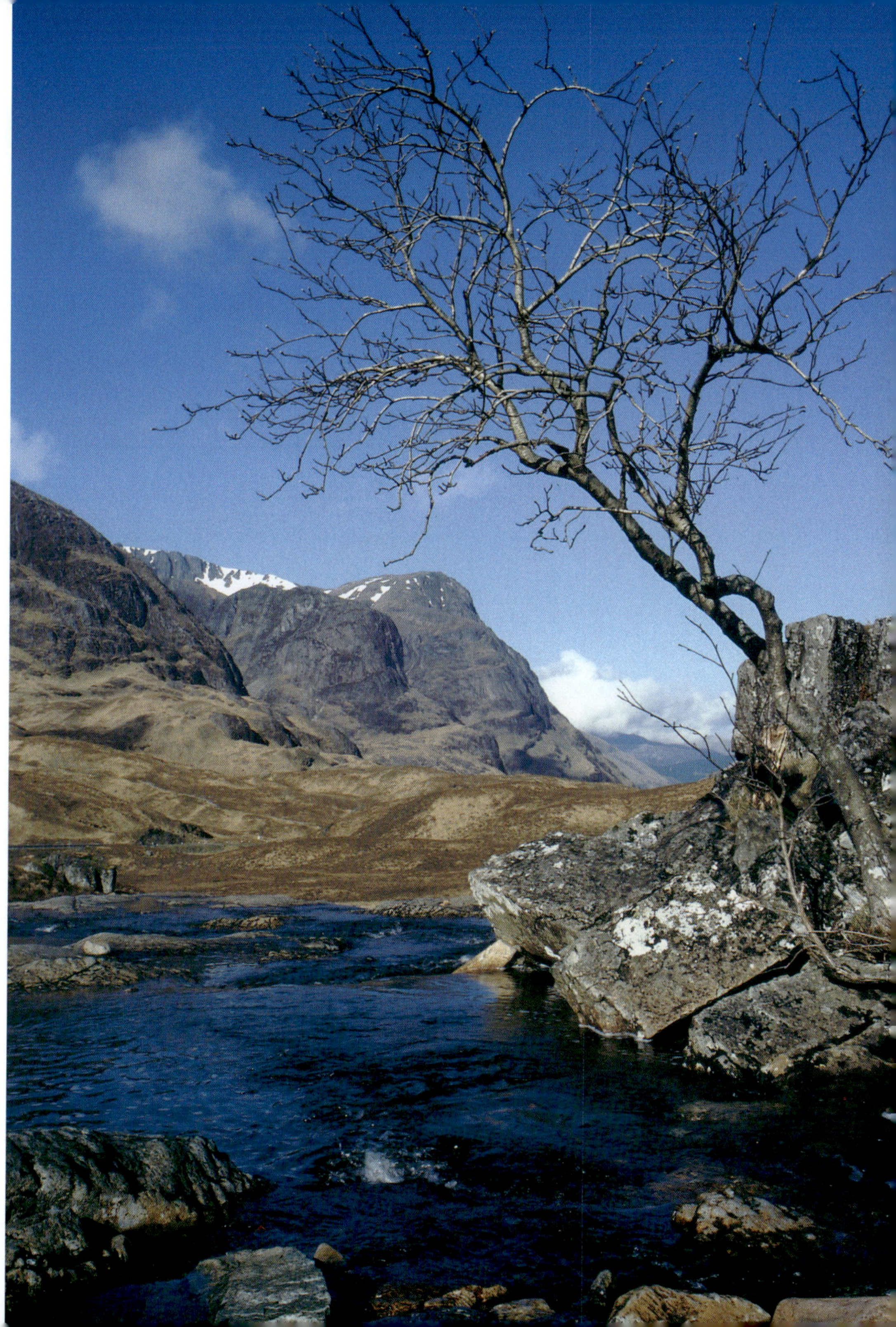

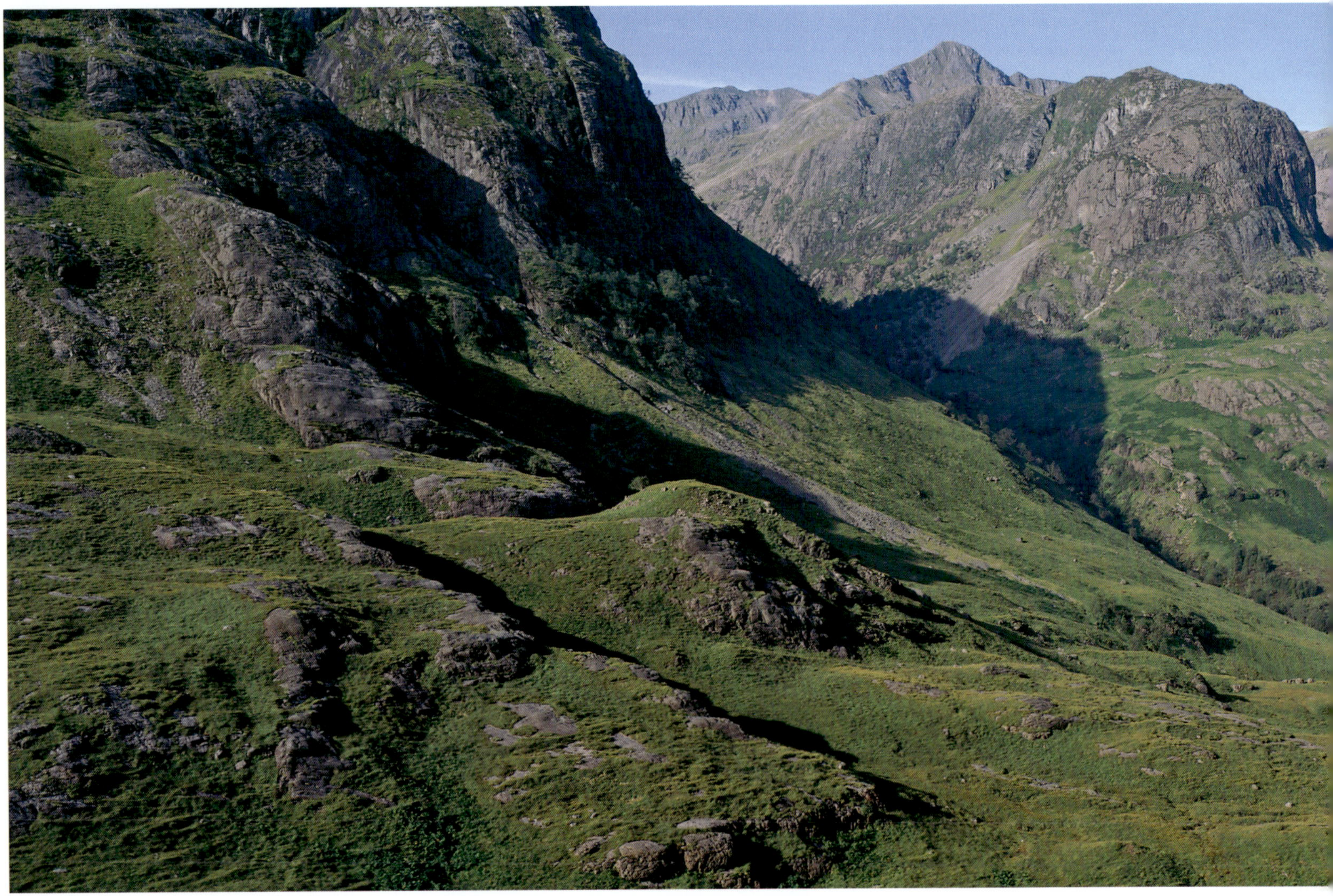

A defining vista.

In this famous view from just above The Study, or Anvil, the A82 sweeps down through Glencoe flanked by the towering craggy architecture of the Bidean nam Bian massif (left) and the jagged ridge of the Aonach Eagach (right). The name Study, is a corruption of Stiddie an old Scots name for Anvil and the Gaelic meaning for the nearby rocky knoll of Inneoin a'Cheathaich, is *Anvil of the Mist*.

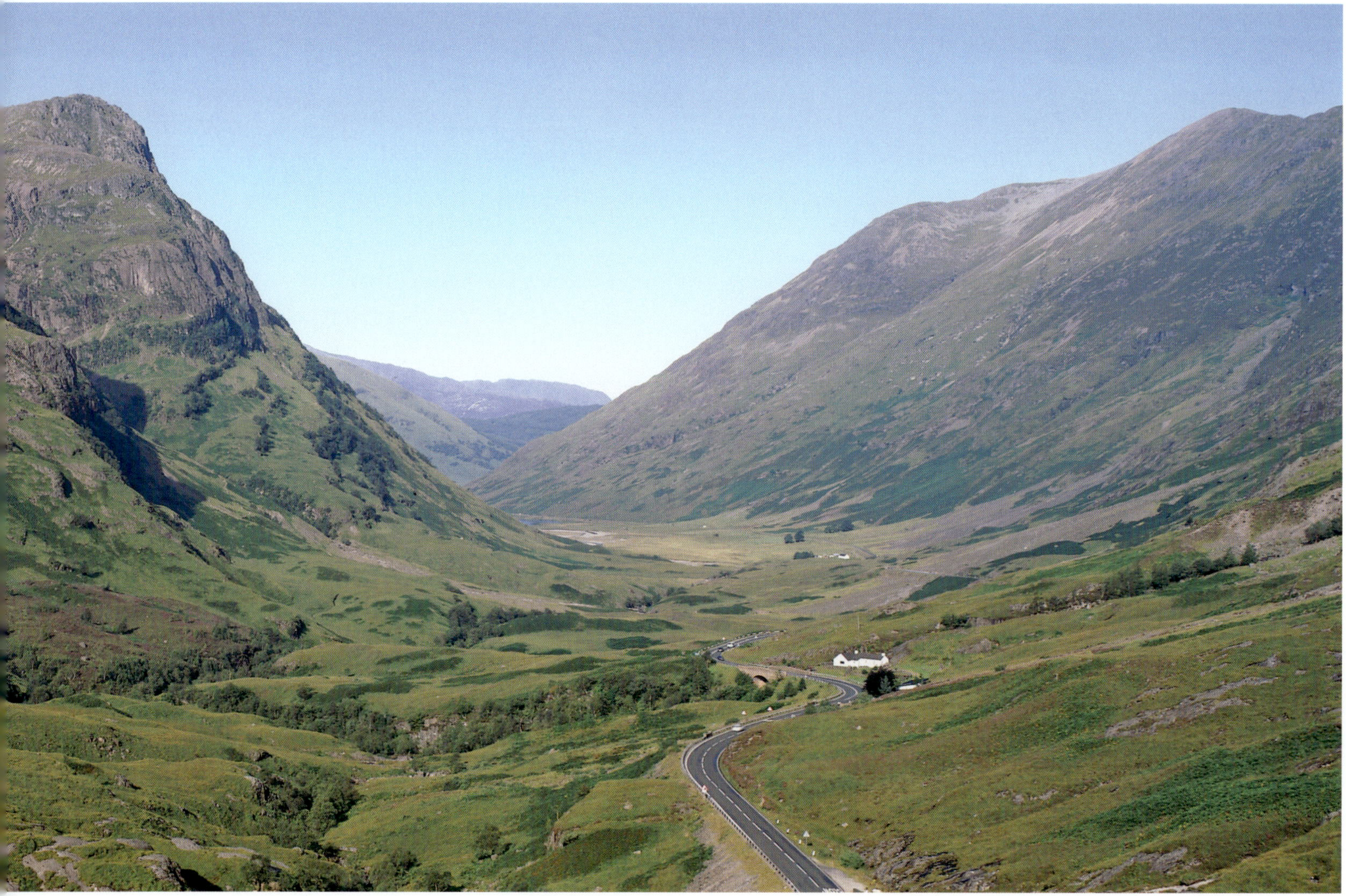

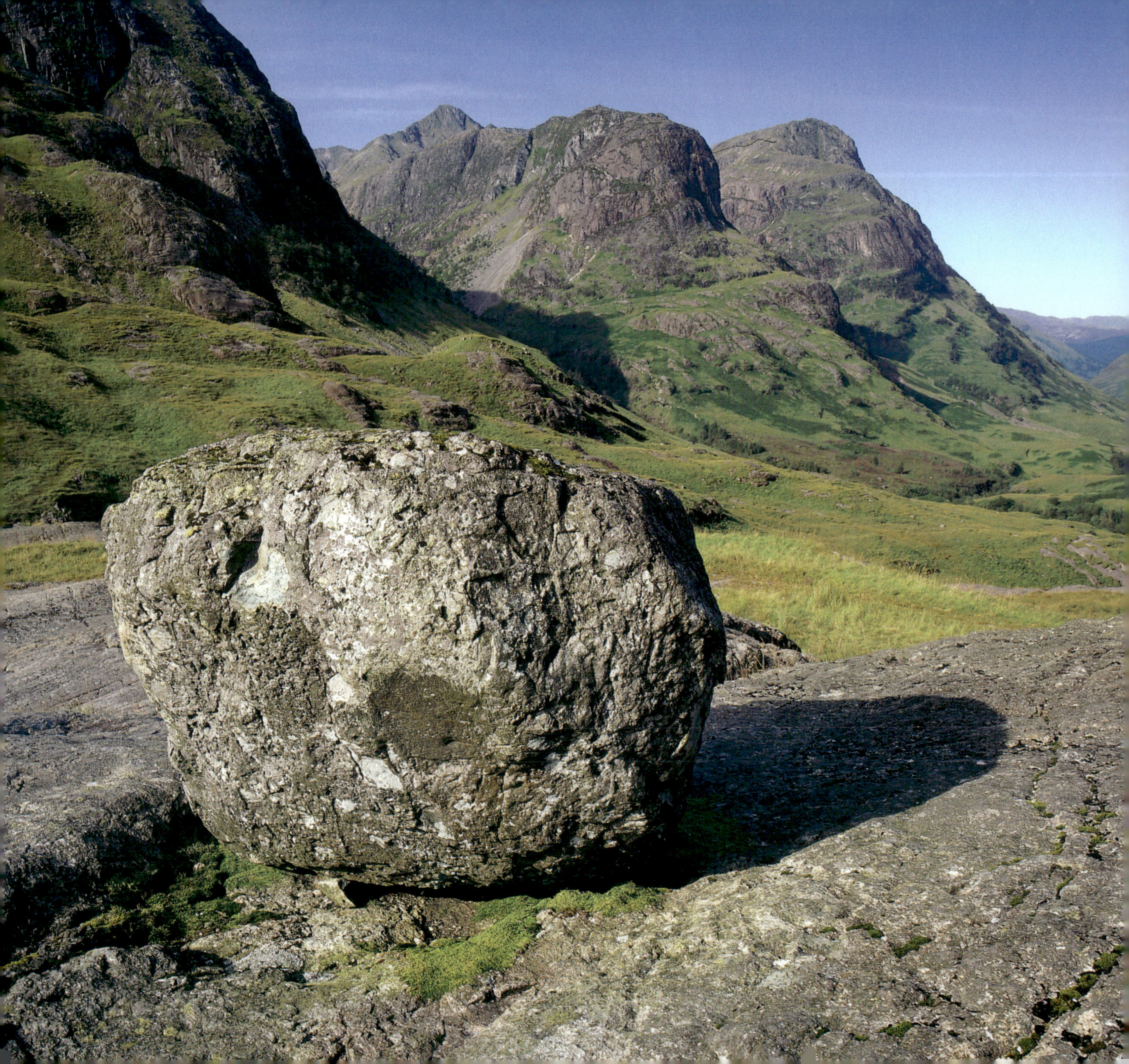

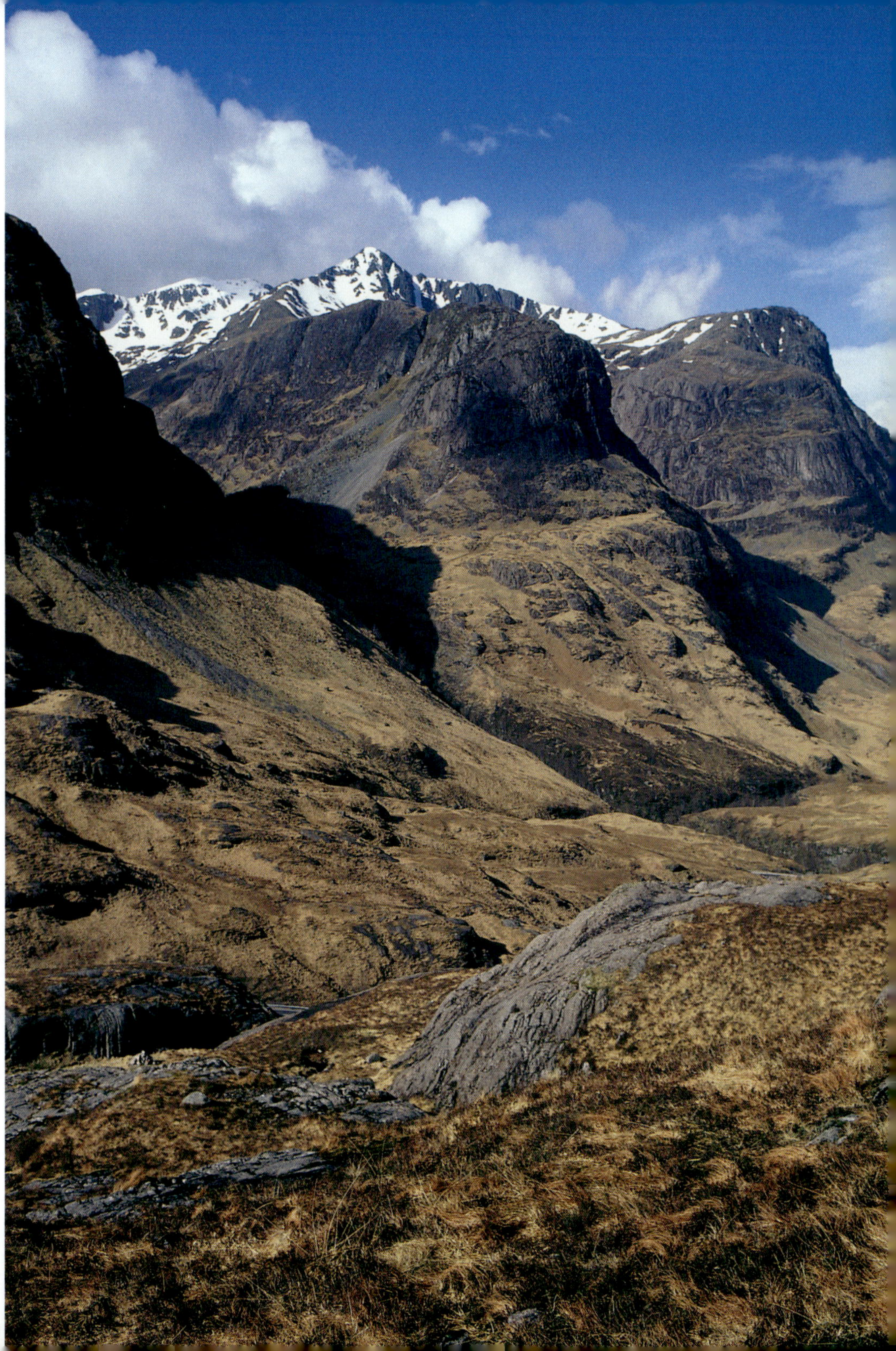

A view from The Study.
The Study, or Anvil rock, above the waters of the Allt Lairig Eilde, provides a great perspective of the snow-covered Bidean nam Bian massif.

Opposite: Erratic boulder.
An erratic boulder beside the old Tyndrum – Glencoe road, forms a classic viewpoint of the Three Sisters. The Sisters – Beinn Fhada, Gearr Aonach *(the slender, lithe-looking one)* and Aonach Dubh – are the craggy ends of long spurs sweeping down from Bidean nam Bian.

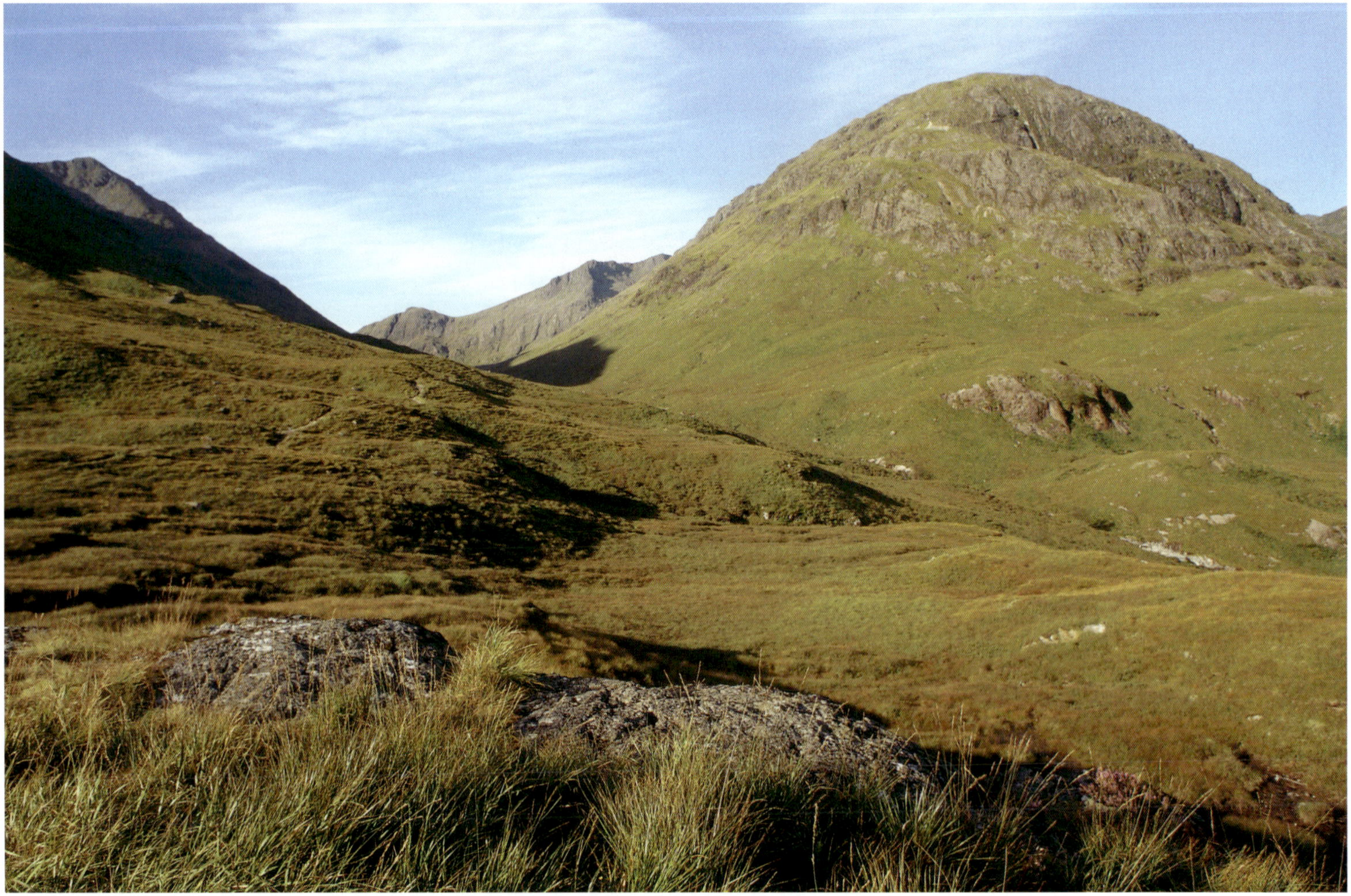

Side valley.
Lairig Eilde (*the pass of the hinds*) separates Beinn Fhada (right) from Buachaille Etive Beag. In this summer view the prominent spur of Sron na Lairig is visible at the head of the valley.

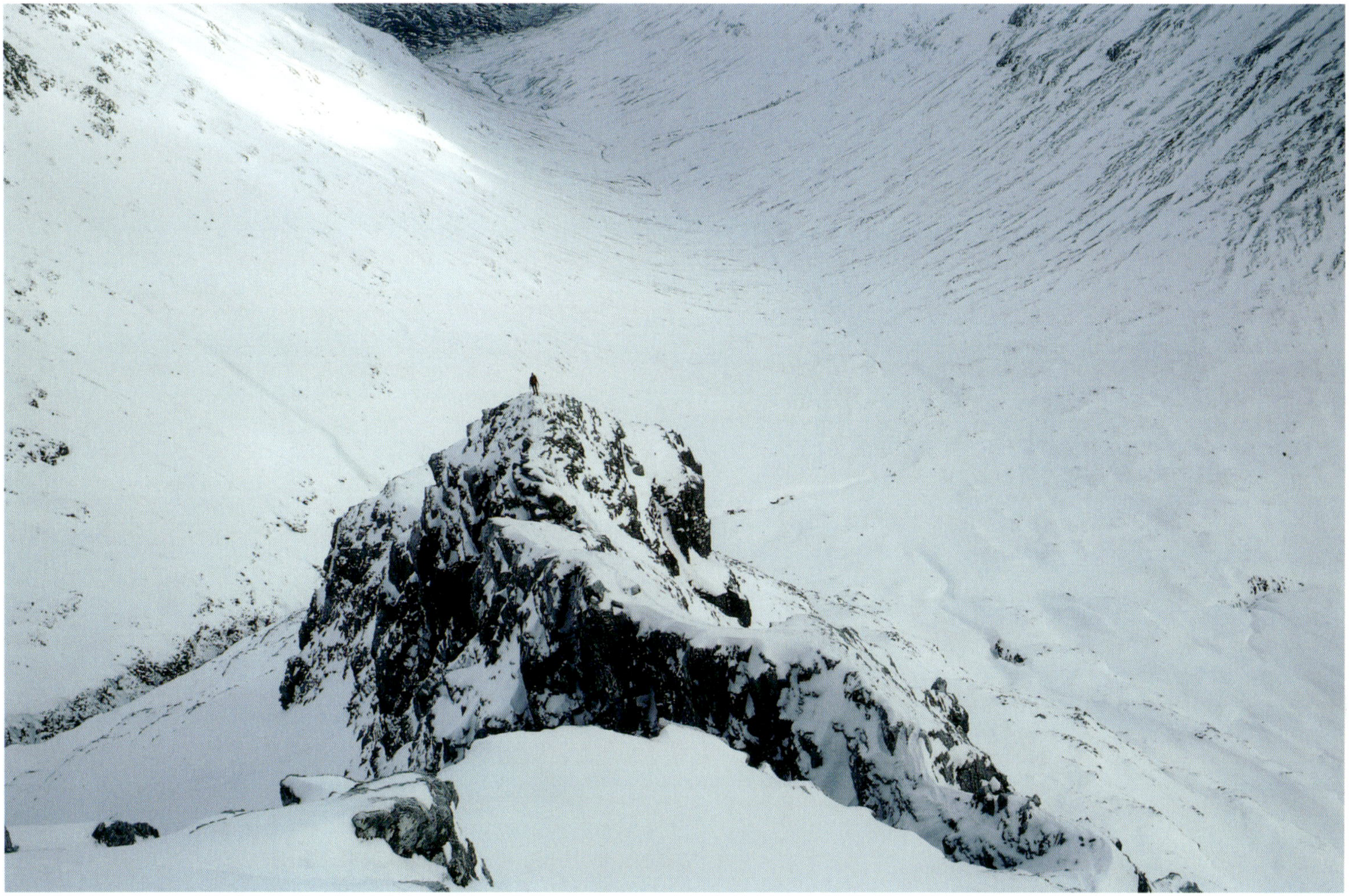

A snowy prospect.
The snowy spur of Sron na Lairig offers a great view down Lairig Eilde.

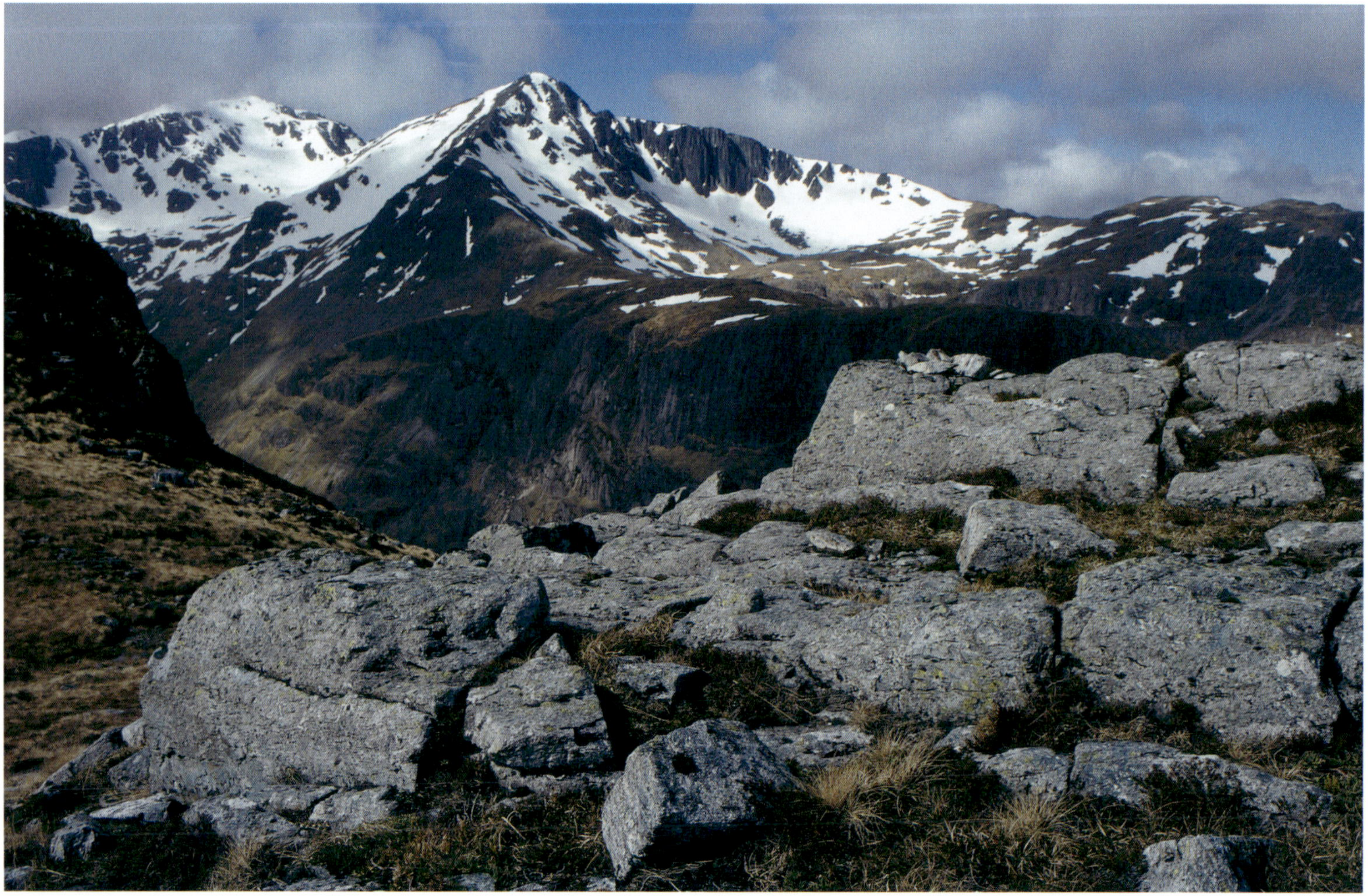

Vista from the ridge.
The rocky ridge of Beinn Fhada is a great place to view the impressive summits and cliff-rimmed corries of Stob Coire nan Lochan and Bidean nam Bian *(peak of the mountains)* rising beyond the trench of Coire Gabhail.

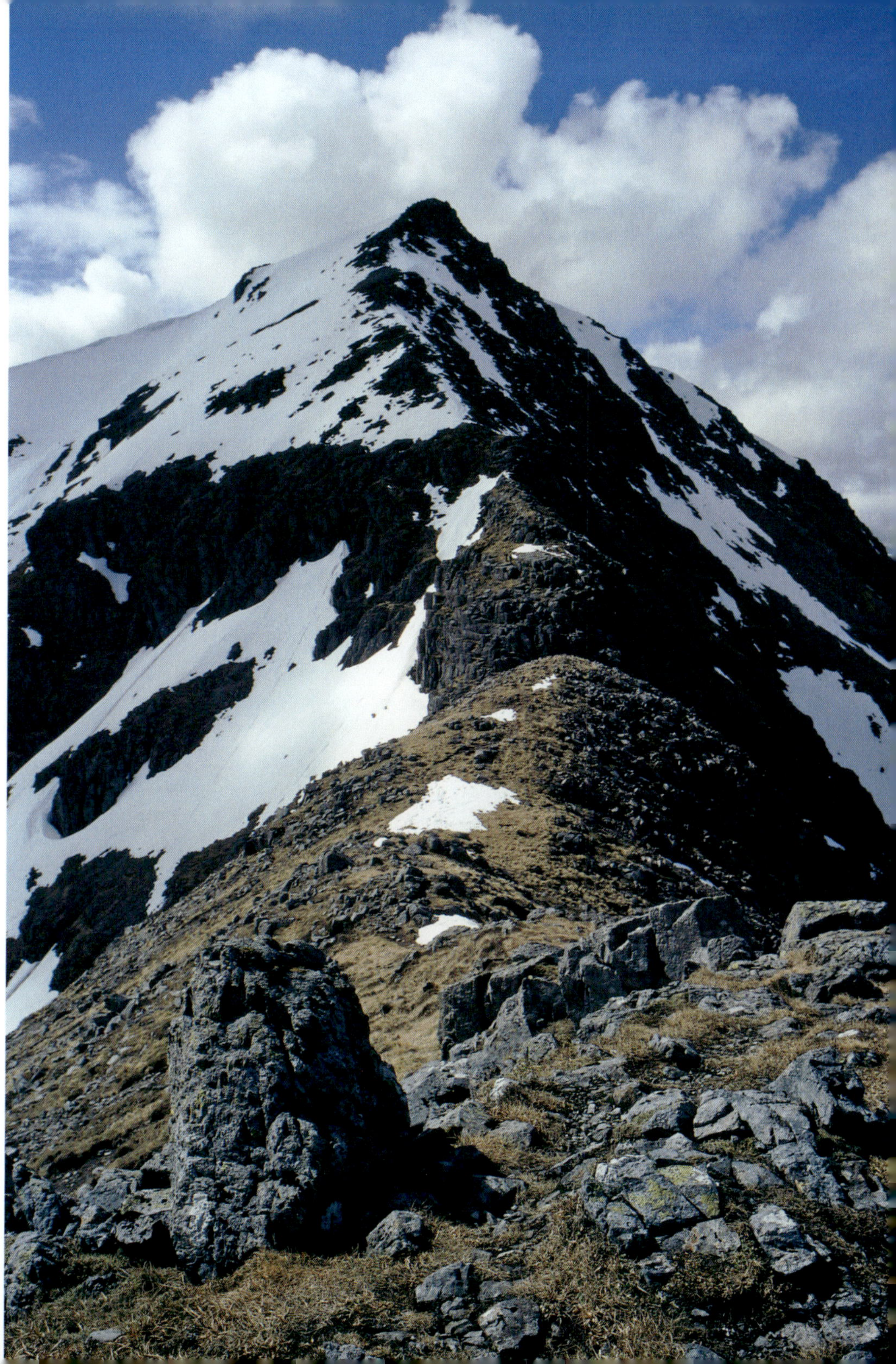

Summit slopes.
The shapely summit of Stob Coire Sgreamhach (*point of the dreadful corrie)* is the high point at the end of the Beinn Fhada ridge.

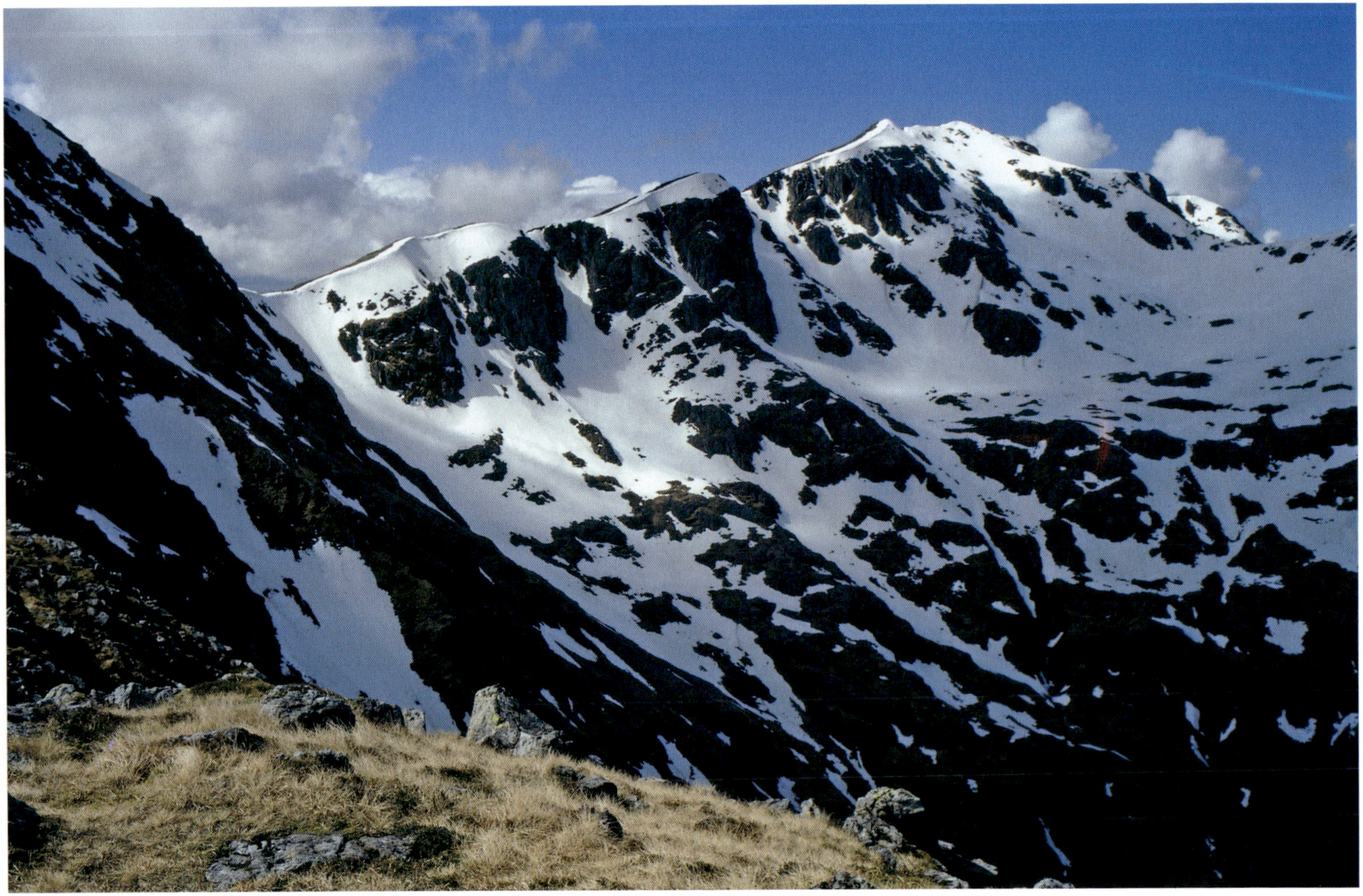

Spring cornices.
Melting snow leaves large cornices on the ridge linking Stob Coire Sgreamhach to Bidean nam Bian, a compact and complex massif with ridges enclosing three fine corries overlooking Glencoe. The summit of Bidean is set well back from Glencoe and is quite hard to see from the valley floor.

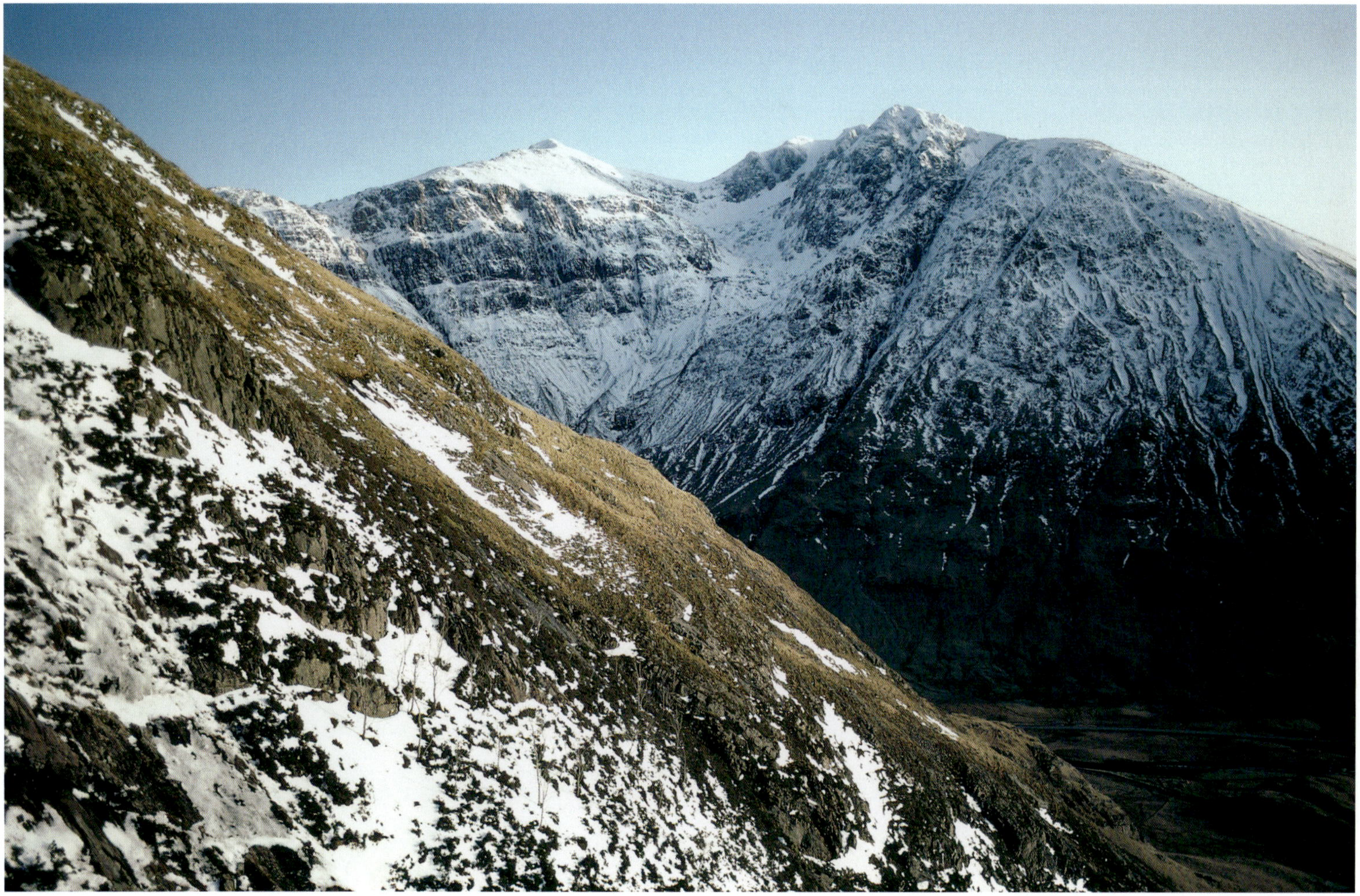

Winter garb.
Bidean nam Bian, one of the finest massifs in the Highlands, looks superb in its winter cloak in this view across the valley from alongside the famous Clachaig Gully.

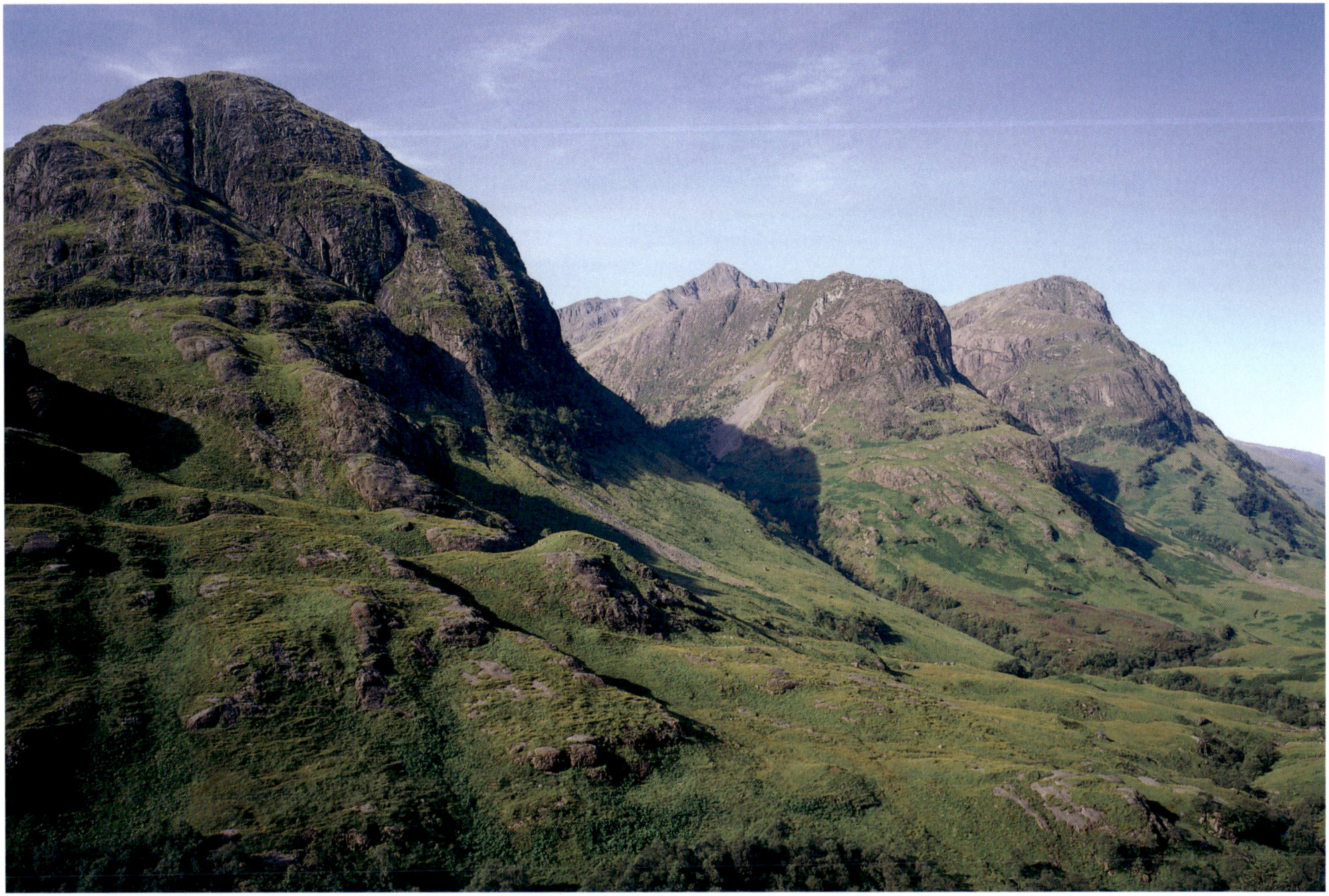

A family affair.
The Three Sisters – Beinn Fhada, Gearr Aonach and Aonach Dubh – dominate the south side of Glencoe.

Opposite: The lost valley.
Situated between the parallel ridges of Beinn Fhada (left) and Gearr Aonach, above the Meeting of Three Waters, is the steep-sided hanging trench of Coire Gabhail (*the corrie of capture*), known as the Lost or Hidden Valley. It has a level valley floor and is reputed to be where the MacDonalds hid rustled cattle.

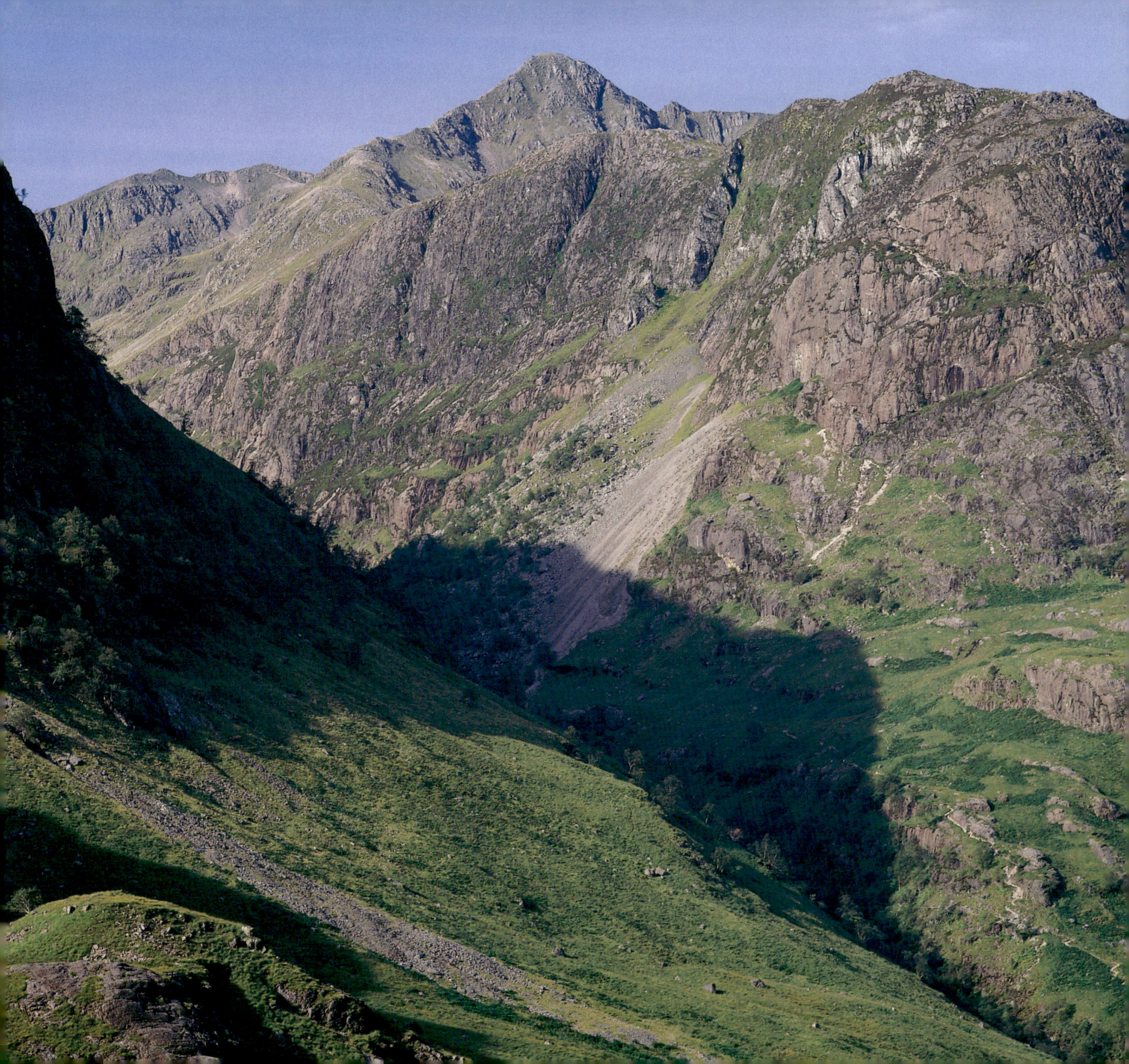

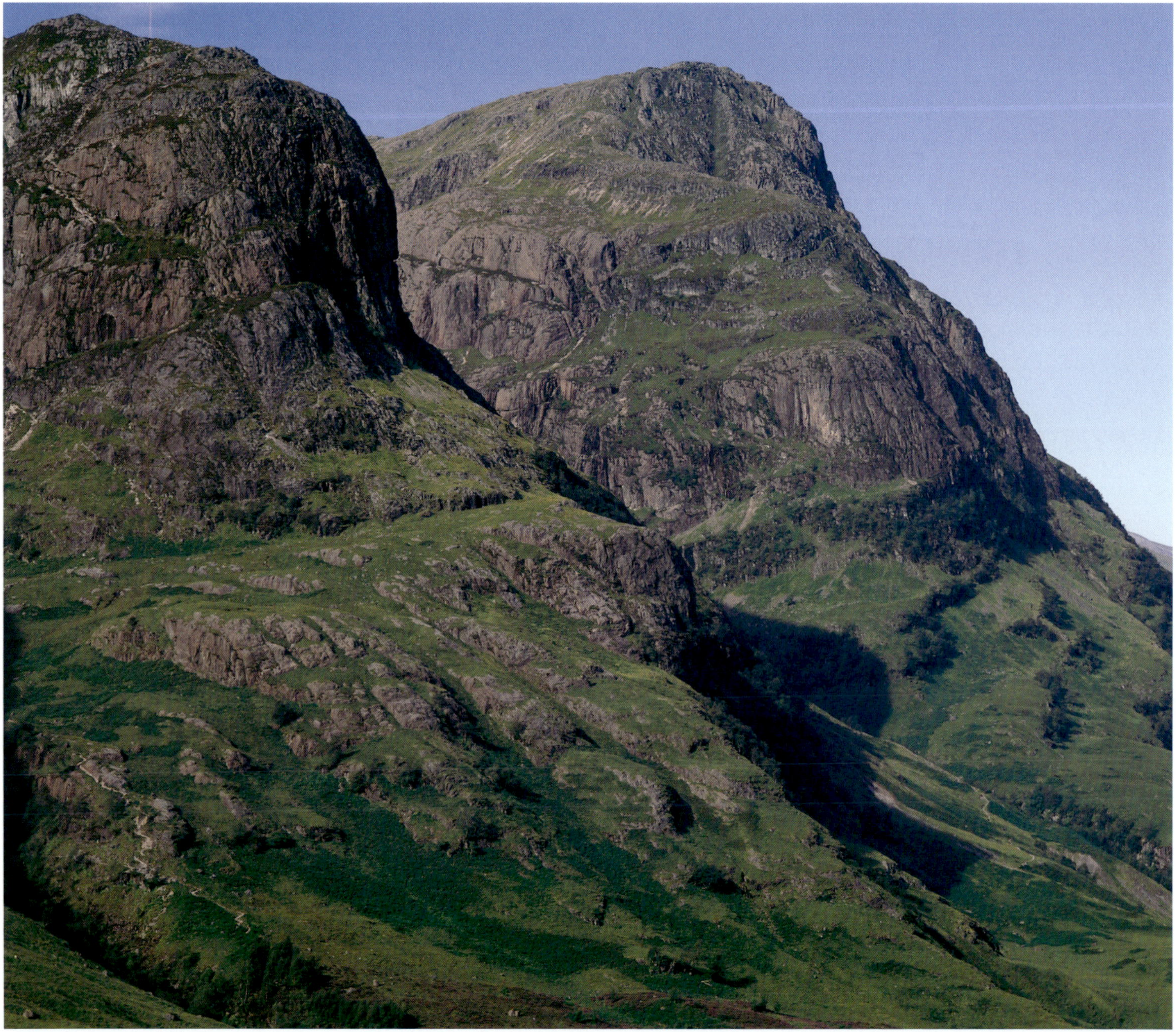

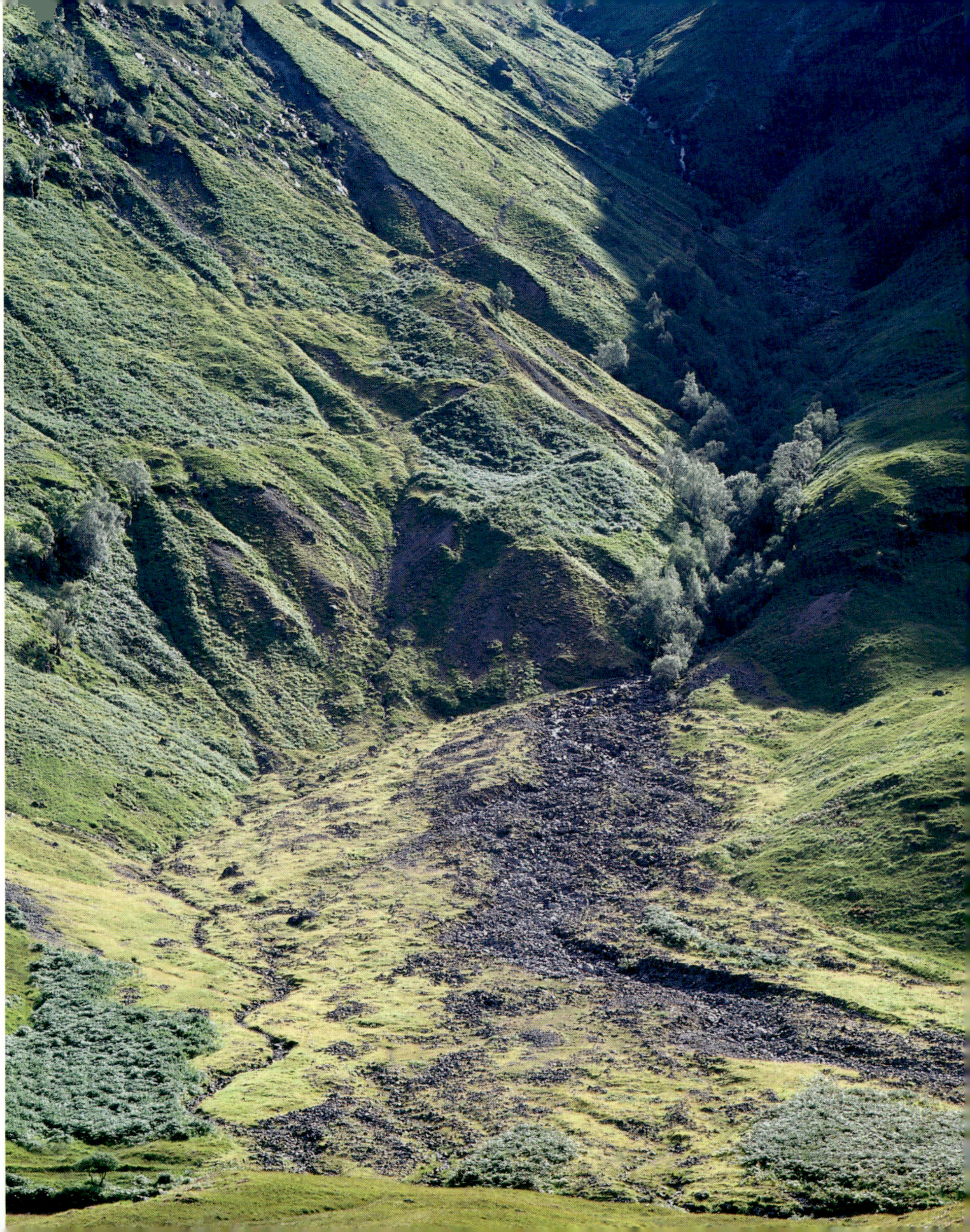

Winding stream.
A stream winds its way down from Coire nan Lochan situated high up between Gearr Aonach and Aonach Dubh.

Opposite: Rocky bastions.
The north facing craggy noses of Gearr Aonach and Aonach Dubh overlook the ancient moraines from Coire Gabhail and Coire nan Lochan. On the front of Aonach Dubh is the huge elongated slit of Ossian's Cave, which can only be reached by a rock climb.

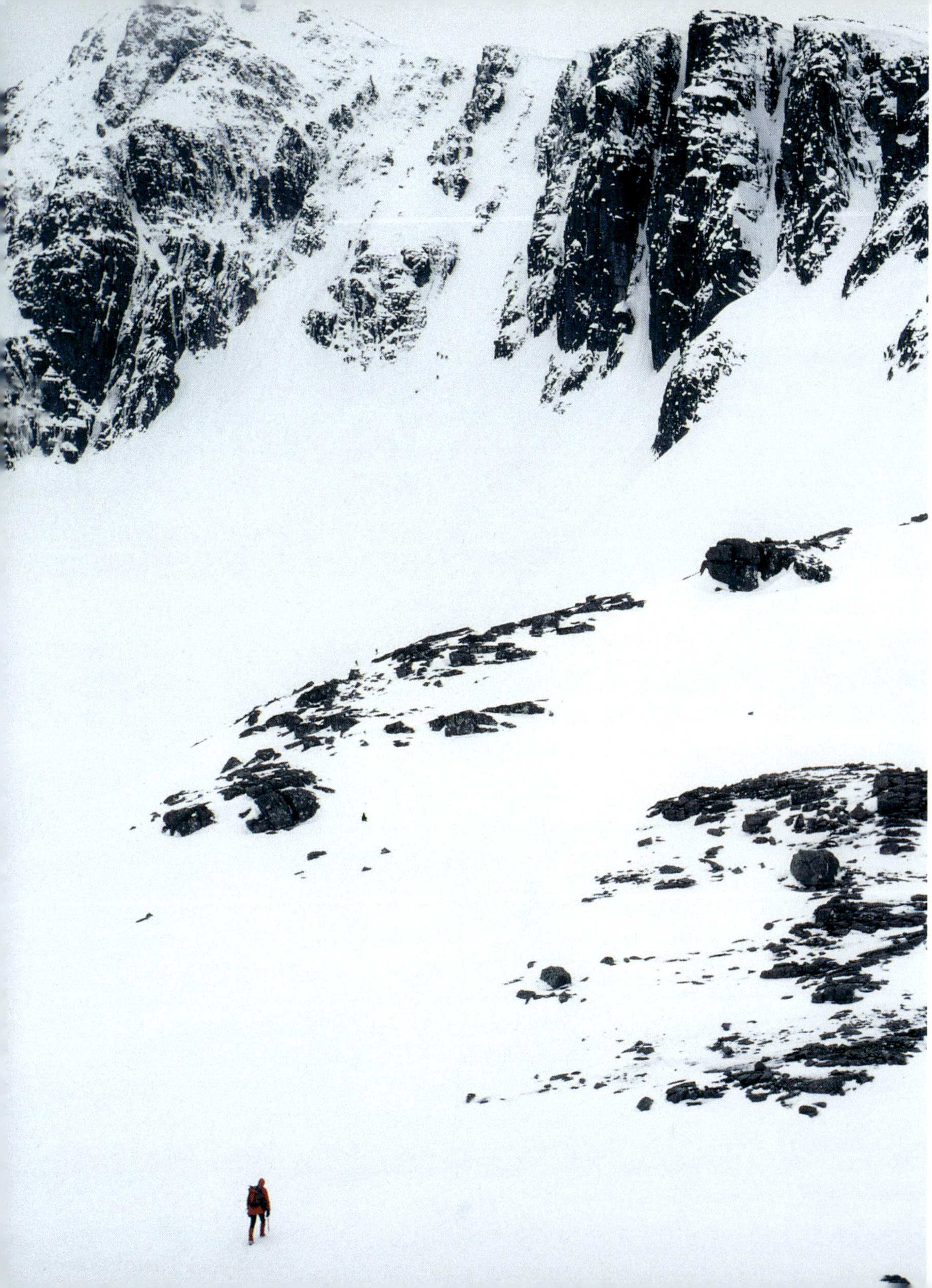

A monochrome landscape.
A lone walker is dwarfed by the icy cliffs of Coire nan Lochan, a superb corrie lying under the shadow of Stob Coire nan Lochan.

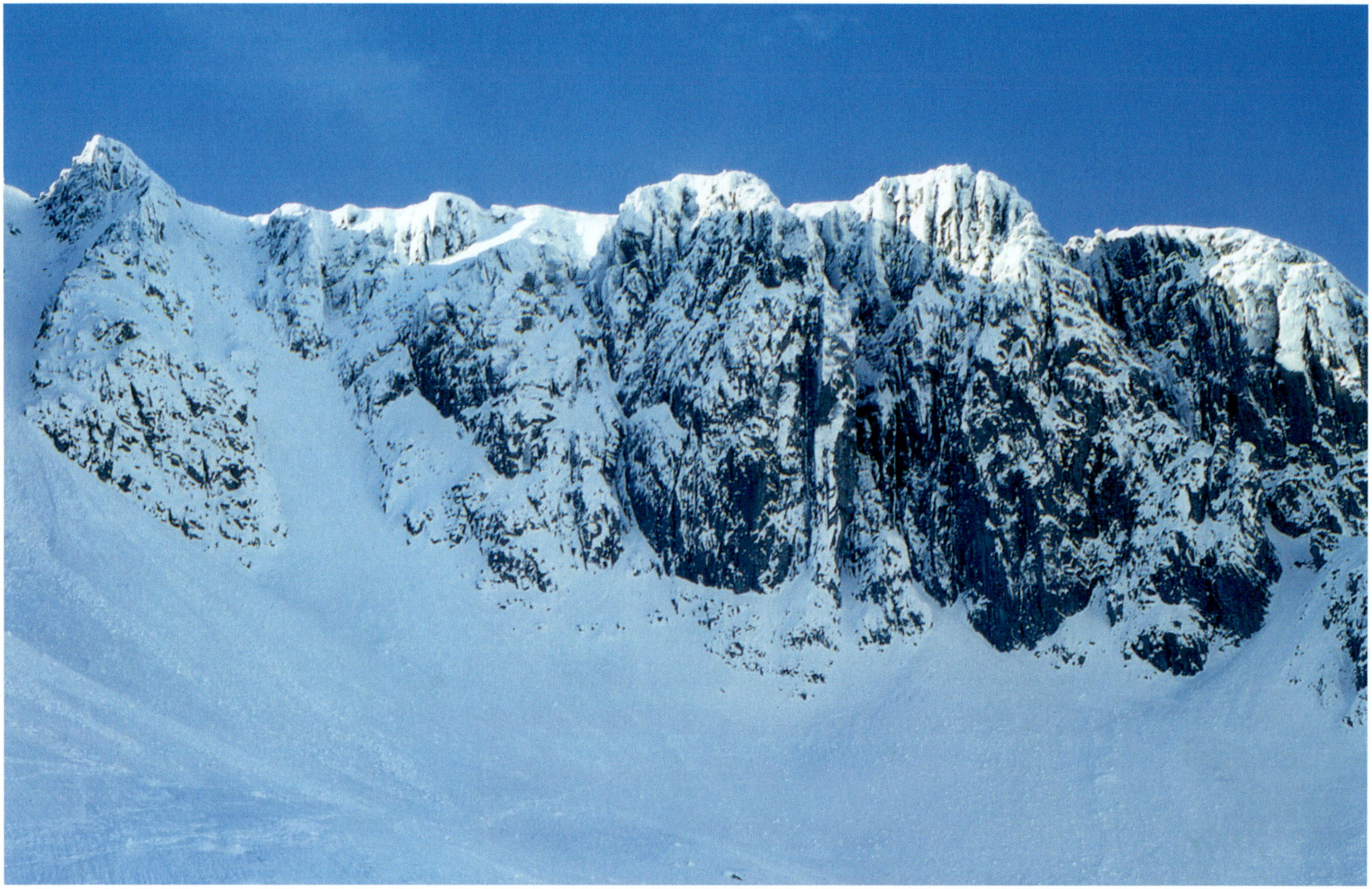

Winter playground.
Sunshine strikes the upper section of the dramatic cliffs and gullies of Coire nan Lochan which are a popular winter playground for climbers.

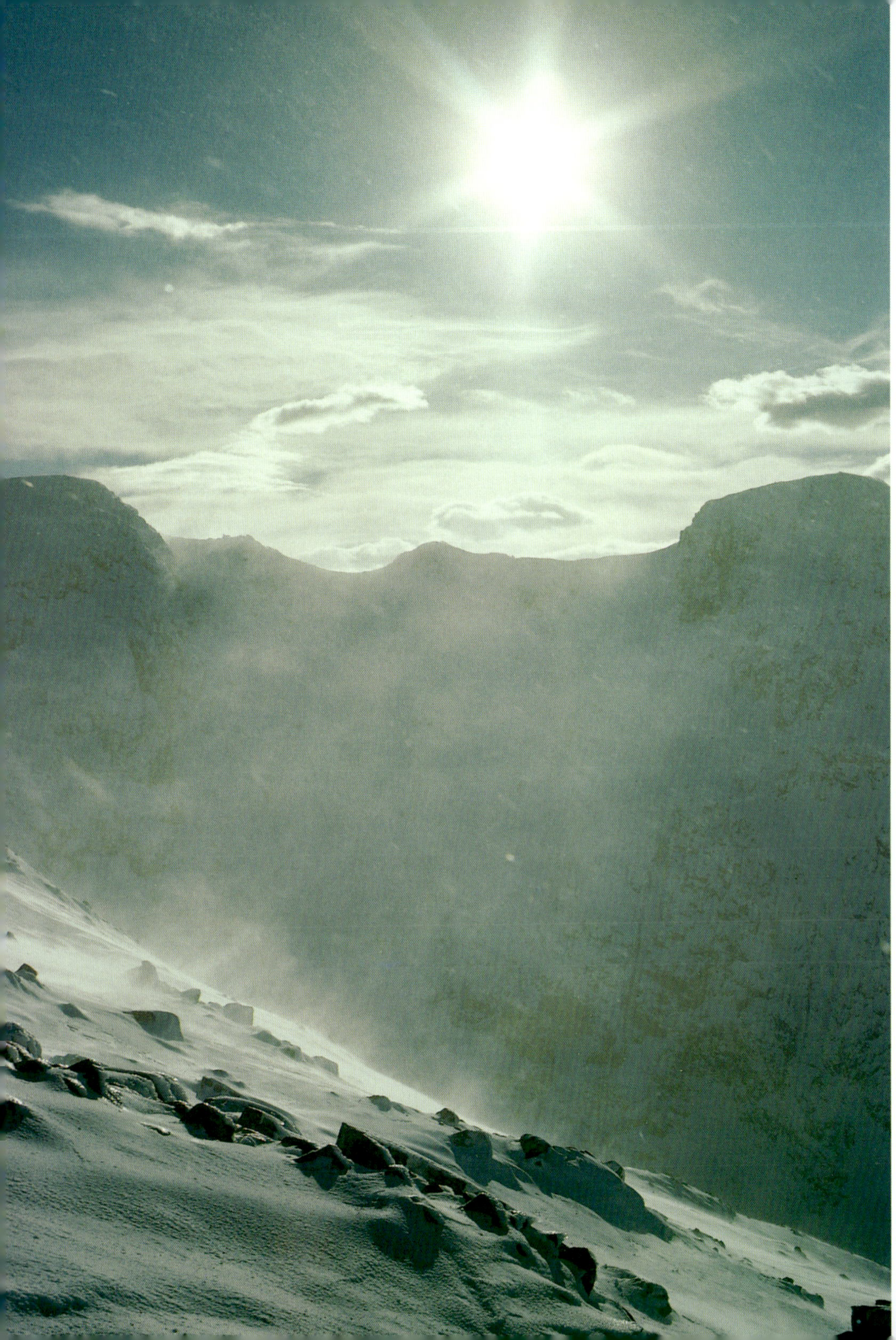

Sunburst.
A fierce wind blows clouds of spindrift (fine ice particles) across the slopes of Stob Coire nan Lochan and Stob Coire nam Beith which is seen in the background.

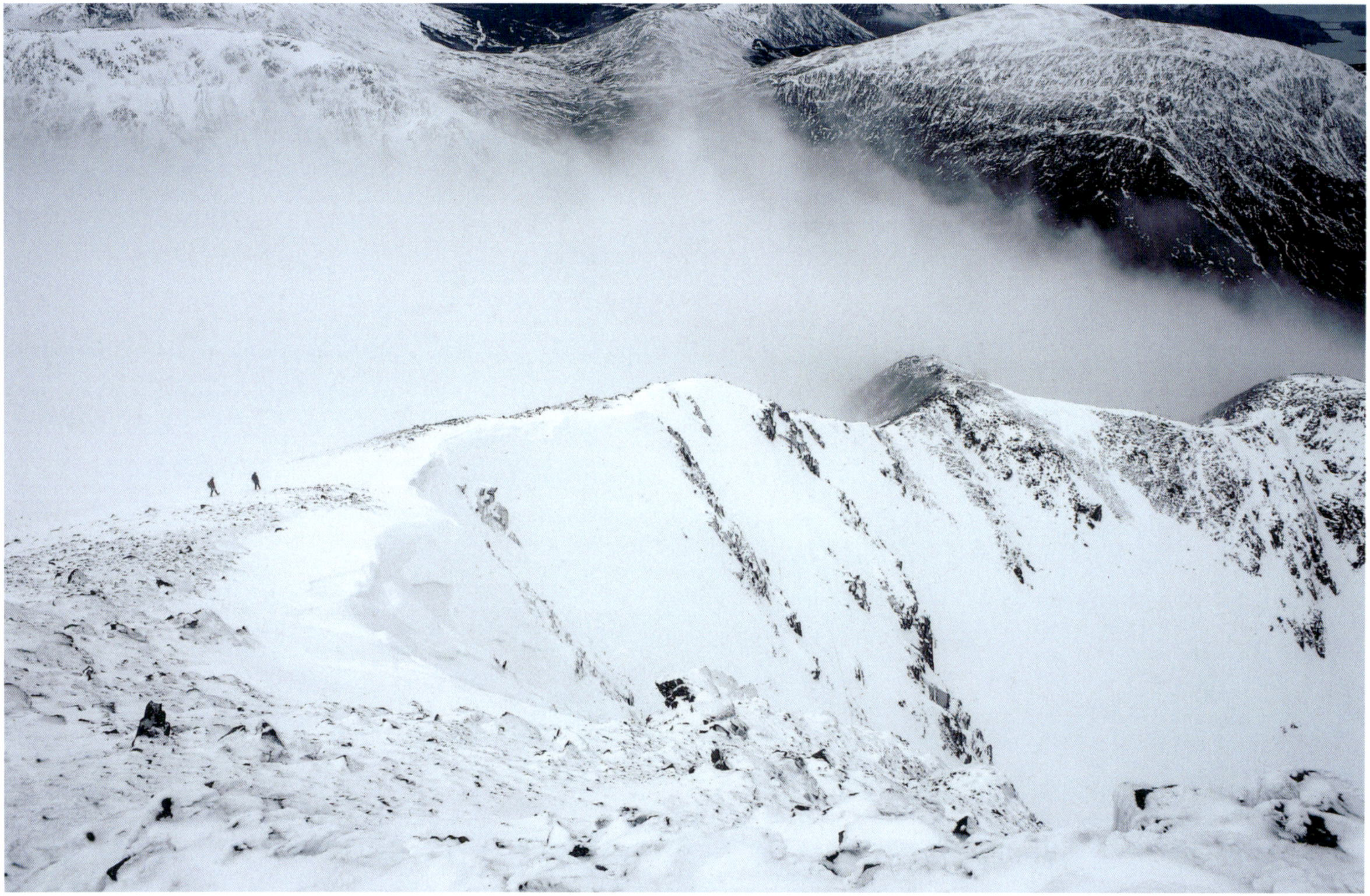

Misty valley.
A snowy ridge sweeps down from Stob Coire nam Beith to a mist-filled Glencoe.

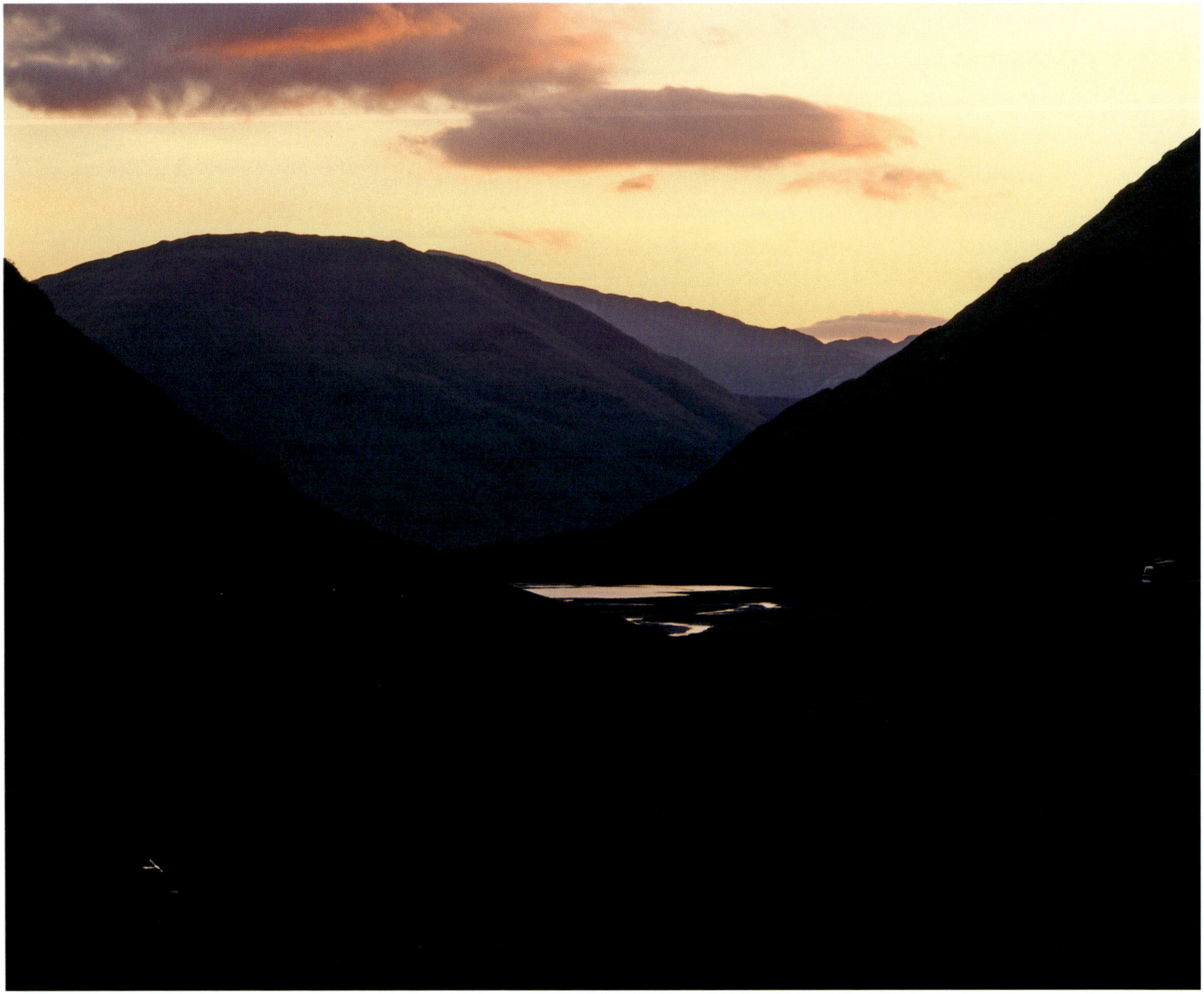

Evening glow.
The setting sun picks out Loch Achtriochtan.

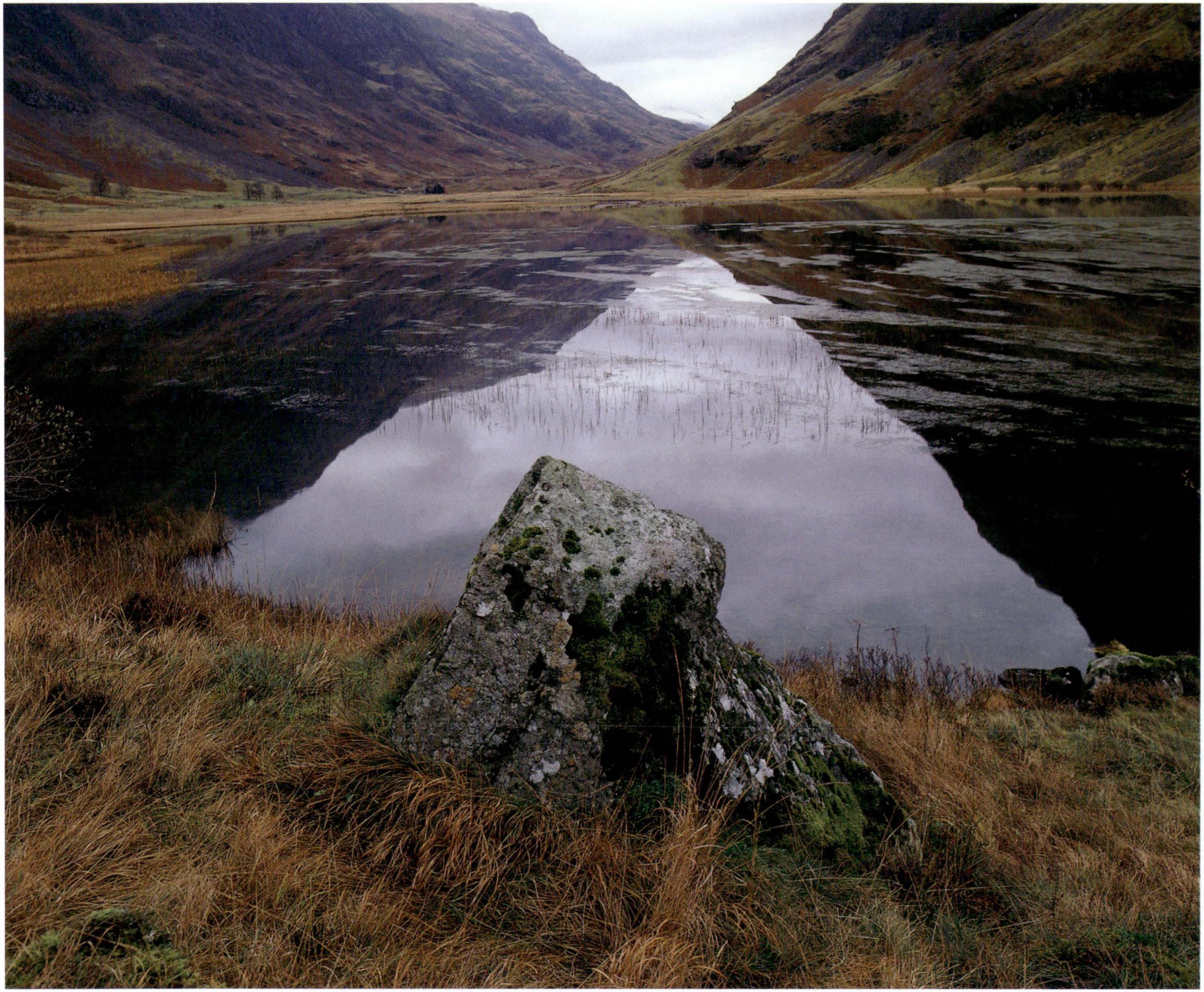

Symmetry.
Looking back up Glencoe reflected in the calm waters of Loch Achtriochtan.

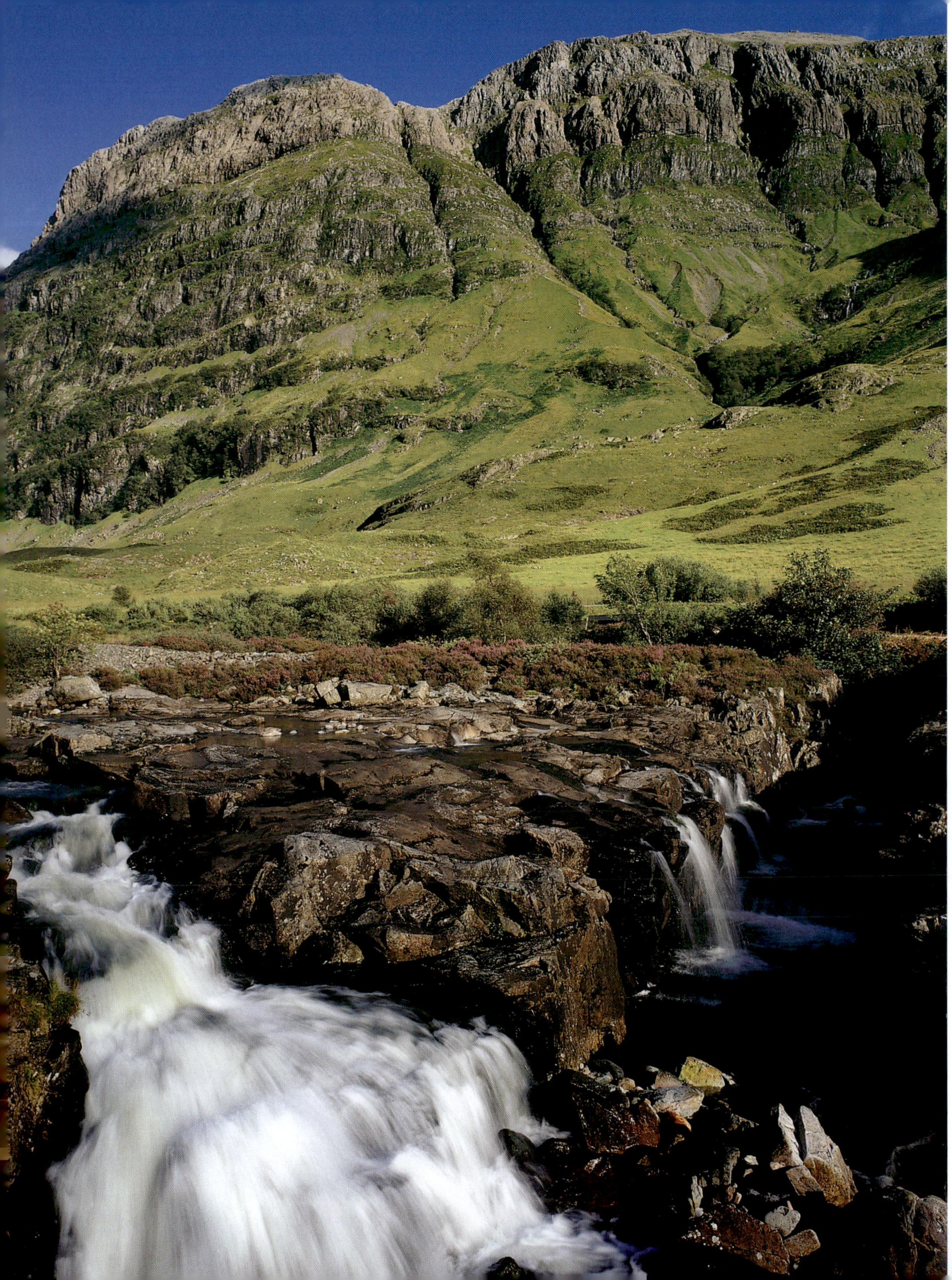

Cascades.
The gully-riven and craggy west face of Aonach Dubh overlooks the cascades of the River Coe near Clachaig.

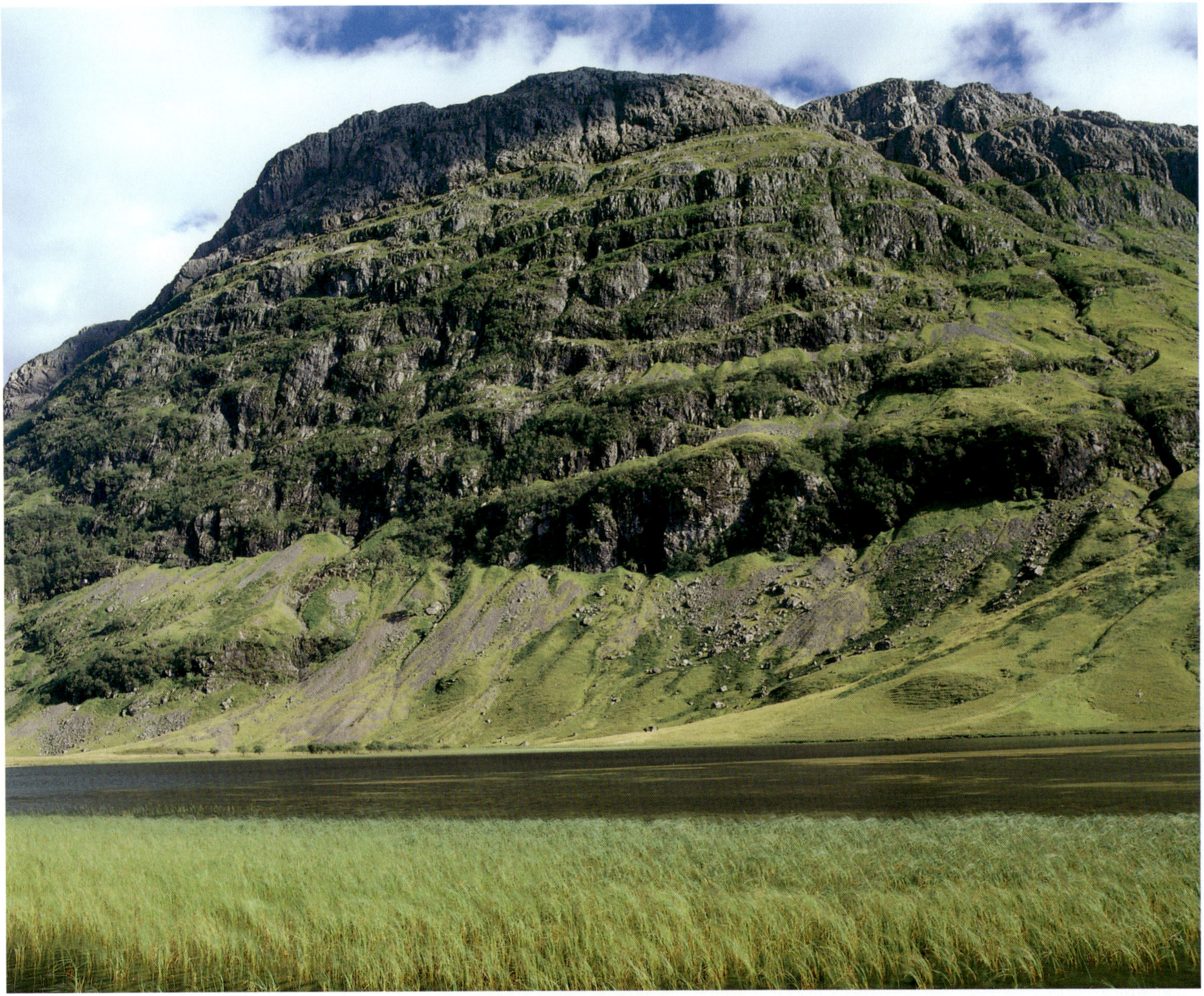

Reeded loch.

The amazing grassy-terraced west face of Aonach Dubh rising above the reed-fringed Loch Achtriochtan.

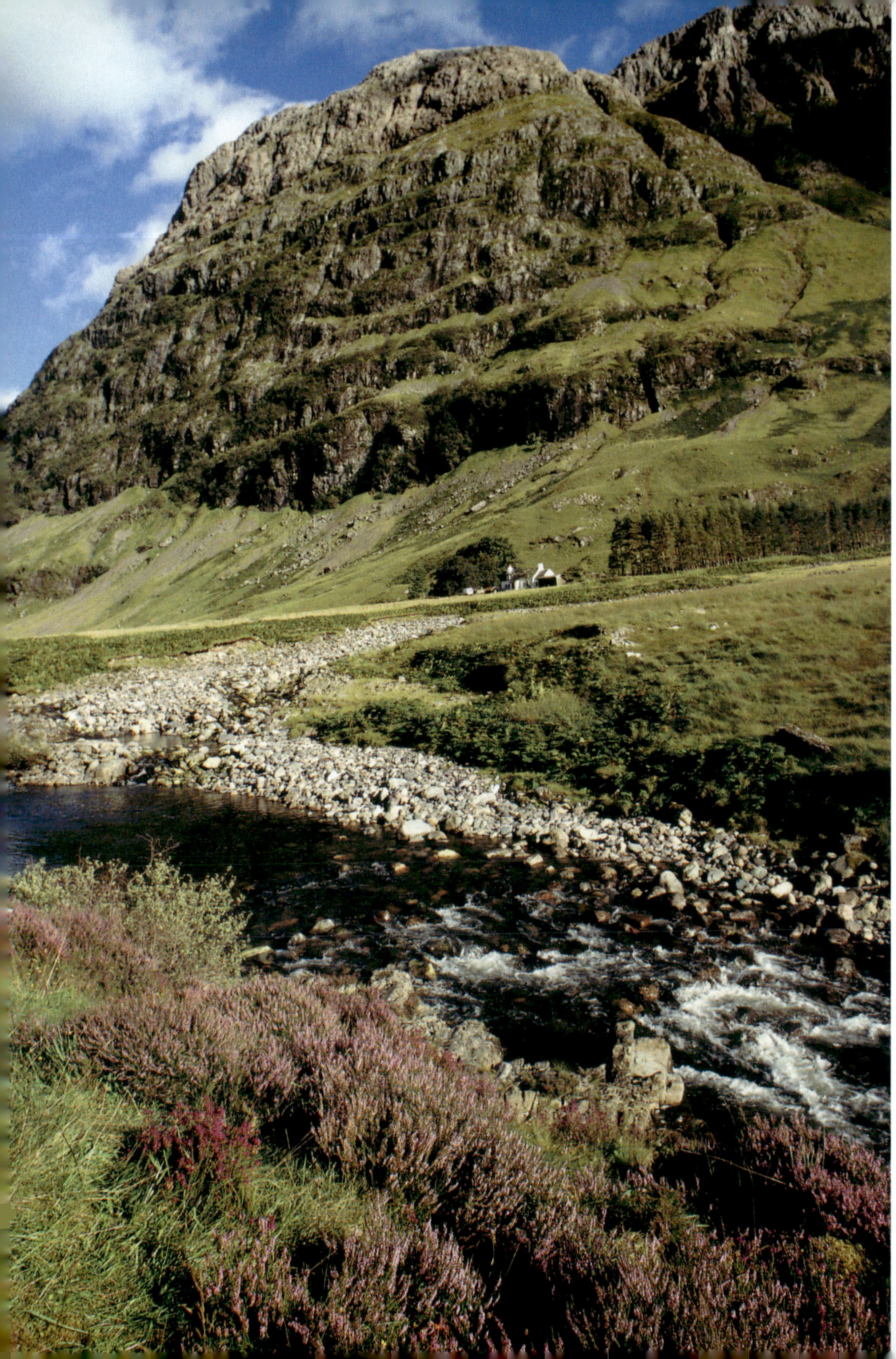

Purple heather.
Summer heather acts as a colourful foreground for this view across the River Coe to Aonach Dubh. The slanting break in the cliffs is known as Dinner Time Buttress, a pleasant approach route for experienced walkers.

River confluence.
Dinner Time Buttress on Aonach Dubh provides a bird's-eye-view of the River Coe. The river drains through Loch Achtriochtan on its short journey to Loch Leven. The village of Glencoe and Loch Leven are visible in the background.

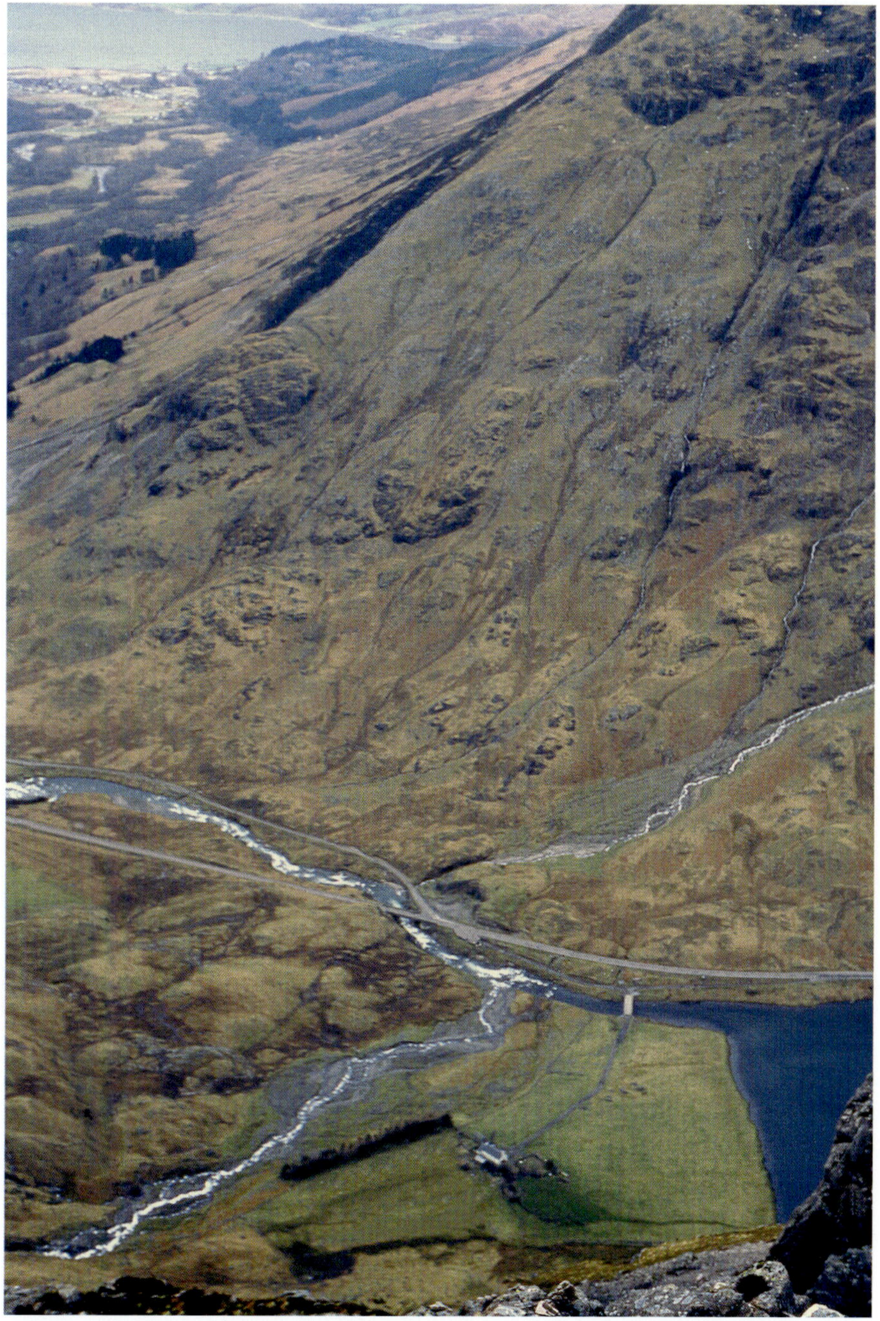

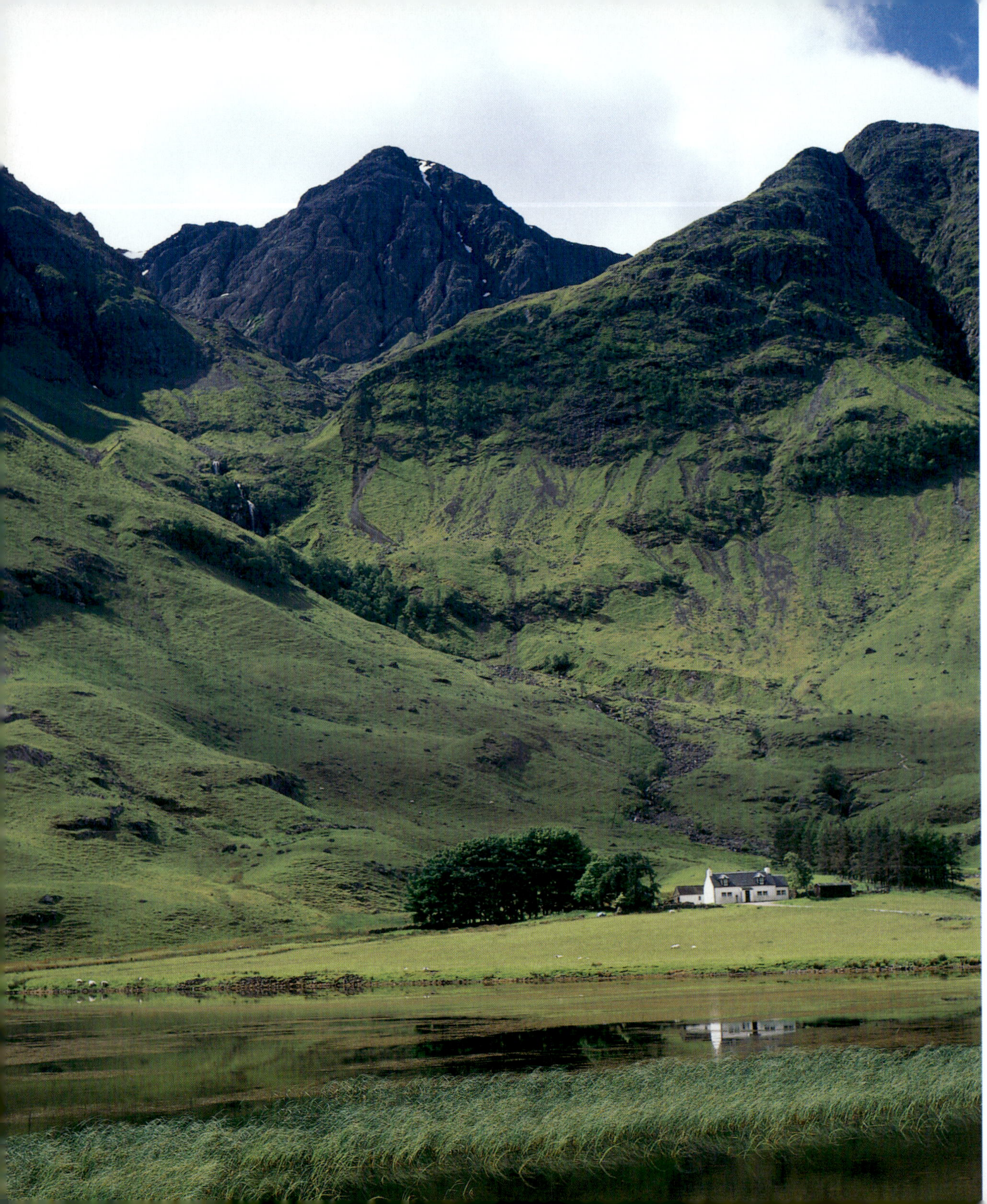

Lonely dwelling.
The impressive craggy cone of Stob Coire nam Beith towers over the farmhouse of Achnambeithach above the outflow of Loch Achtriochtan.

Opposite: Misty tops.
Low cloud cloaks the Aonach Eagach in this reflected view across the calm waters of Loch Achtriochtan.

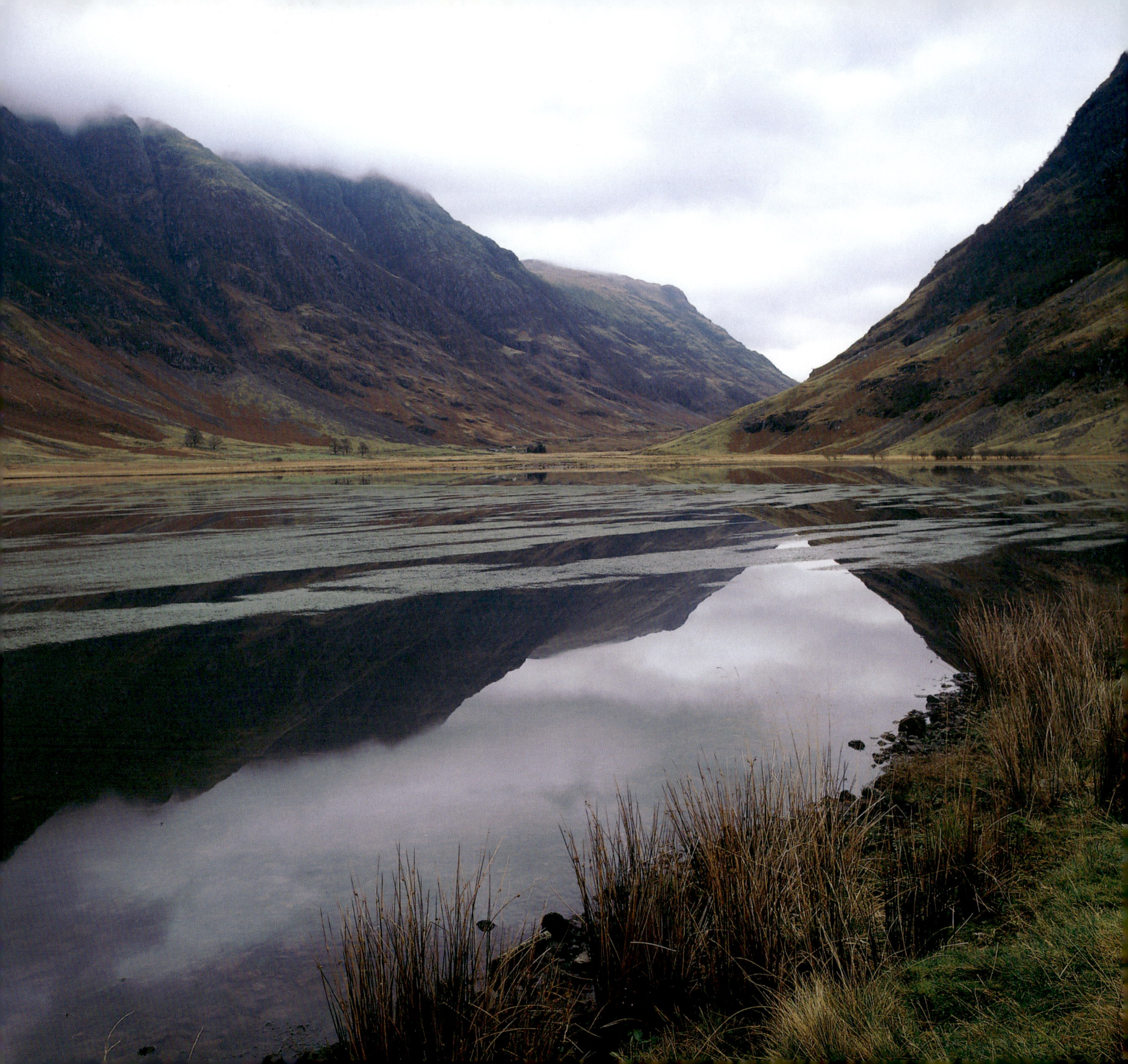

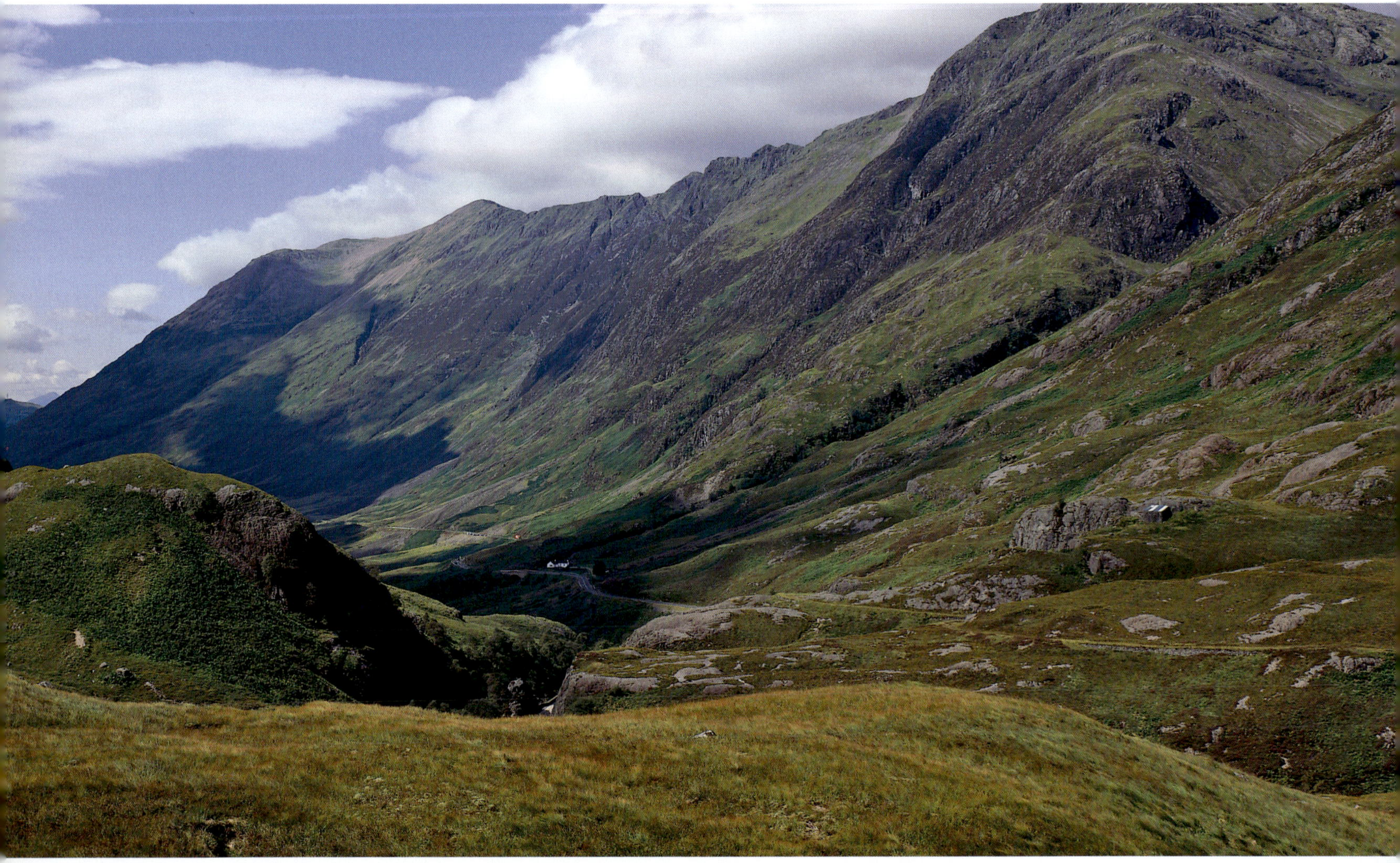

The notched ridge.

The north side of Glencoe is closely hemmed in the jagged ridge of the famous Aonach Eagach (*notched ridge*).

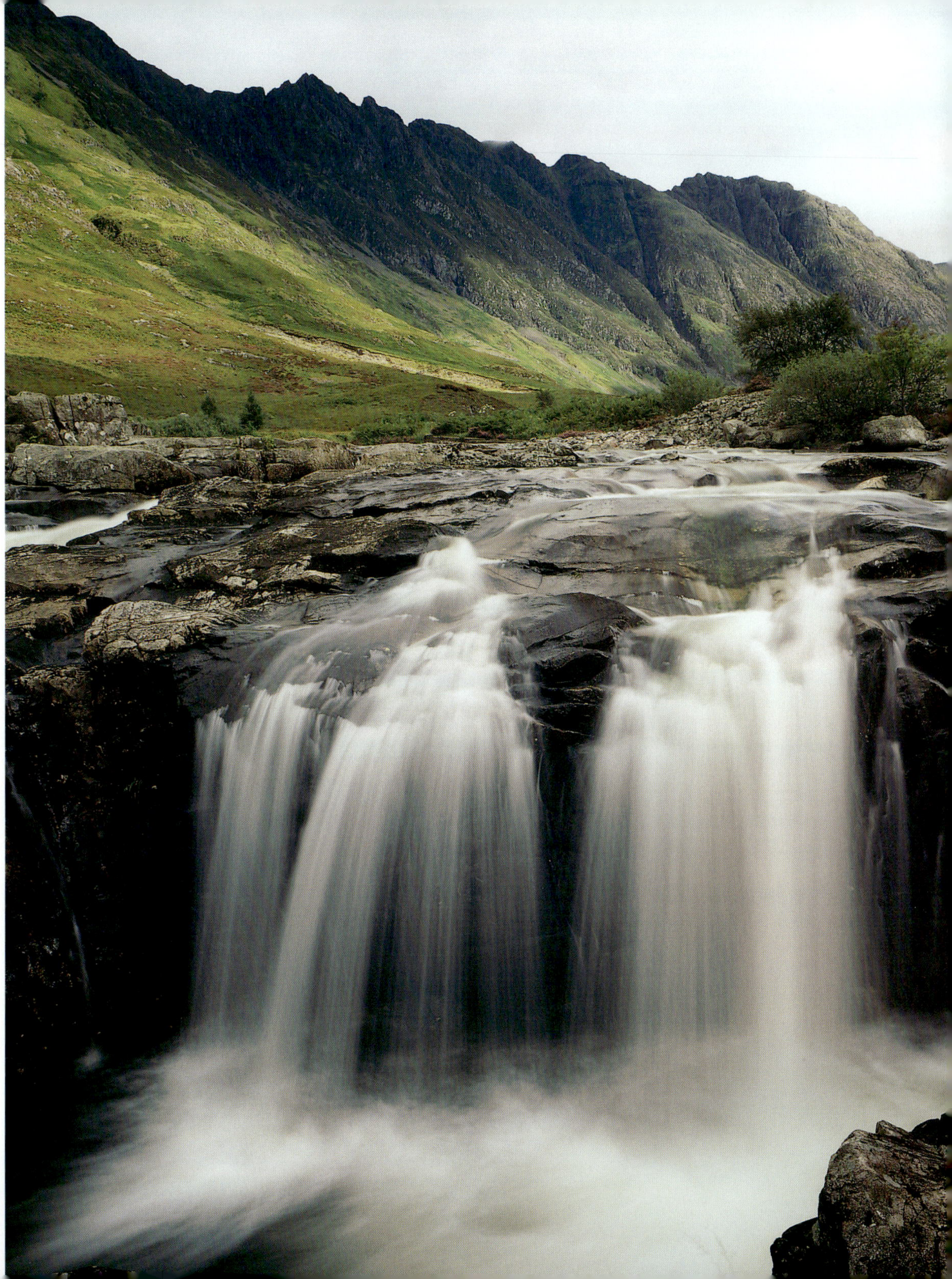

Waterfall.
The cascades of the River Coe near Clachaig provide a dramatic foreground for this classic view of the Aonach Eagach.

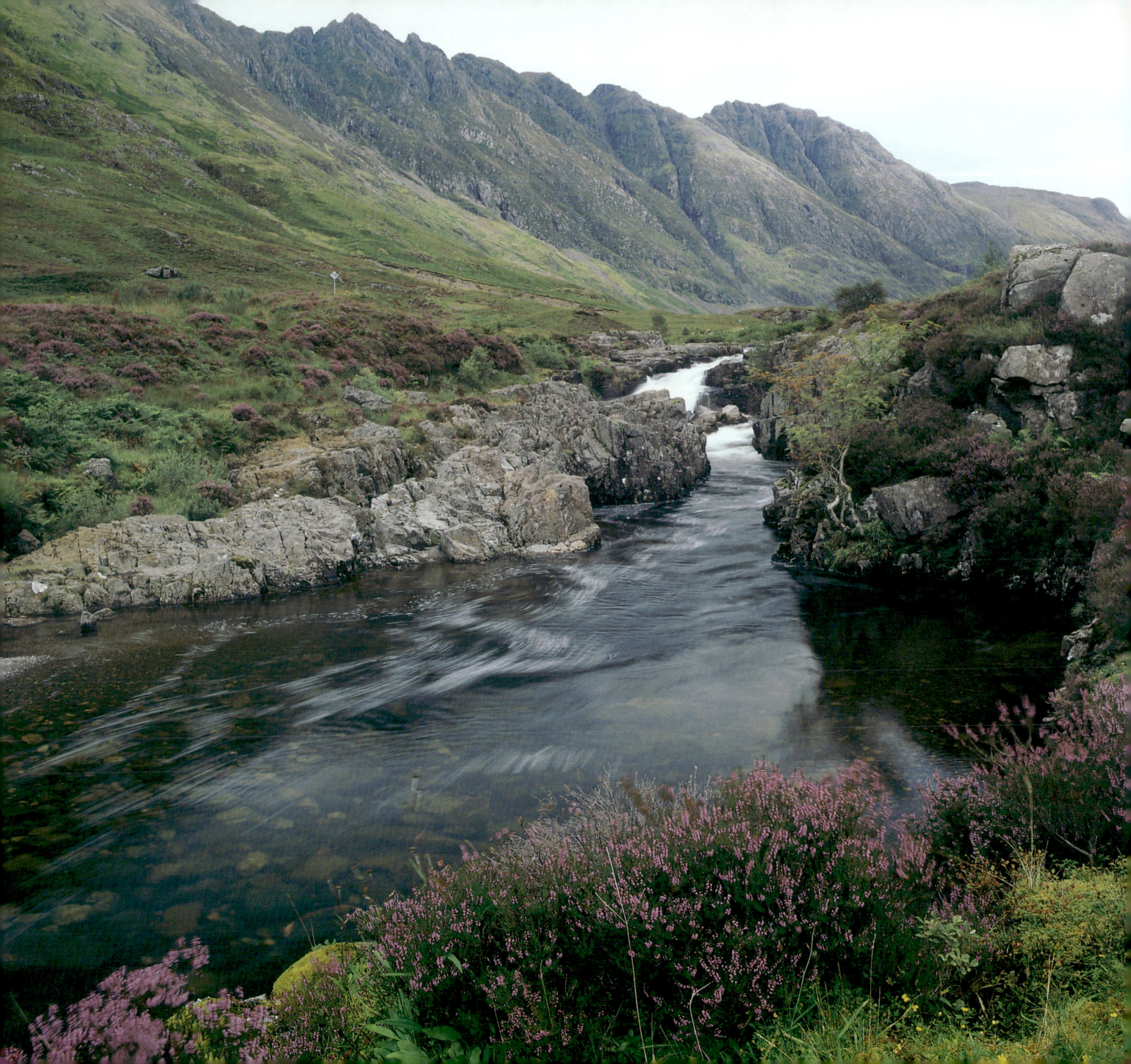

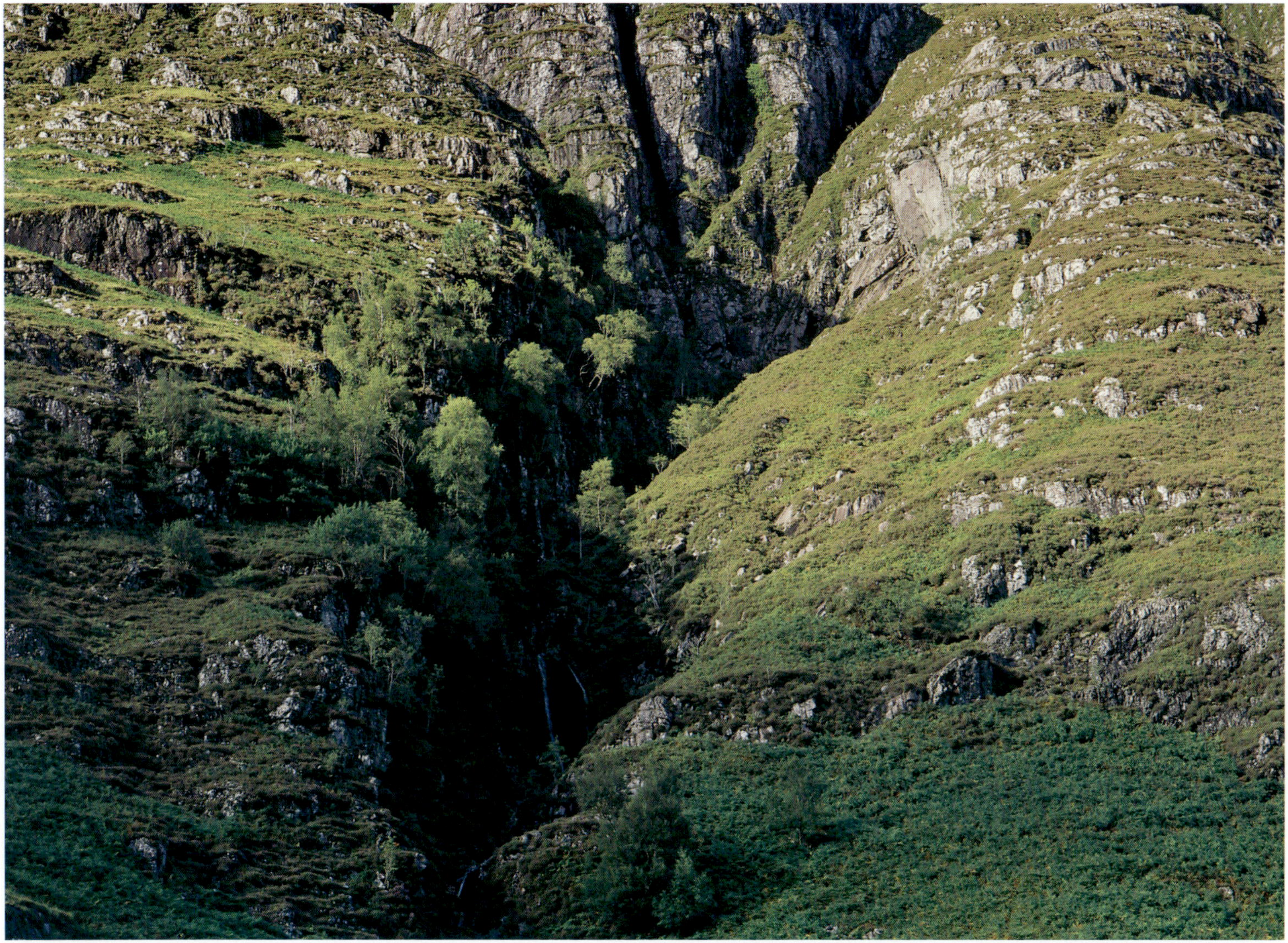

Shelter.
A craggy ravine on the lower slopes of Aoanach Eagach, provides welcome protection for a group of trees.

Opposite: Westering river.
In this summer view, the gently flowing River Coe near Clachaig swings towards the green strath of Achnacon (*the field of dogs*).

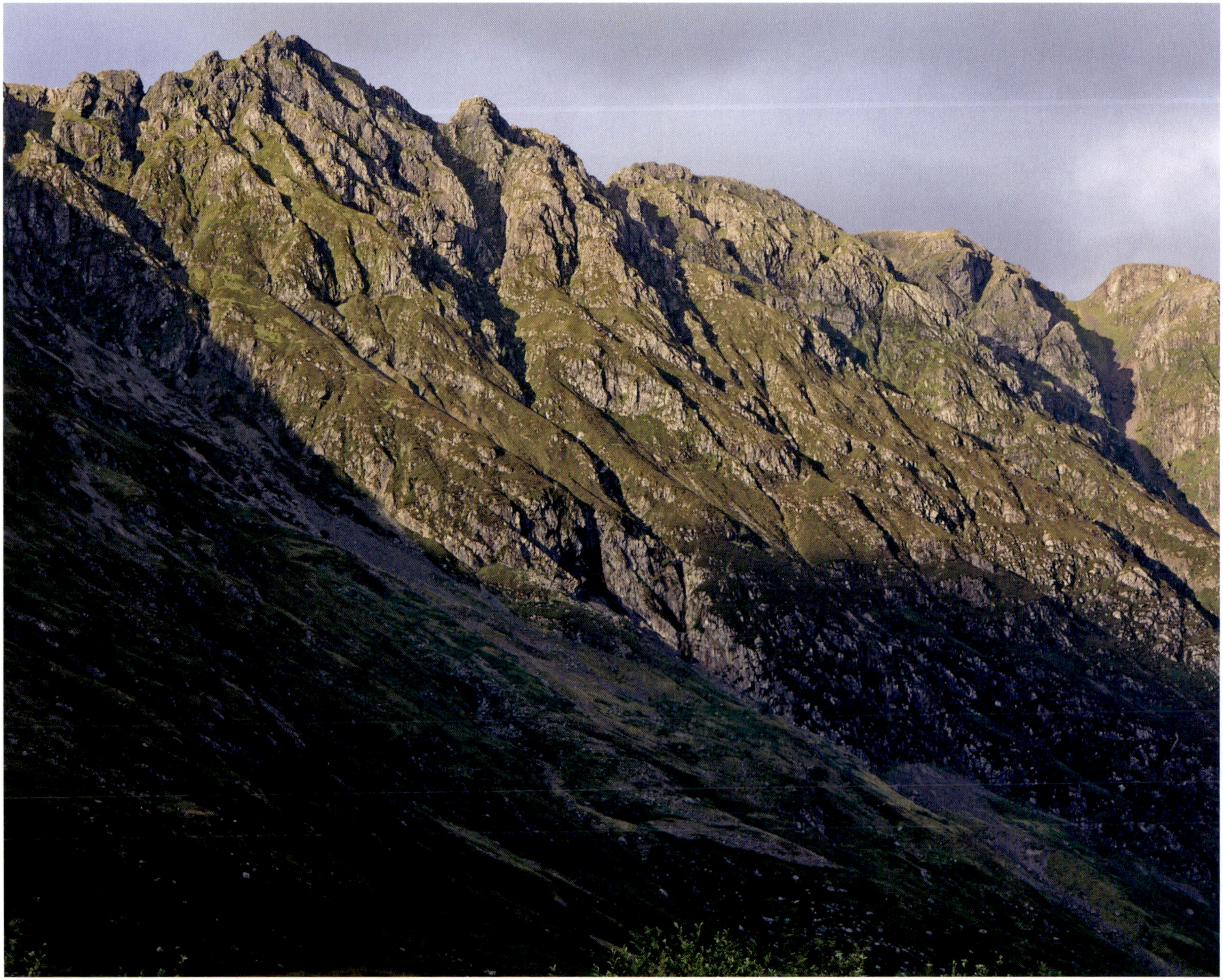

Jagged skyline.
Late afternoon sunshine illuminates the switch-back ridge of the Aonach Eagach. This exposed narrow ridge is a delight to traverse but you need a head for heights.

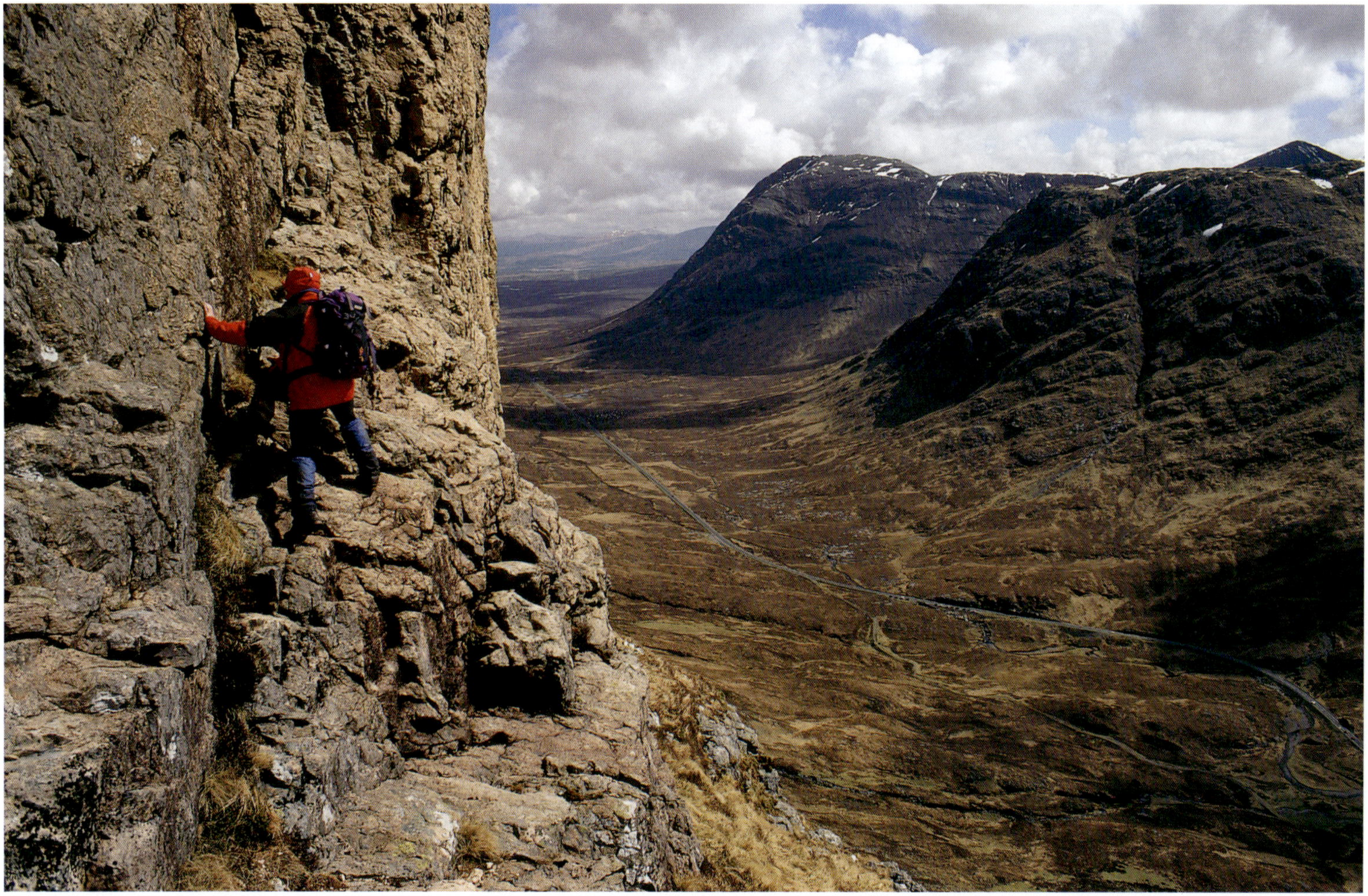

Exposure.
The steep south face of A' Chailleach (*the old woman*), situated high above The Study, offers an alternative scrambling approach to the start of a traverse of the Aonach Eagach. Buachaille Etive Mor is visible further up Glencoe.

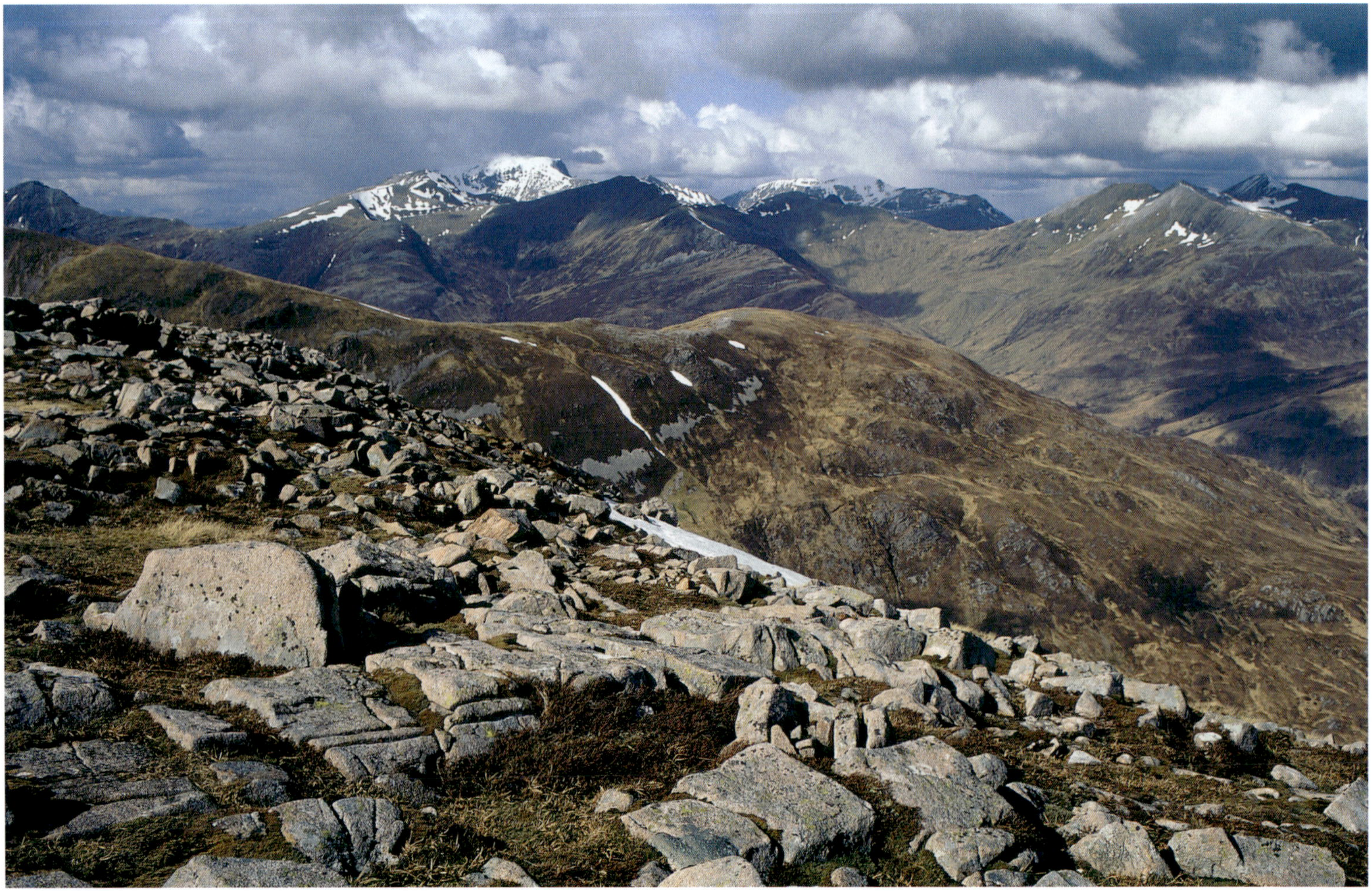

Pink rocks.

The rocks on Sron Gharbh above A' Chailleach act as foreground for this northern view of bulky Ben Nevis and the Mamores.

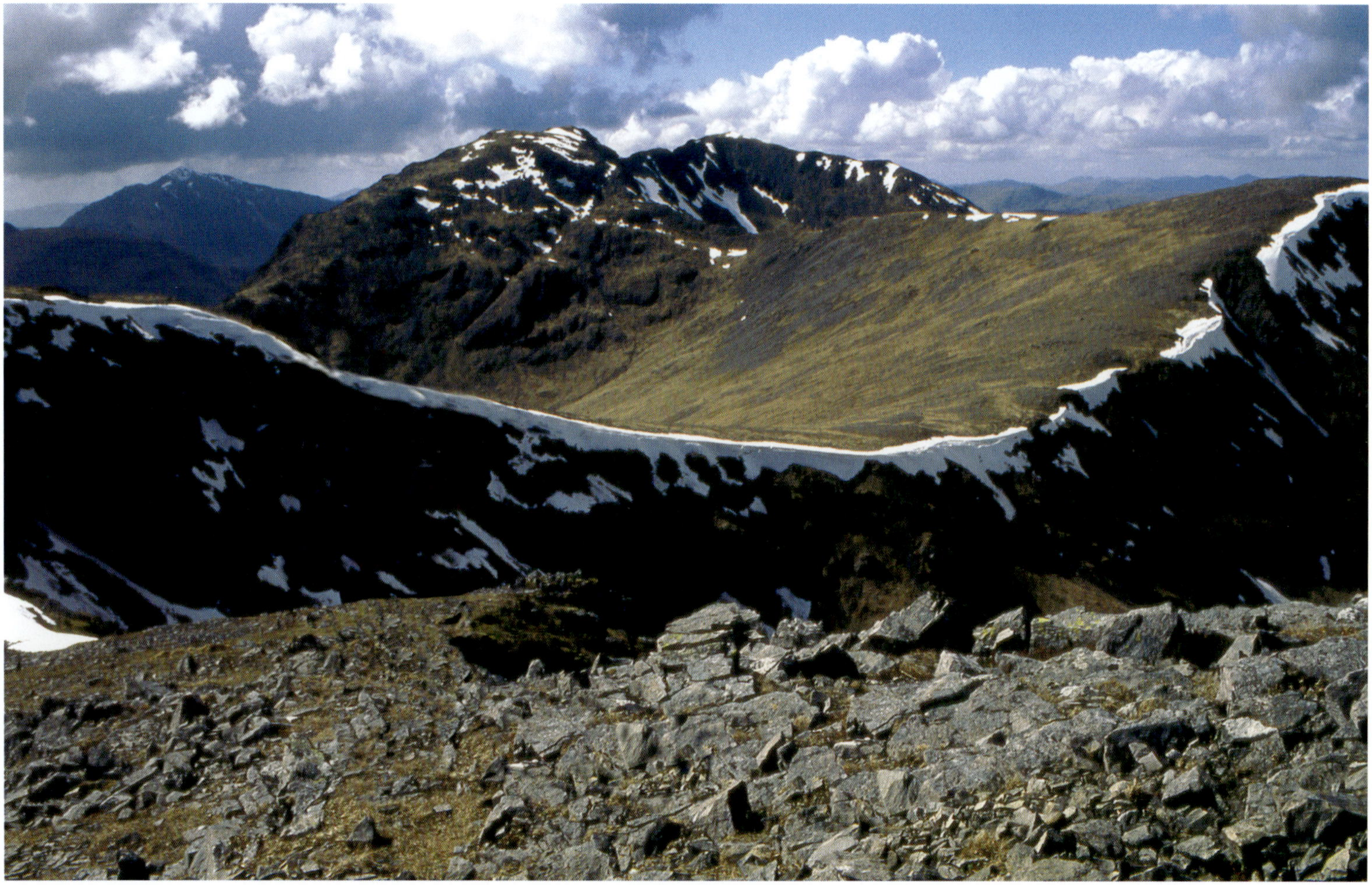

Vantage point.
Looking west from Sron Gharbh towards Am Bodach the usual start for a traverse of the Aonach Eagach.

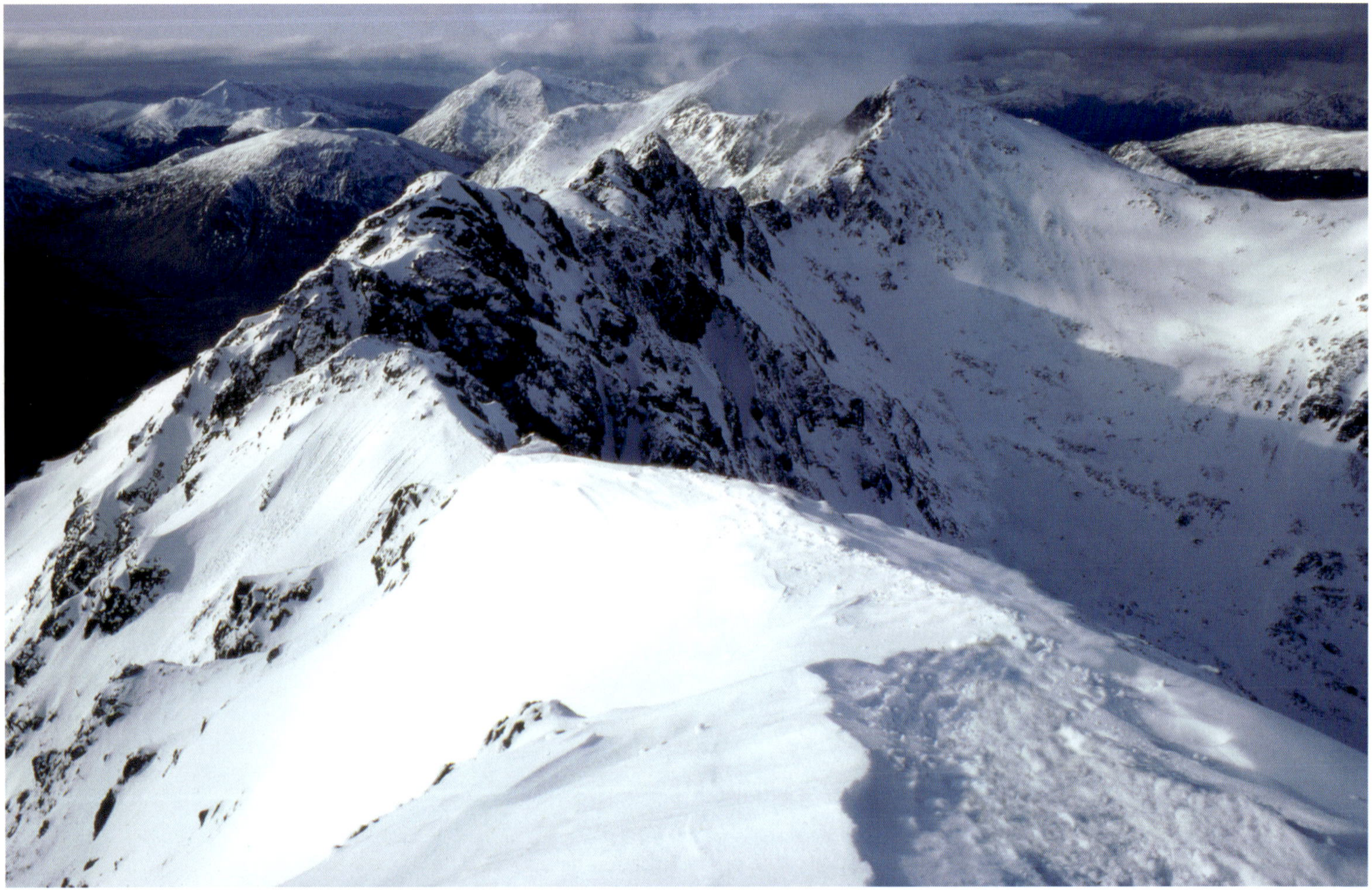

A challenging ridge.

Looking west along the magnificent Aonach Eagach towards a distant Sgorr nam Fiannaidh. In its full winter mantle, the Aonach Eagach is one of the most challenging ridge traverses in Scotland and is exposed and continuously narrow. Once started there is no escape route from the narrow crest.

Snowy summit.
The shapely peak of Stob Coire Leith is one of the high points on the Aonach Eagach.

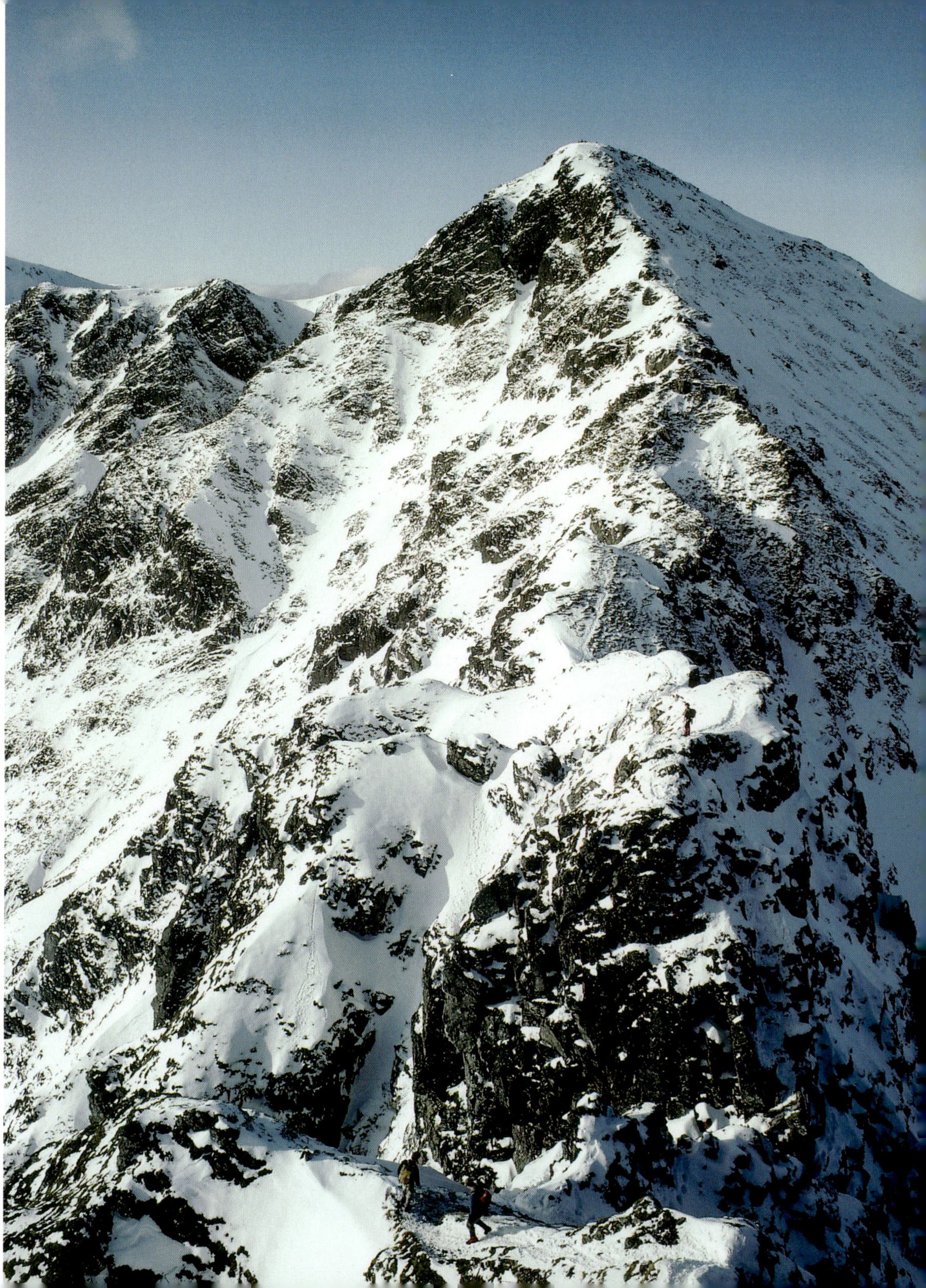

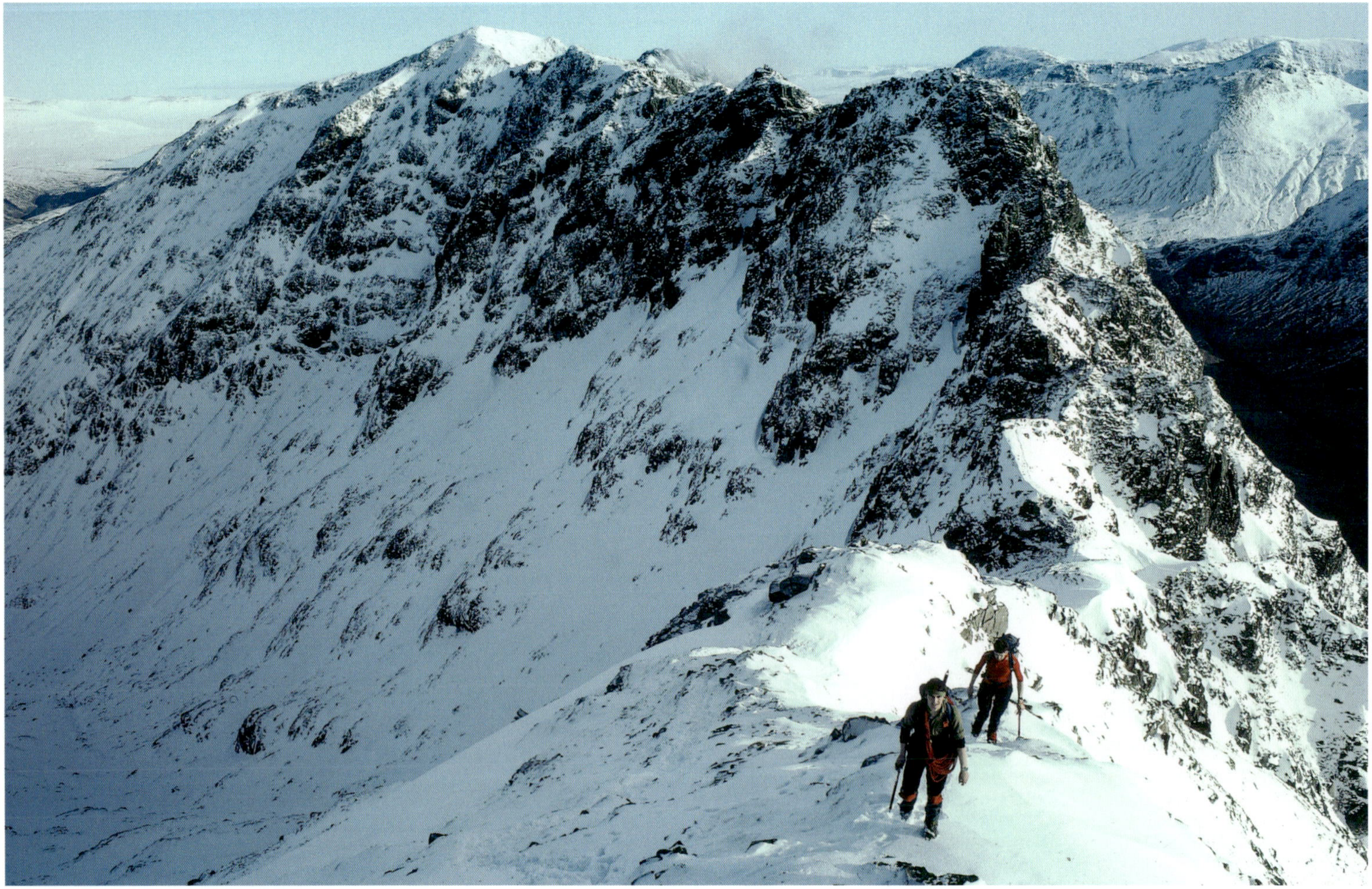

Nearing the finish.
A dramatic eastern view along the jagged crest of the Aonach Eagach. The descent alongside the Clachaig Gully is not recommended and most walkers continue along the ridge towards the Pap of Glencoe.

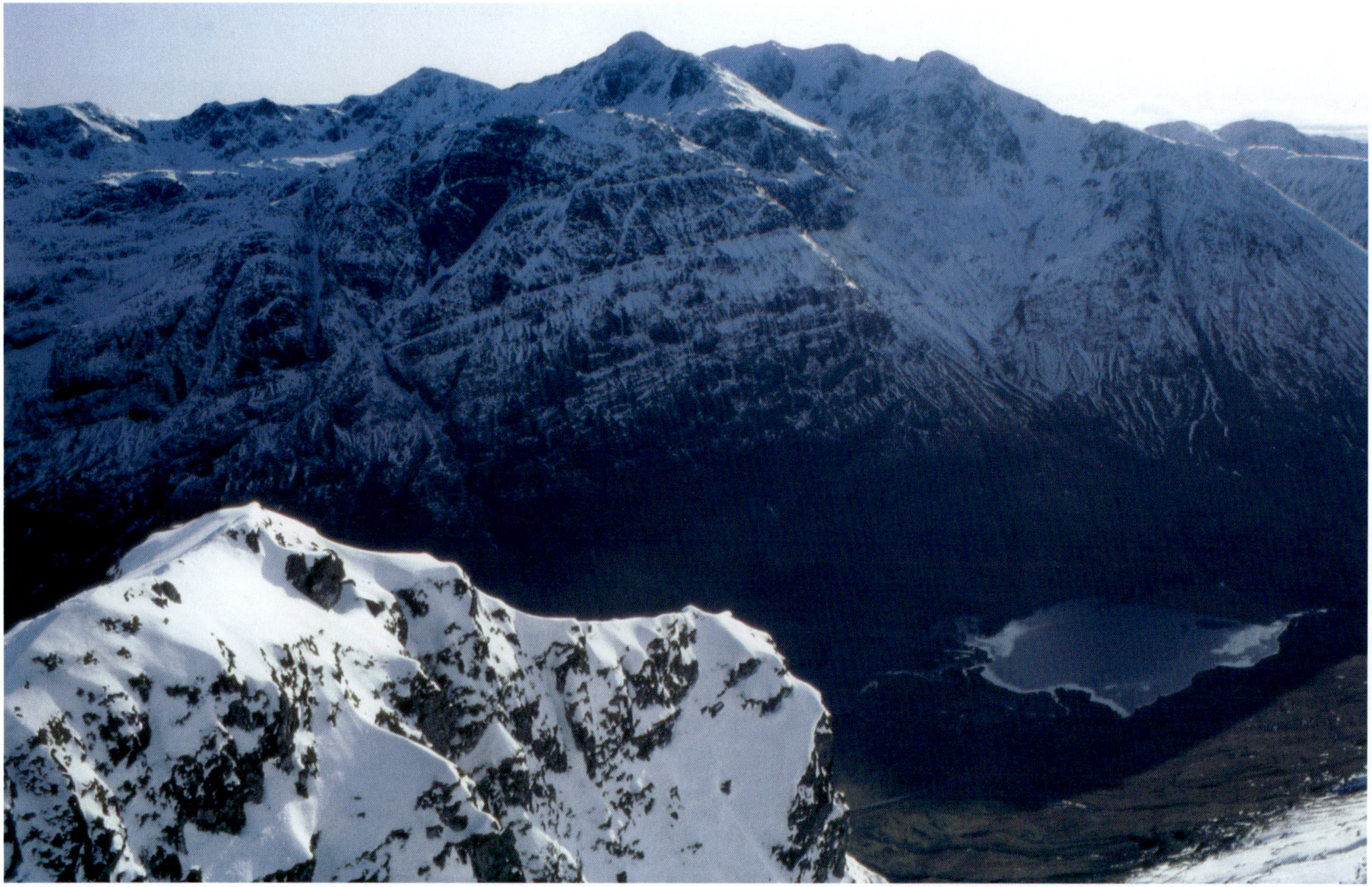

Across the glen.
From the Aonach Eagach you have a superb view across Glencoe to Loch Achtriochtan under the shadowy bulk of the Bidean nam Bian massif.

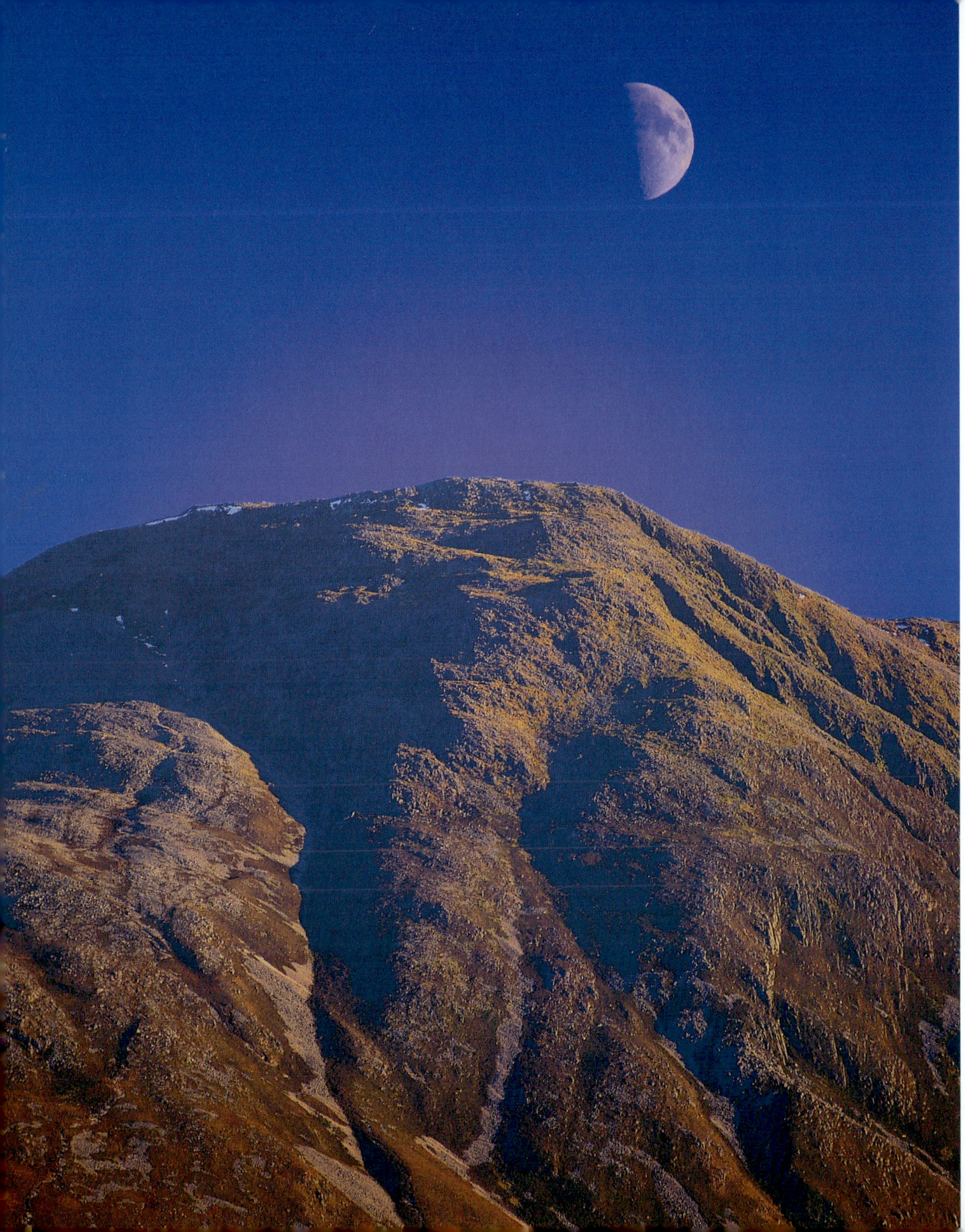

Moonrise.
The moon rises over Sgorr nam Fiannaidh (*peak of the Fian warriors*) at the western end of the Aonach Eagach.

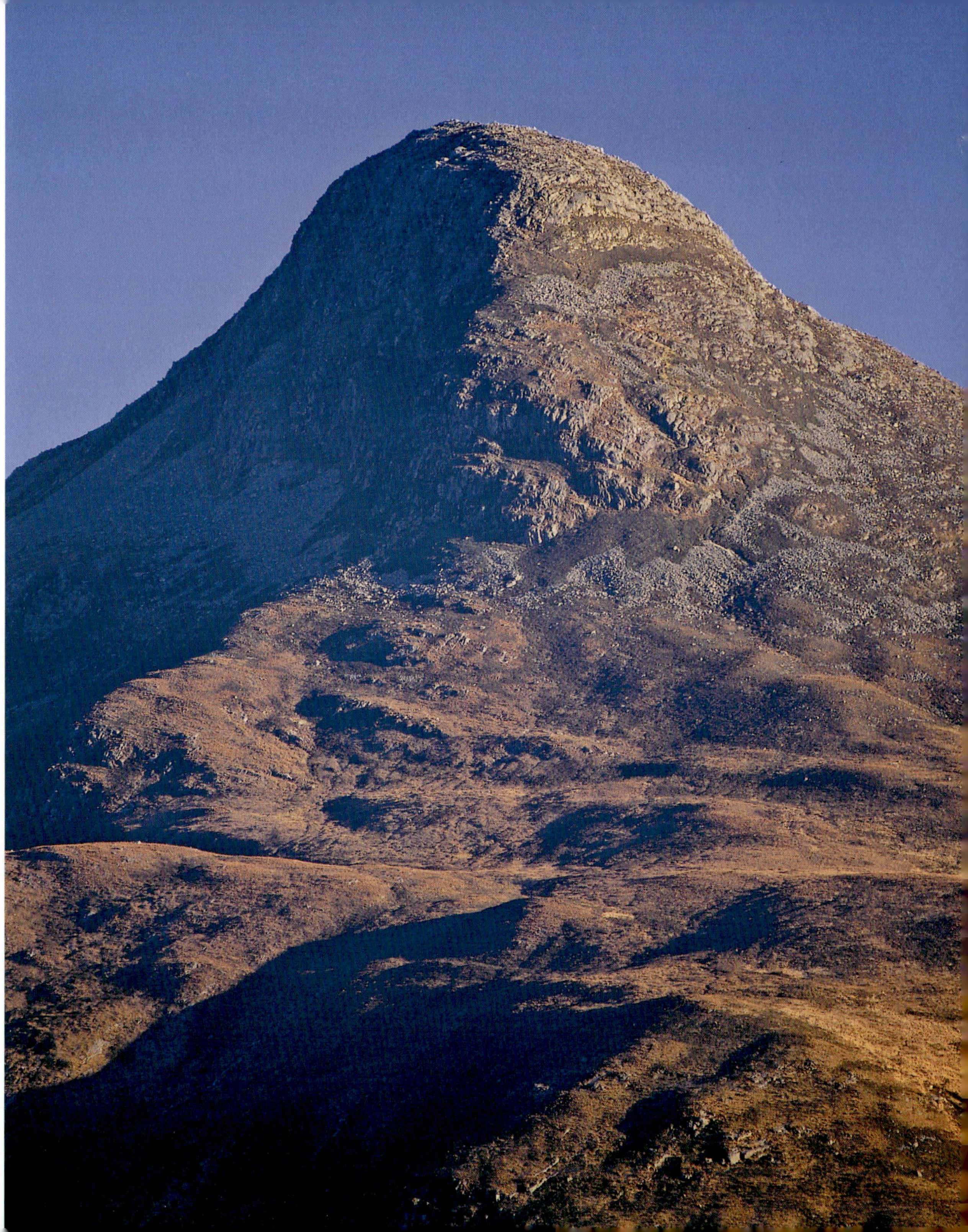

Sentinel peak.
The distinctive cone of Sgorr na Ciche (*Pap of Glencoe*), sentinel to Glencoe. The rounded summit cone is made up of quartzite scree and boulders.

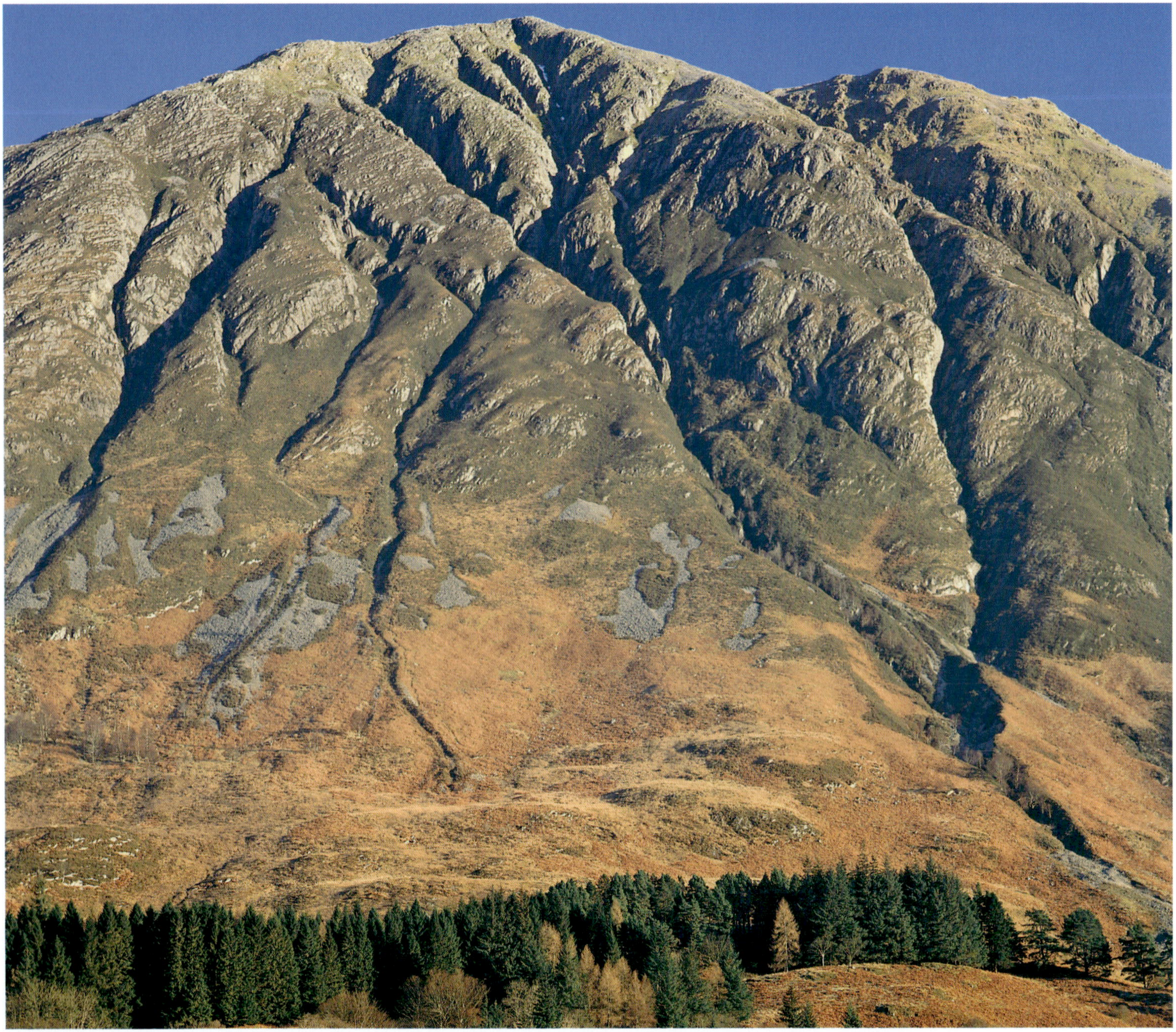

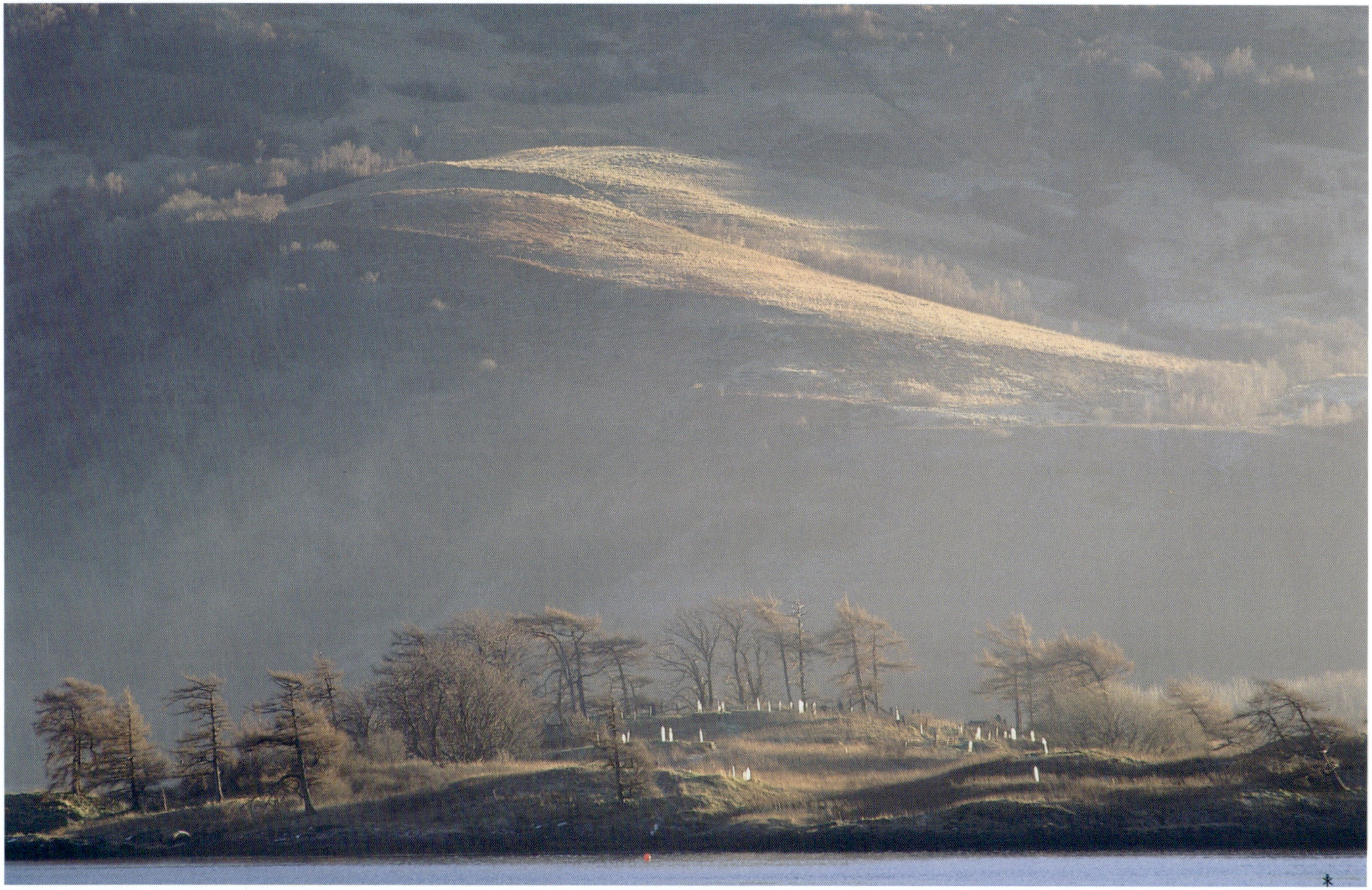

Burial island.

Evening sunshine across Loch Leven highlights the gravestones on Eilean Munde (St Munda's Island) the ancient burial isle of the MacDonalds of Glencoe. The ruins of the island's chapel can still be seen.

Opposite: An etched face.

The deeply cut Clachaig Gully splits the south face of Sgorr nam Fiannaidh. At the foot of the gully is the Clachaig Inn and the nearby Signal Rock. Although there is no historical evidence, according to legend, a fire was lit on Signal Rock to commence the Massacre of Glencoe. Beyond the woods the old road winds through woodland to Glencoe village in upper Carnoch.

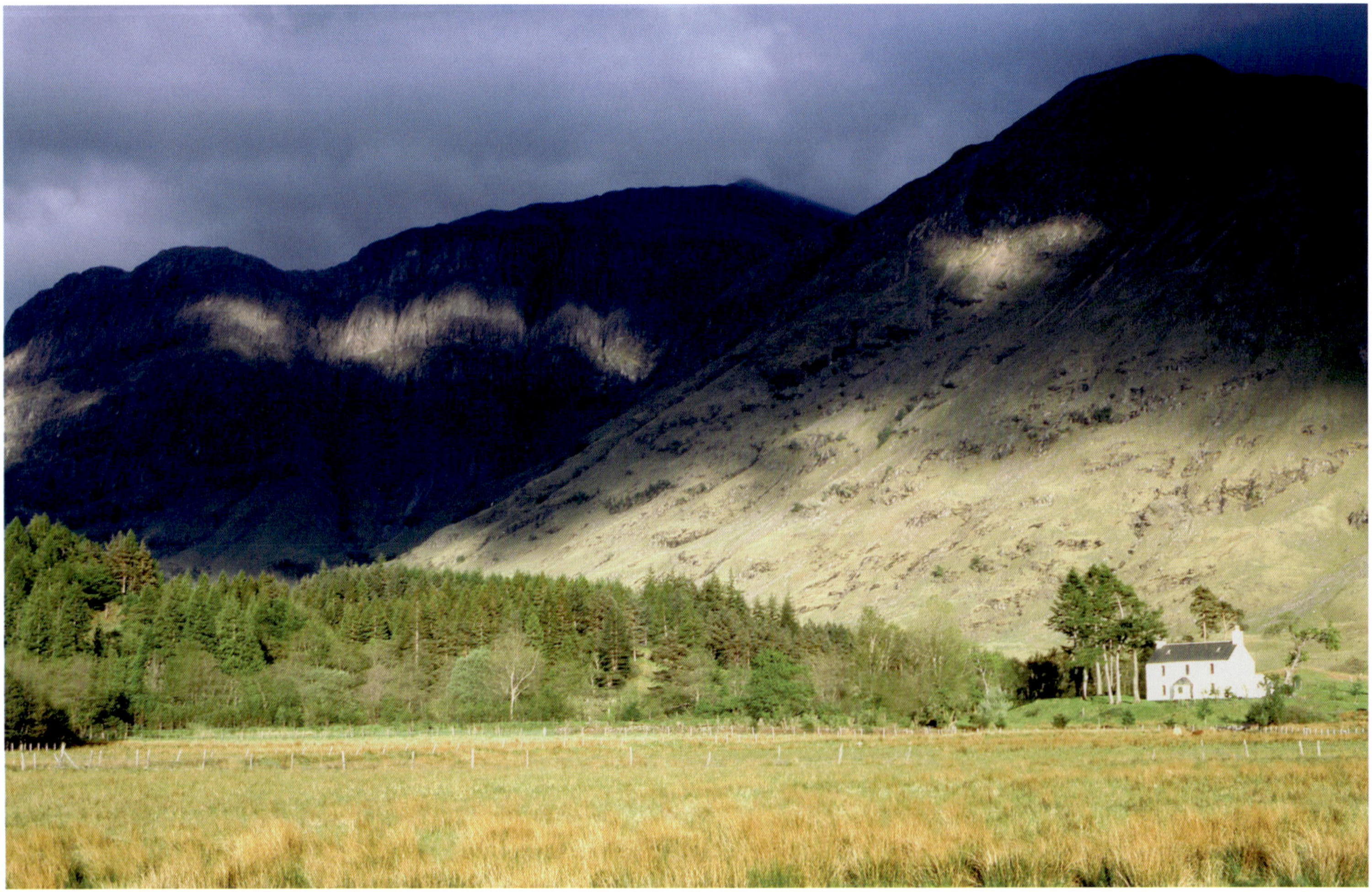

Glowering skies.

A break in the storm clouds over Aonach Dubh allows a patch of sunshine to pick out the farmhouse at Achnacon.

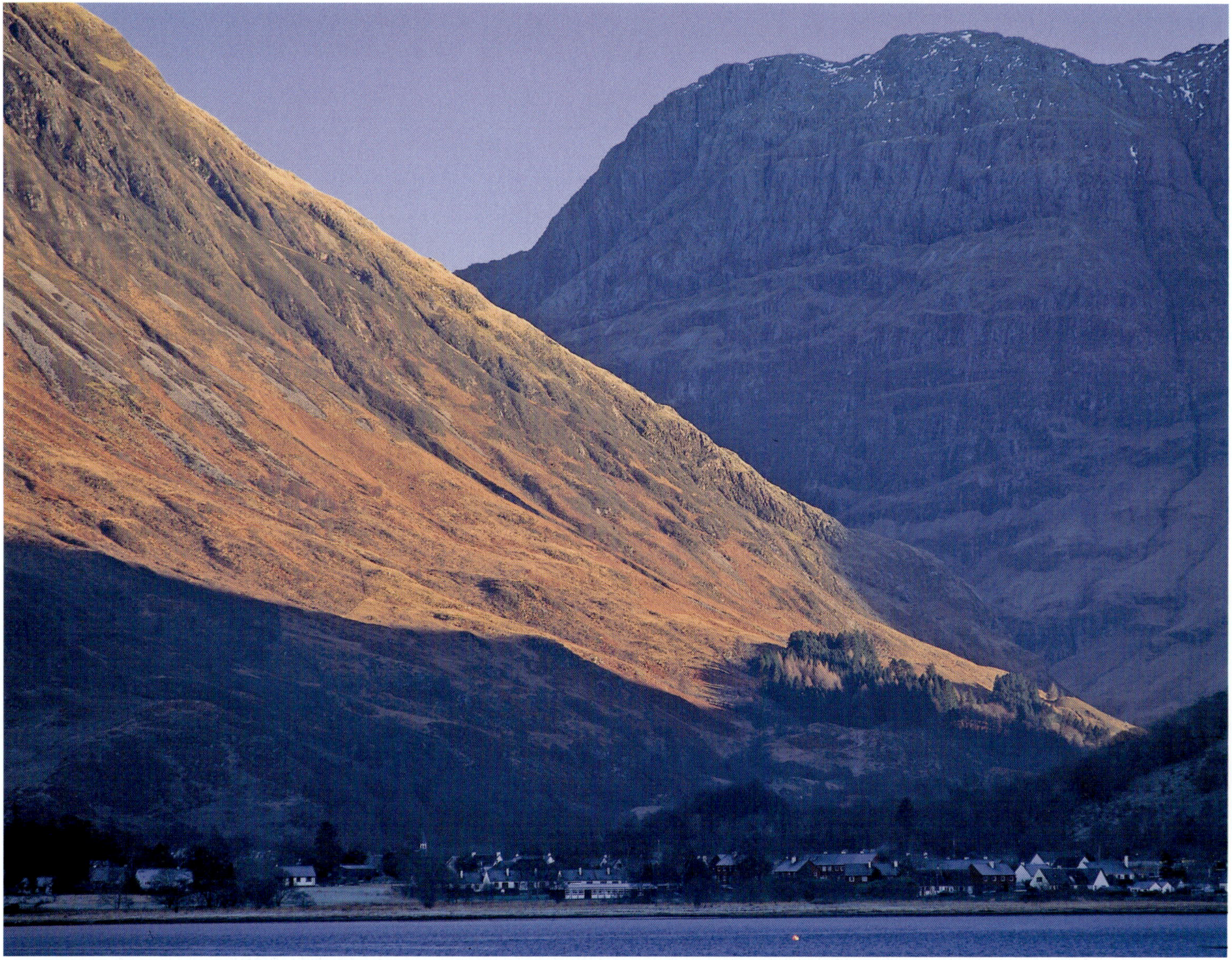

Dusk.

Twilight descends on Glencoe village seen across the sea loch of Loch Leven. At the end of the village, near the Old Bridge of Coe is a Celtic cross erected in 1884 in memory of MacIan, Chief of the Clan MacDonald of Glencoe, who fell with his people in the Massacre of Glencoe.

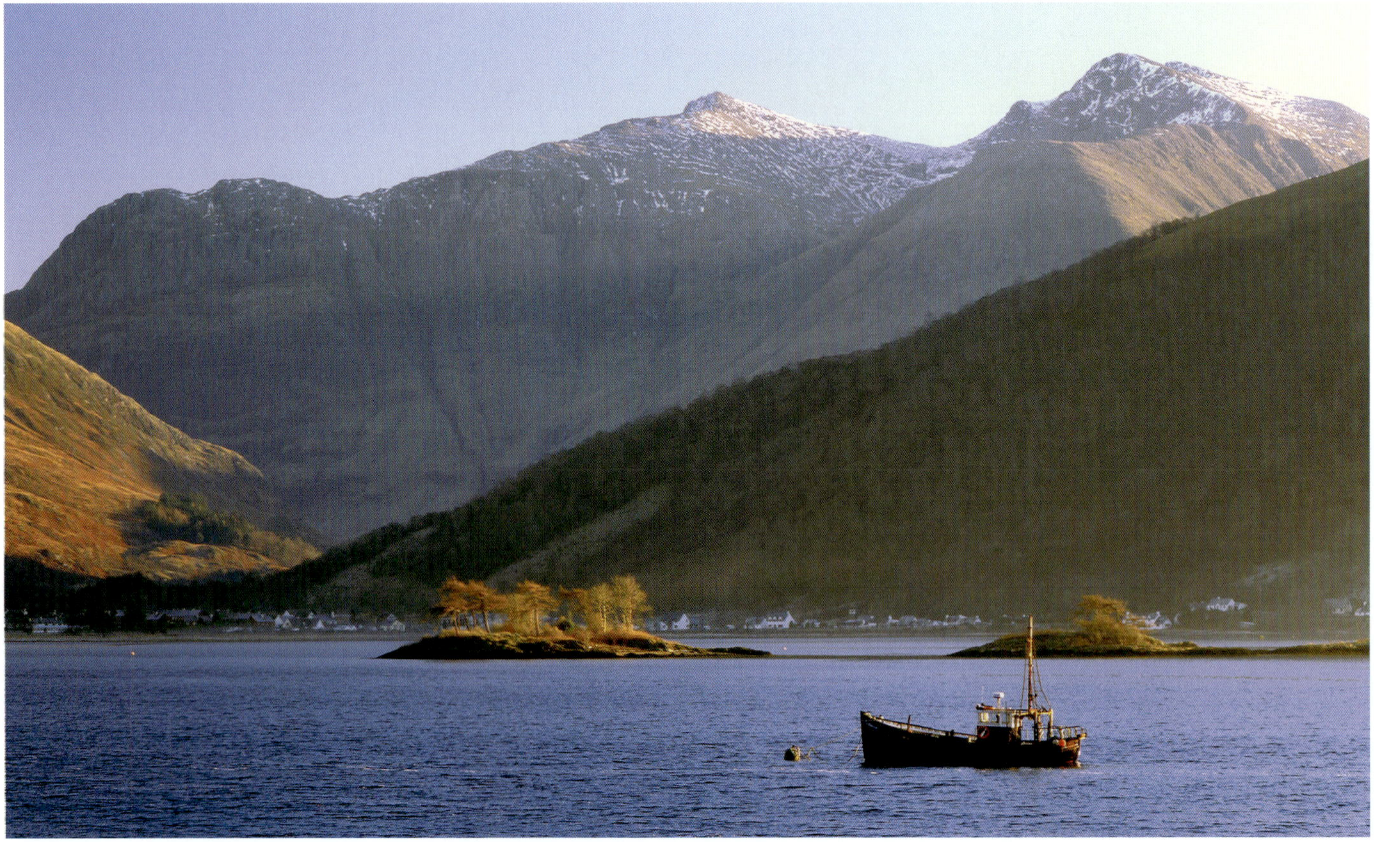

Across the Loch.
The entrance to the Pass of Glencoe looks dramatic in this view across Loch Leven.
The setting sun illuminates the tops of Stob Coire nam Beith and Stob Coire nan Lochan.

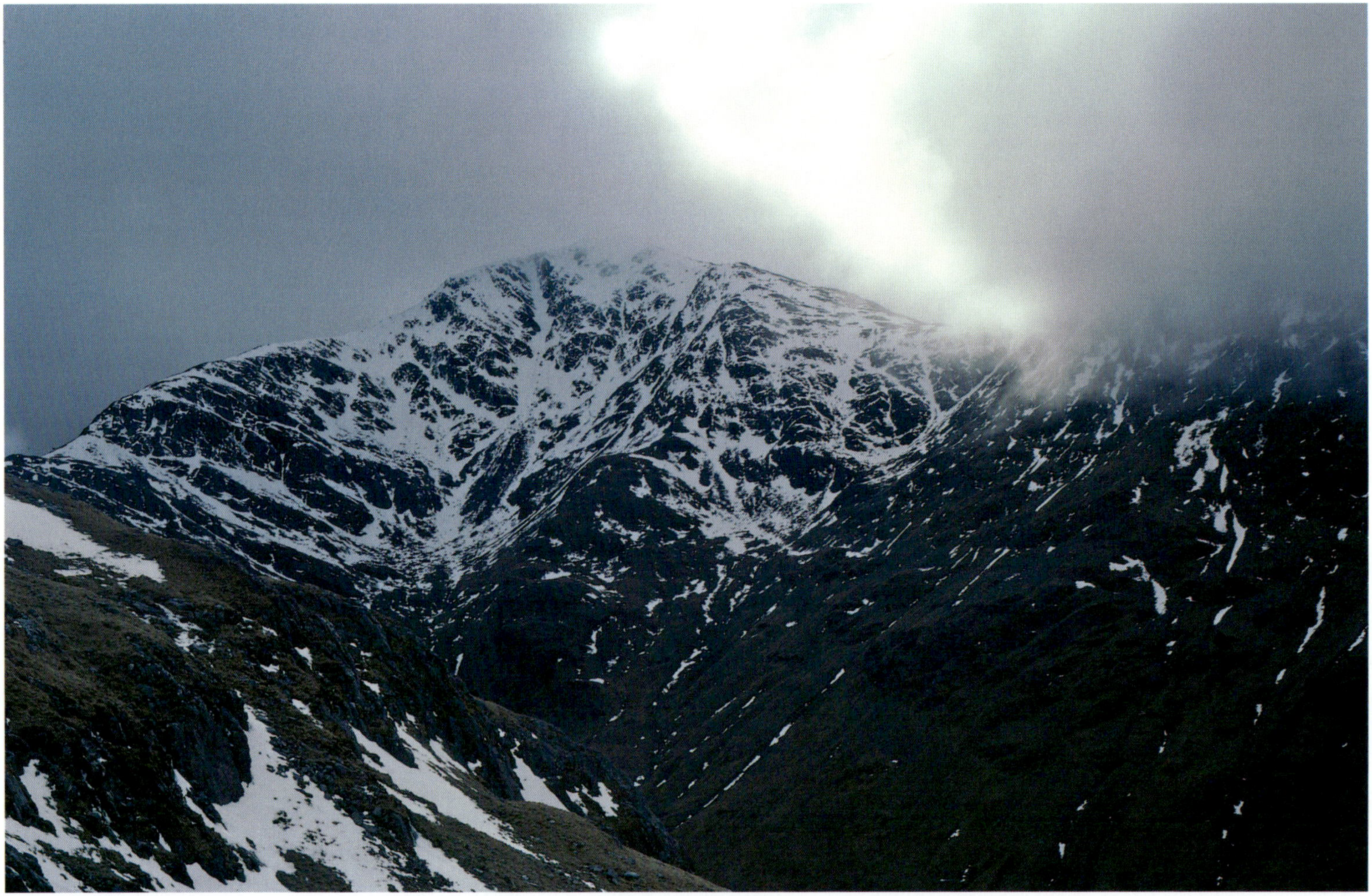

Hidden treasure.
A shaft of light cuts through the storm clouds on Sgor na h-Ulaidh (*peak of treasure*), a neglected hill hidden from the main road at the western end of the Glencoe.

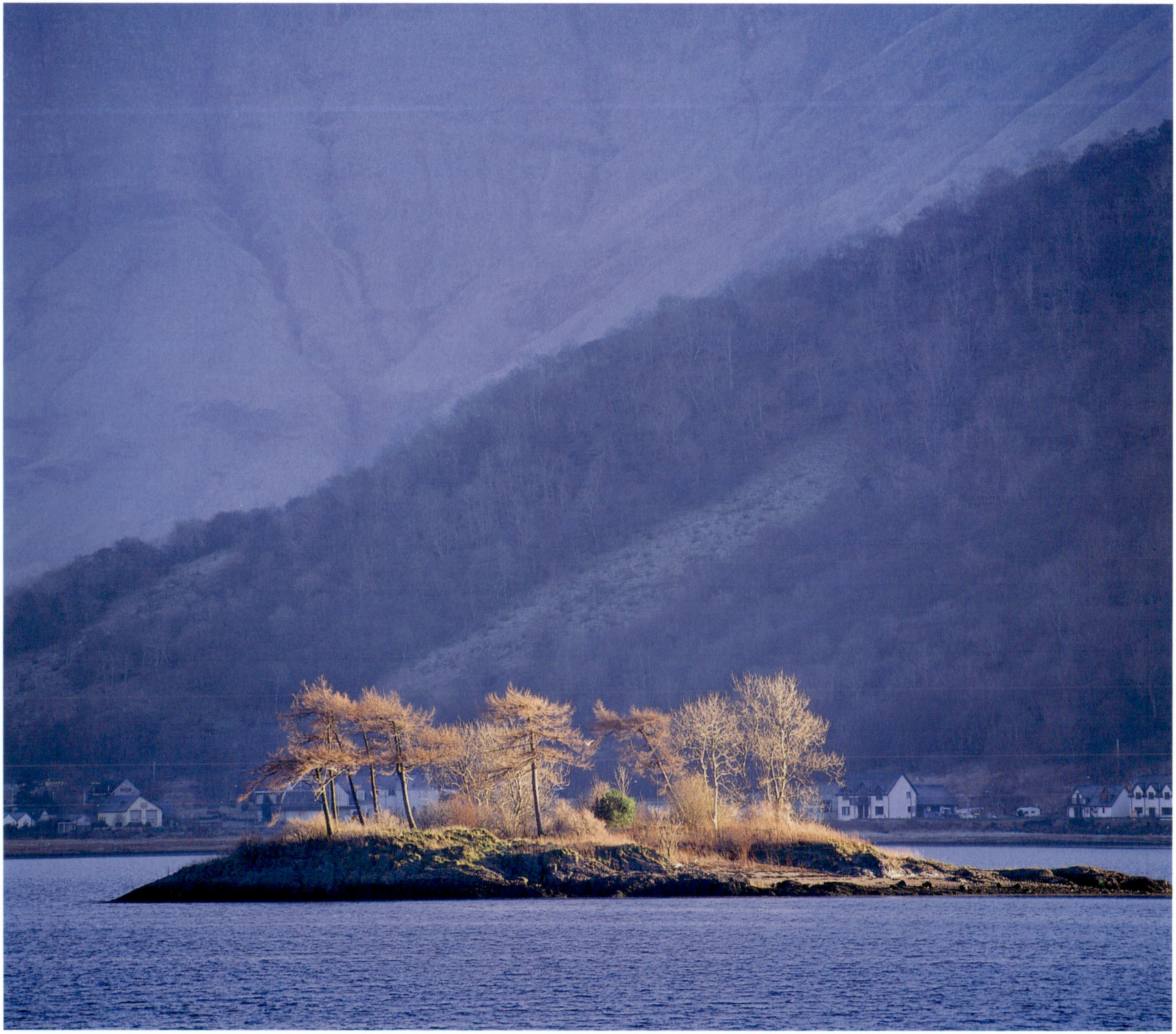

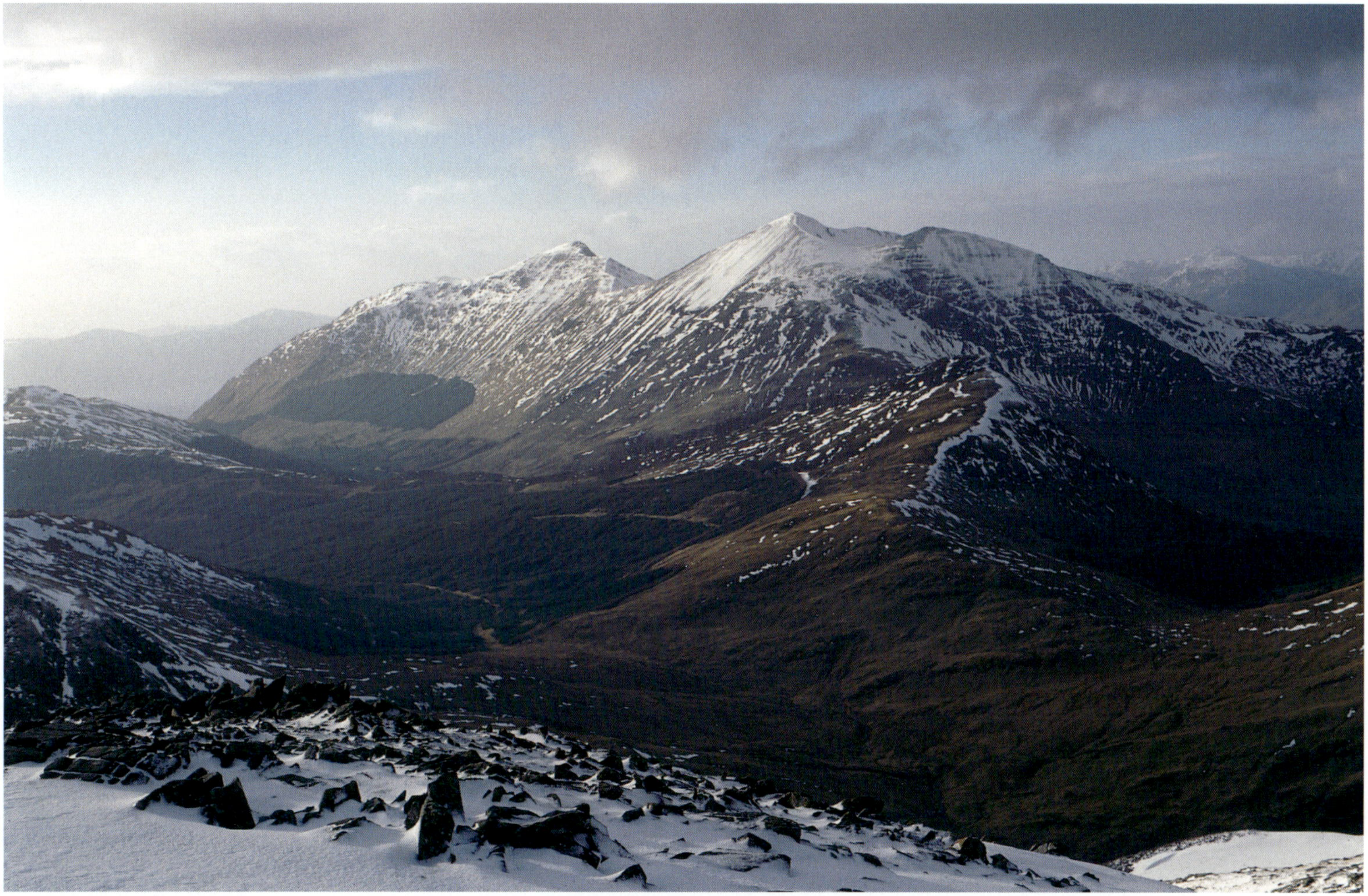

Ballachulish horseshoe.
This fine horseshoe range of hills, linked by graceful ridges, is seen in this western view from the slopes of Sgor na h-Ulaidh. The range sweeps up from the former slate village of Ballachulish on the shore of Loch Leven.

Opposite: Sunlit island.
Evening light picks out one of several small wooded islands on Loch Leven.

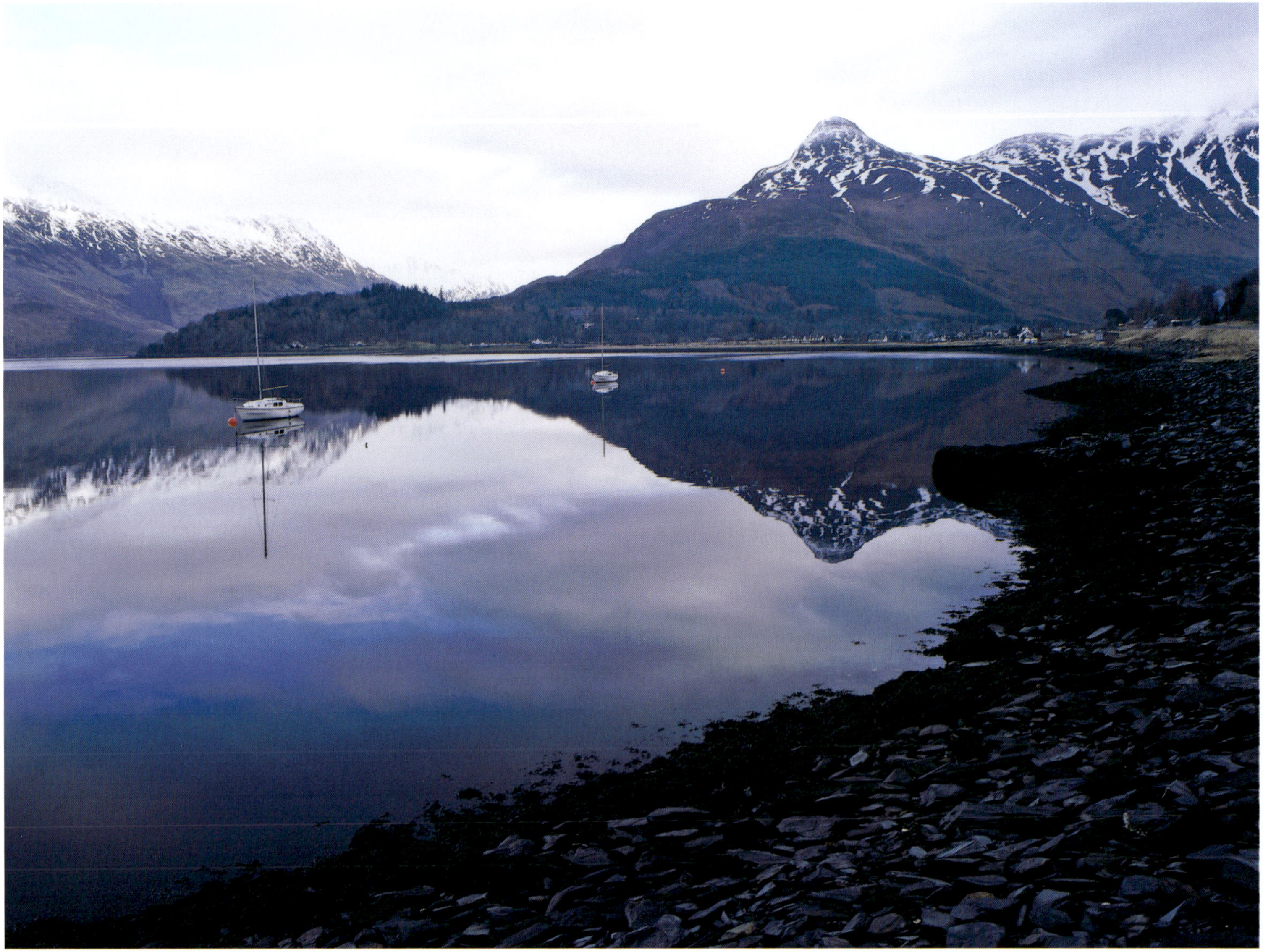

Winter reflections.

Sgor na Ciche (Pap of Glencoe) and the Mamores reflected in an unusually calm Loch Leven seen from near Ballachulish. The fjord-like Loch Leven extends for about 14km from Ballachulish Bay at its western end, to its head at the village of Kinlochleven. Once famous for its aluminium smelting works until their closure in 2000, the village is now an important centre for outdoor activities and provides a gateway into the Mamores

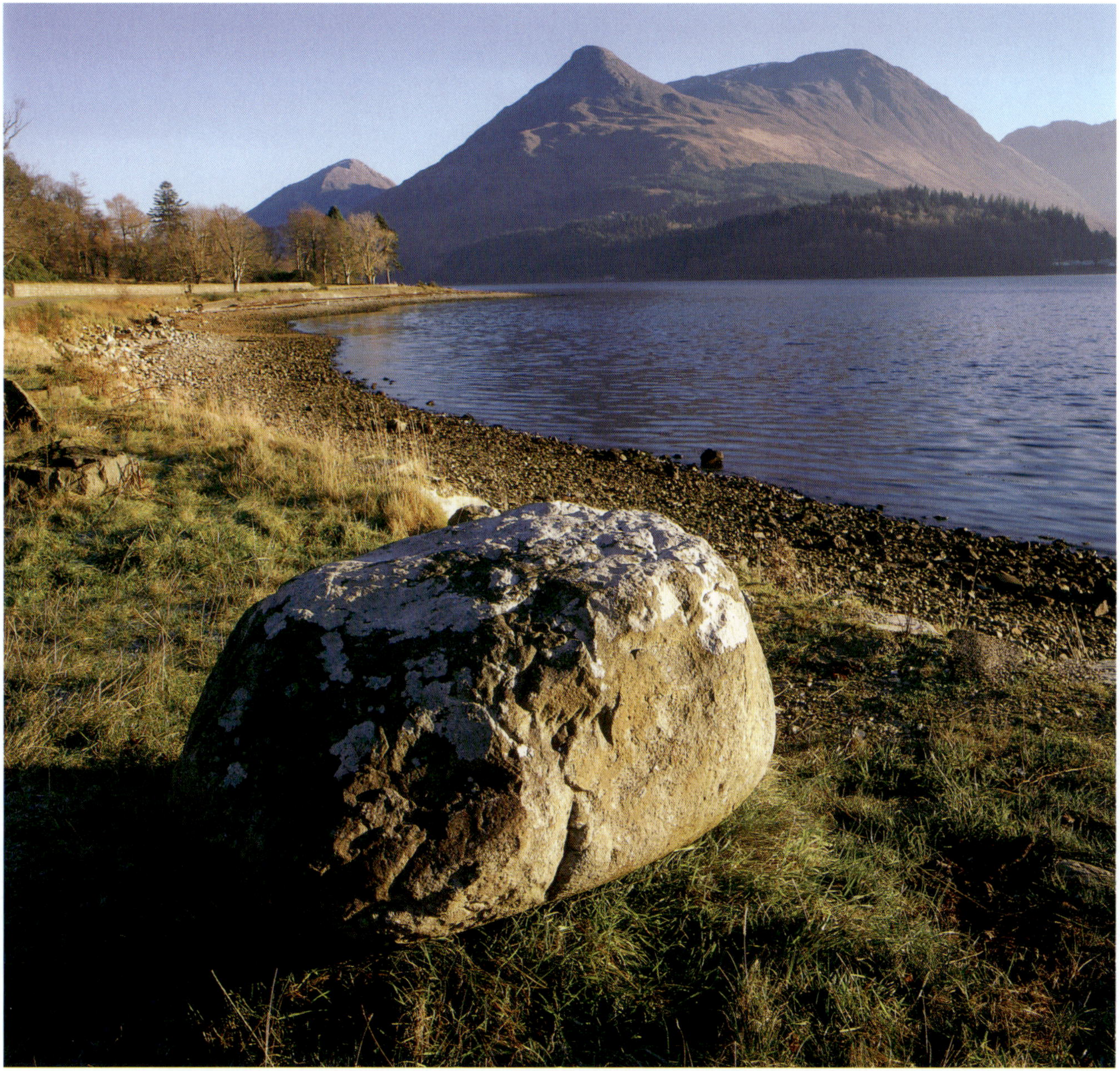

Across the loch.
A large boulder provides a foreground for a view of the Pap of Glencoe and Sgorr nam Fiannaidh across Loch Leven.

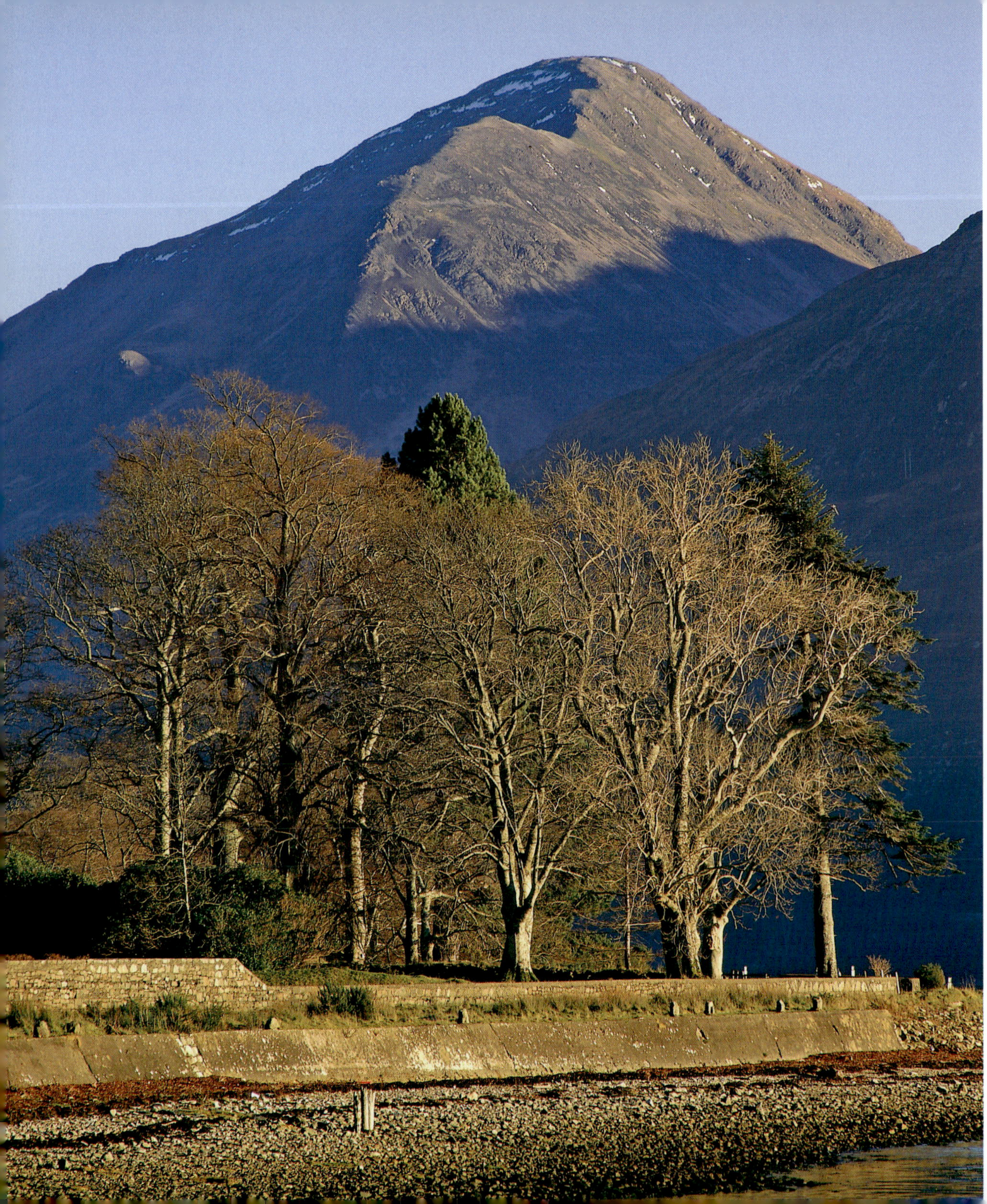

Bulky hill.
The shapely peak of Garbh Bheinn rising from the north shore of Loch Leven is a wonderful sight in autumn sunlight.

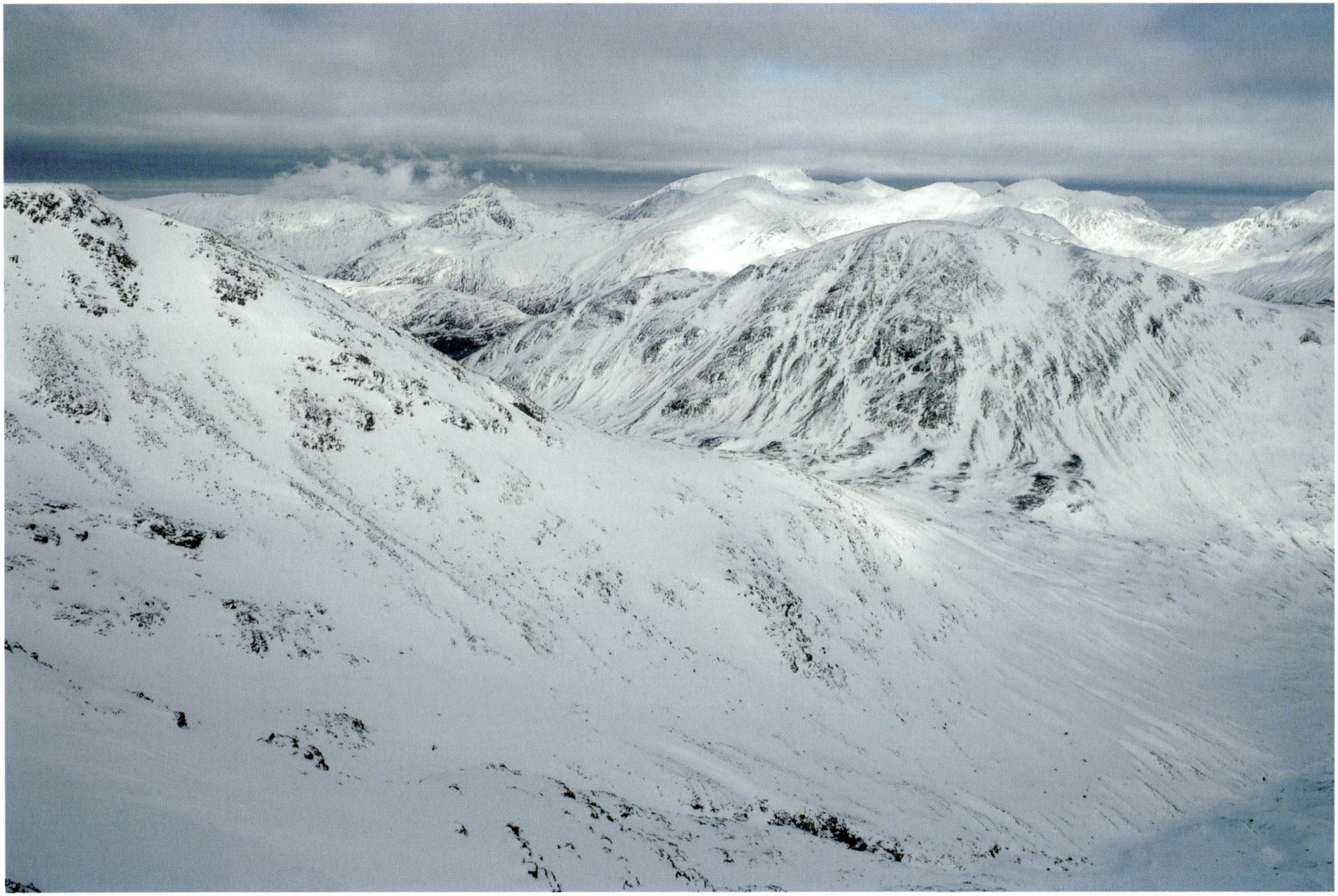

A bleak midwinter.
Patches of sunshine pick out Ben Nevis and the Mamores in this view across Garbh Bheinn.

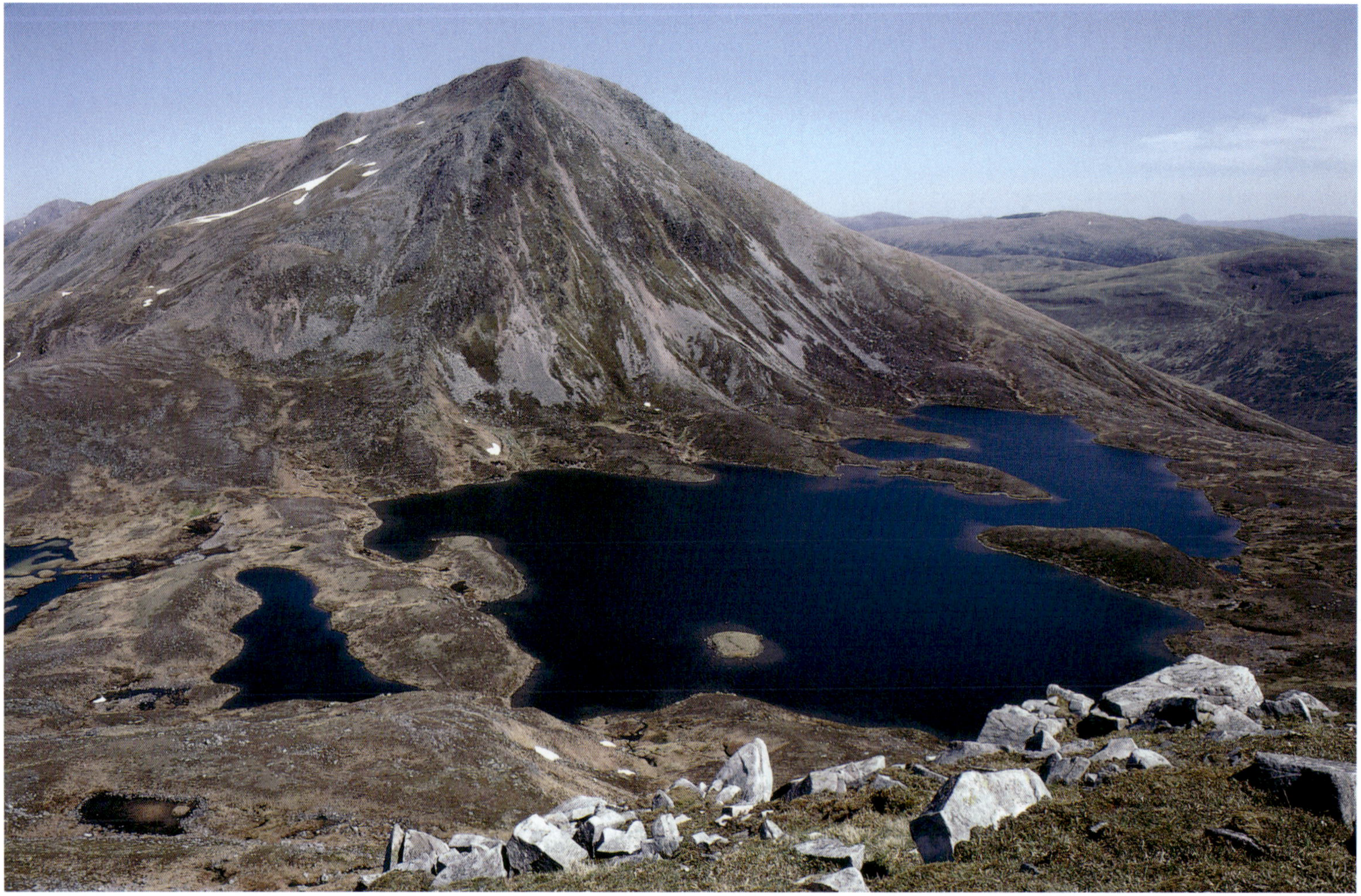

Isolation.

Situated between Loch Leven and Glen Nevis, the Mamores are one of the finest ranges in Scotland.
The conical peak of Sgurr Eilde Mor (*big peak of the hinds)* above Coire an Lochain, is one of the remotest hills in the range.

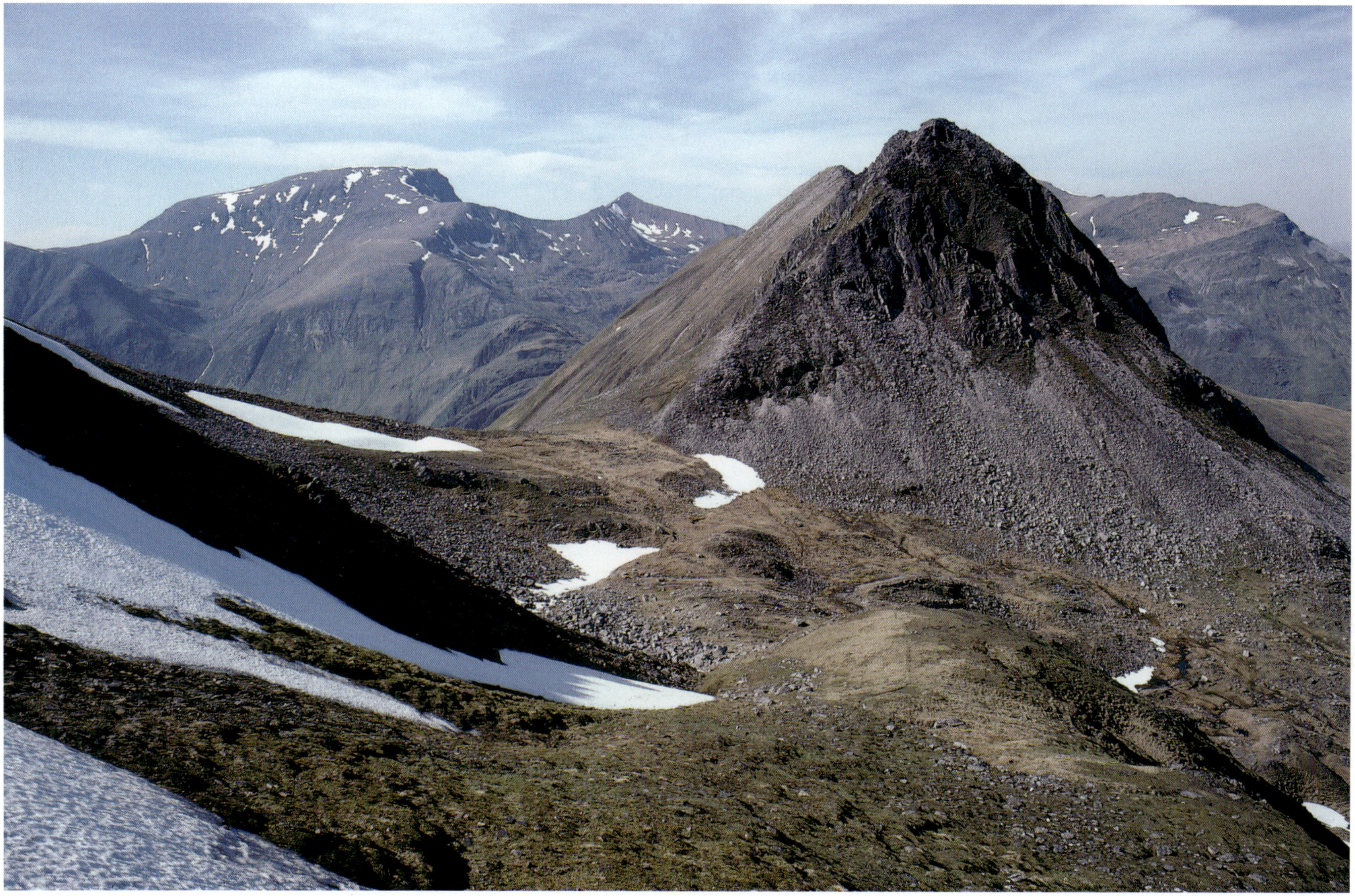

Pointed peak.
The rocky peak of An Garbhanach *(the complainer)* in the Mamores acts as a foreground for this view of Ben Nevis rising beyond the trench of Glen Nevis.

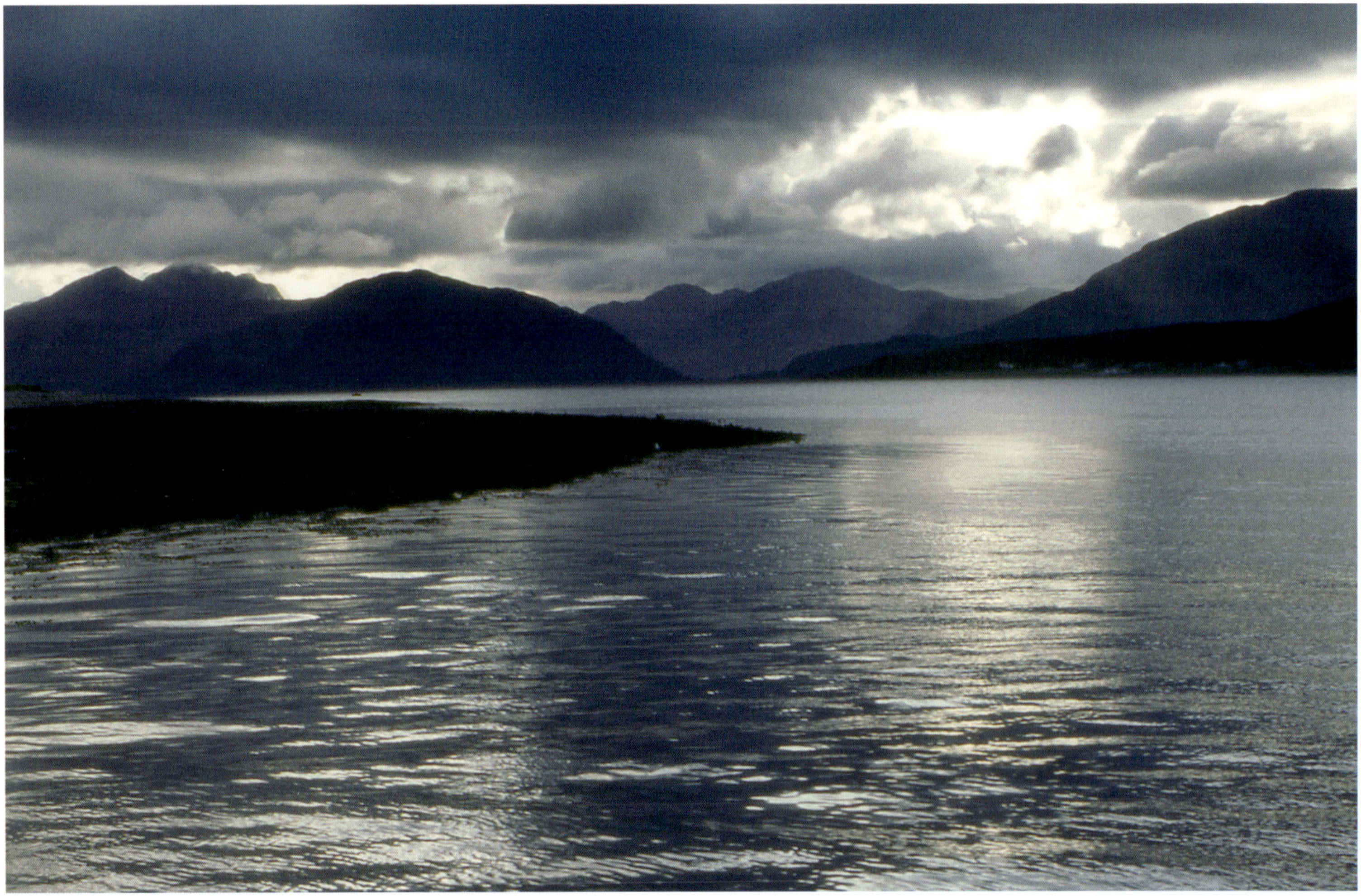

Gathering storm.

Dark clouds sweep across Loch Linnhe backed by the Ardgour hills. The dramatic light gives the scene atmosphere and mood.

Opposite: Dawn over Loch Linnhe.

Winter sunshine at dawn illuminates the craggy buttresses of Garbh Bheinn seen from Onich on the shore of Loch Linnhe.

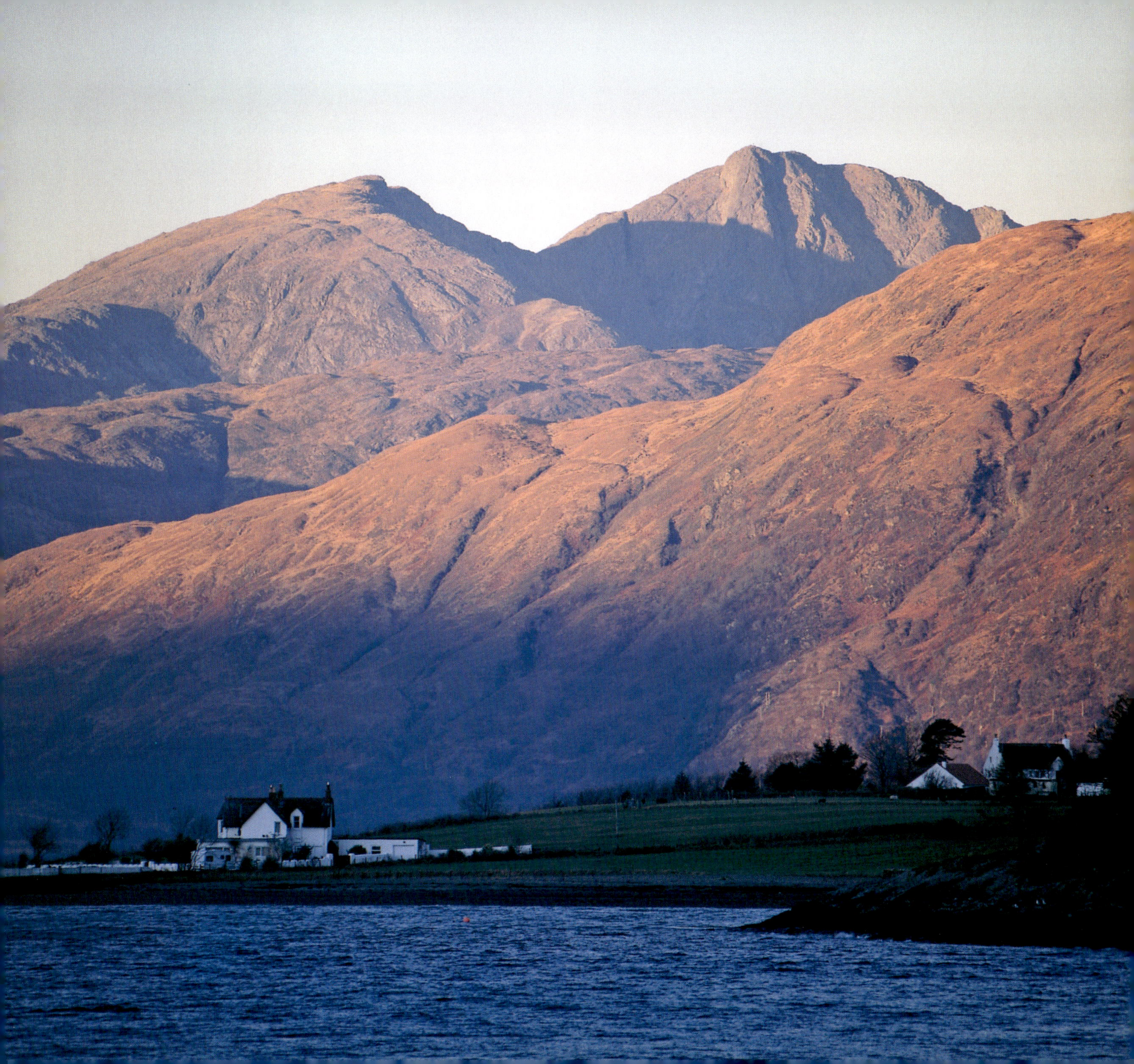

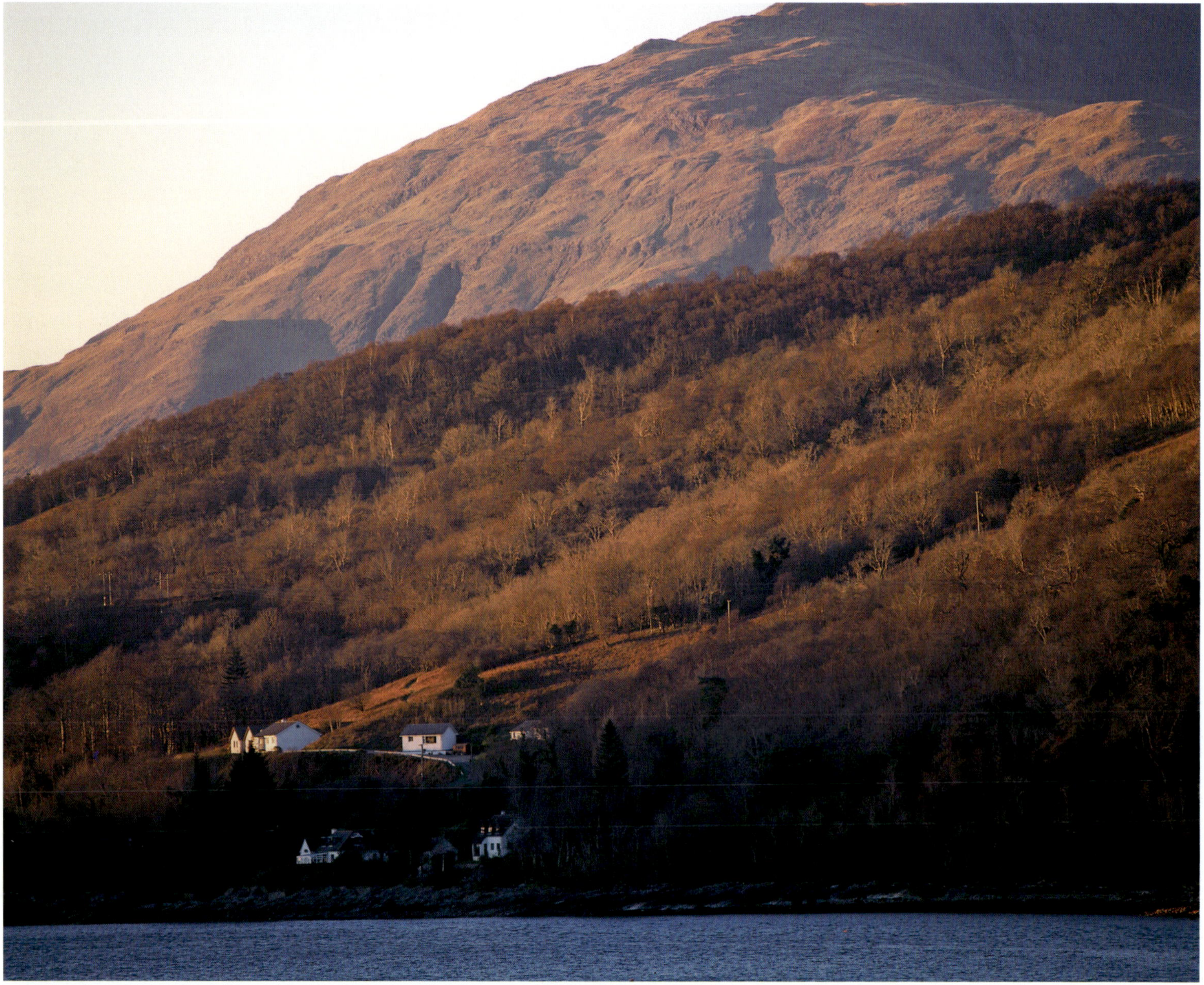

Golden glow.
Light from the setting sun illuminates the wooded hillside above the village of Onich beside Loch Linnhe.

Nature's patterns.
The setting winter sun creates fantastic bands of colour across Loch Linnhe.

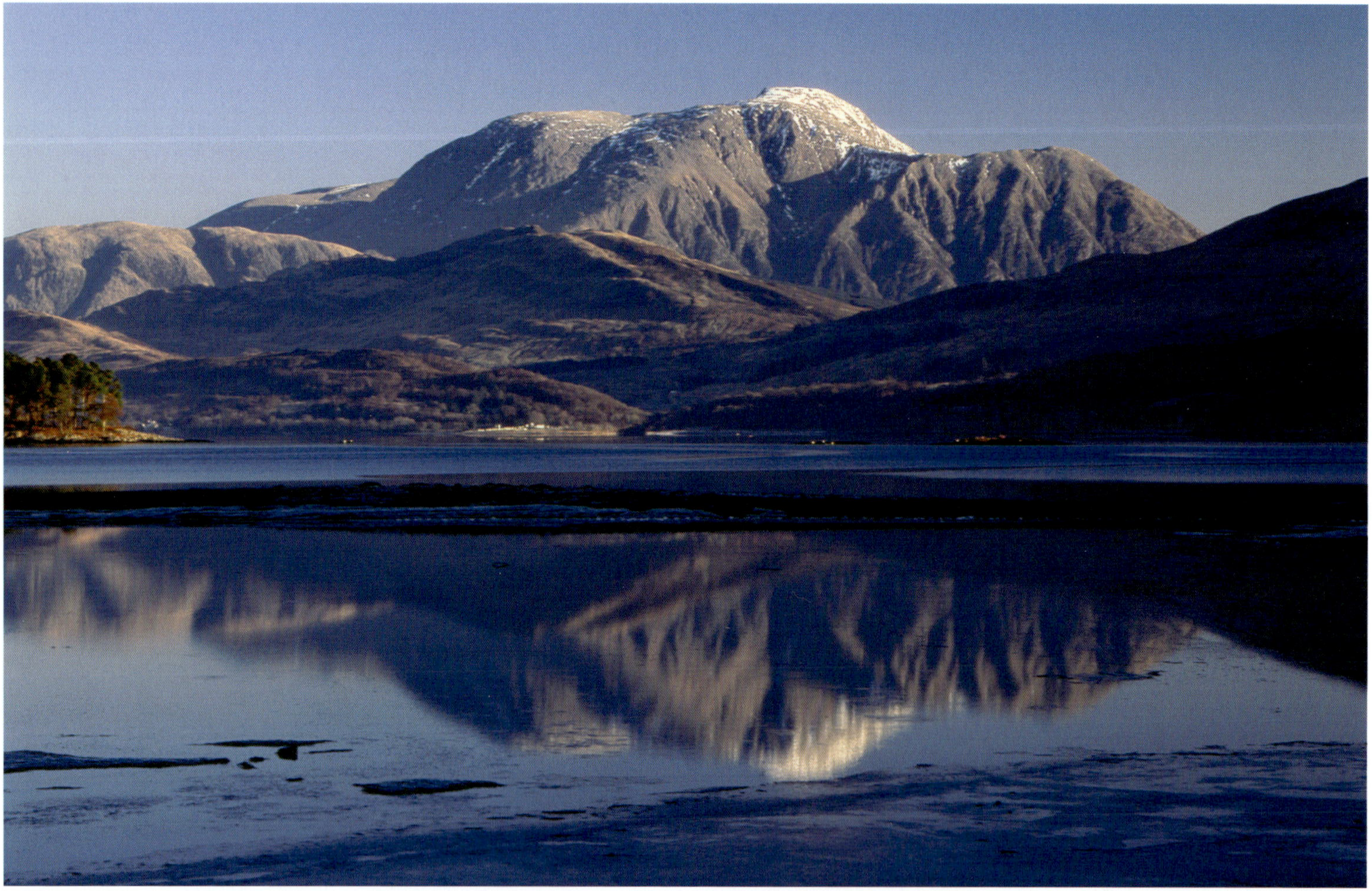

Sleeping giant.
Inverscaddle Bay, on the western shore of Loch Linnhe just north of the Corran ferry crossing, provides a great viewpoint for this unusual perspective of the great flanks and rounded dome of Ben Nevis, Britain's highest mountain.

Opposite: Boats on Loch Linnhe.
Late afternoon sunshine picks out colourful boats on Loch Linnhe, with Fort William in the background.

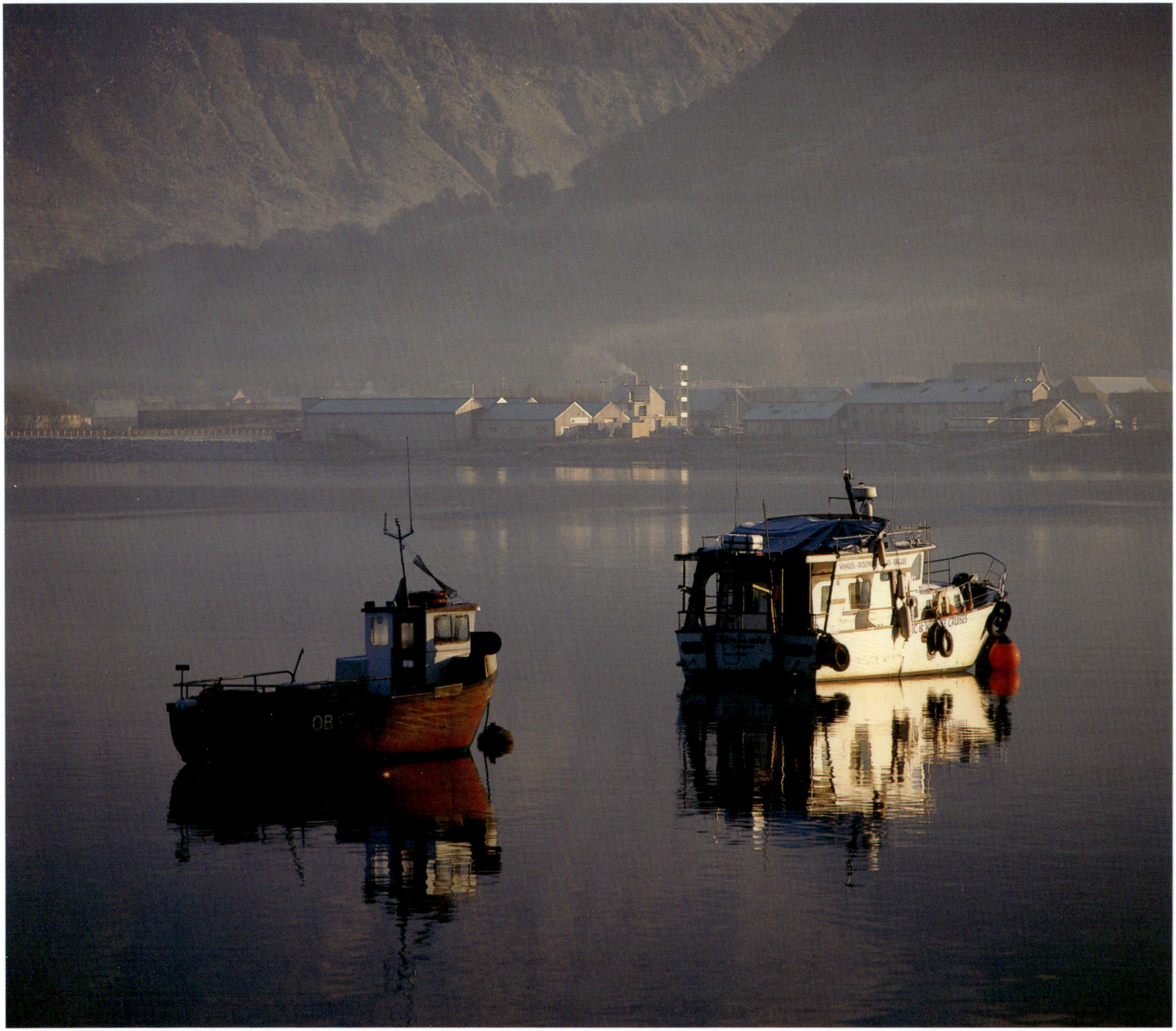

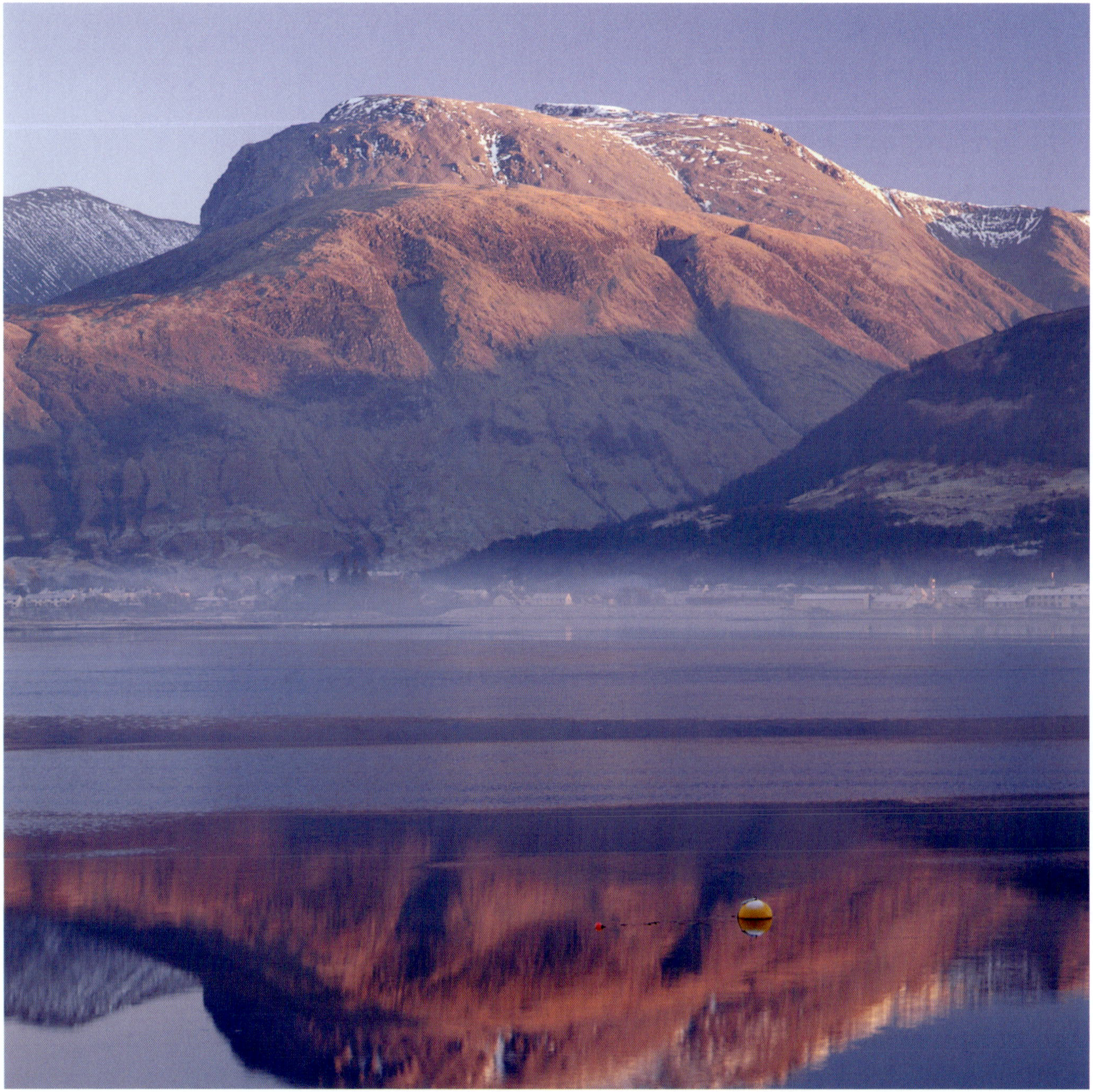

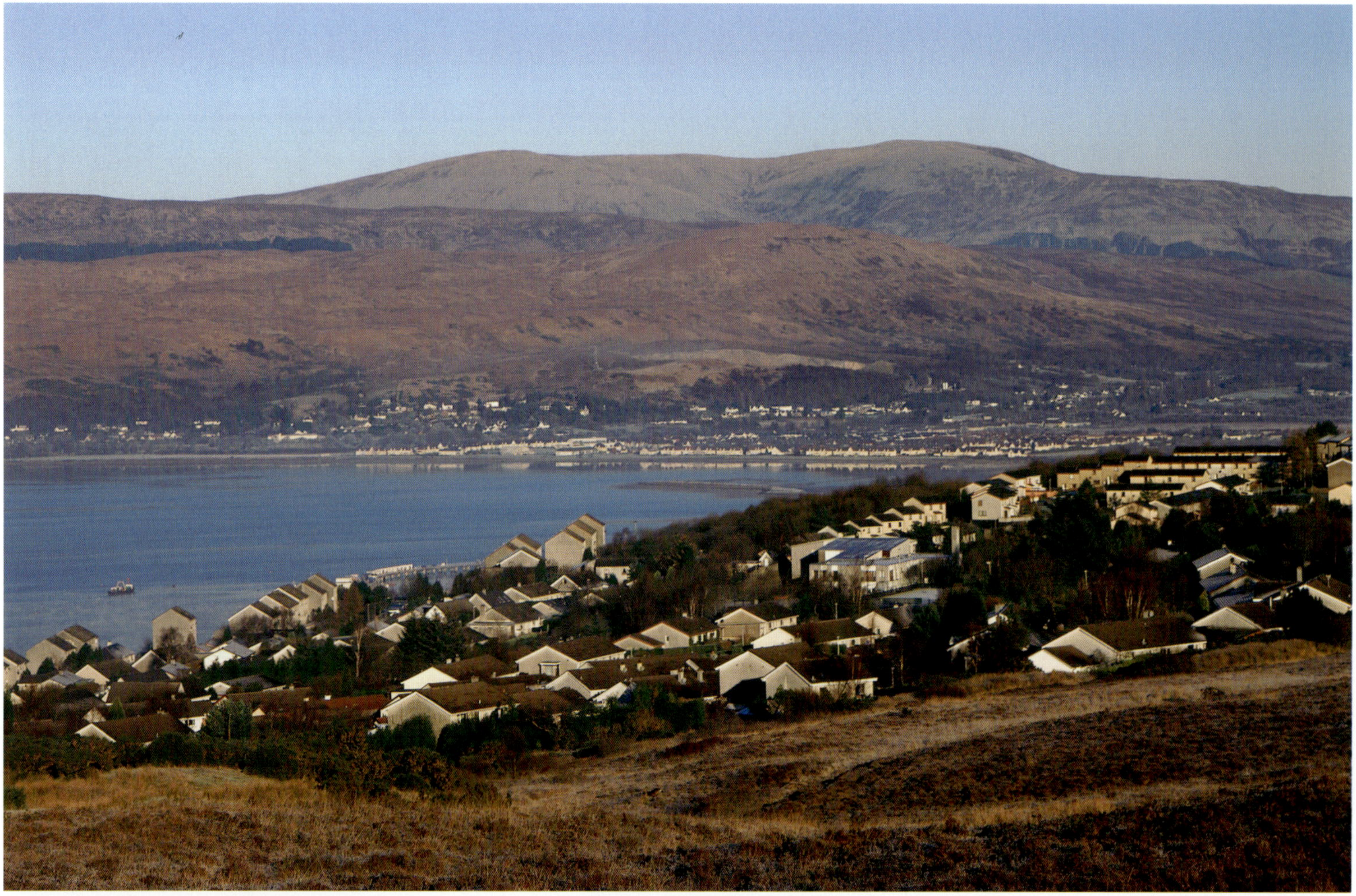

A town with a view.

The slopes of Fort William provide a great view over Loch Linnhe to the Druim Fada hills. Named after the fort built there in the seventeenth century during the reign of King William III (William of Orange) to control the rebellious Highland Clans, Fort William is now famous as being the 'Outdoor Capital of the UK'. Just north of the town is the Nevis Range ski complex and miles of superb mountain bike tracks.

Opposite: Dominant mountain.

The enormous bulk of Ben Nevis looms over the town of Fort William at the head of Loch Linnhe.

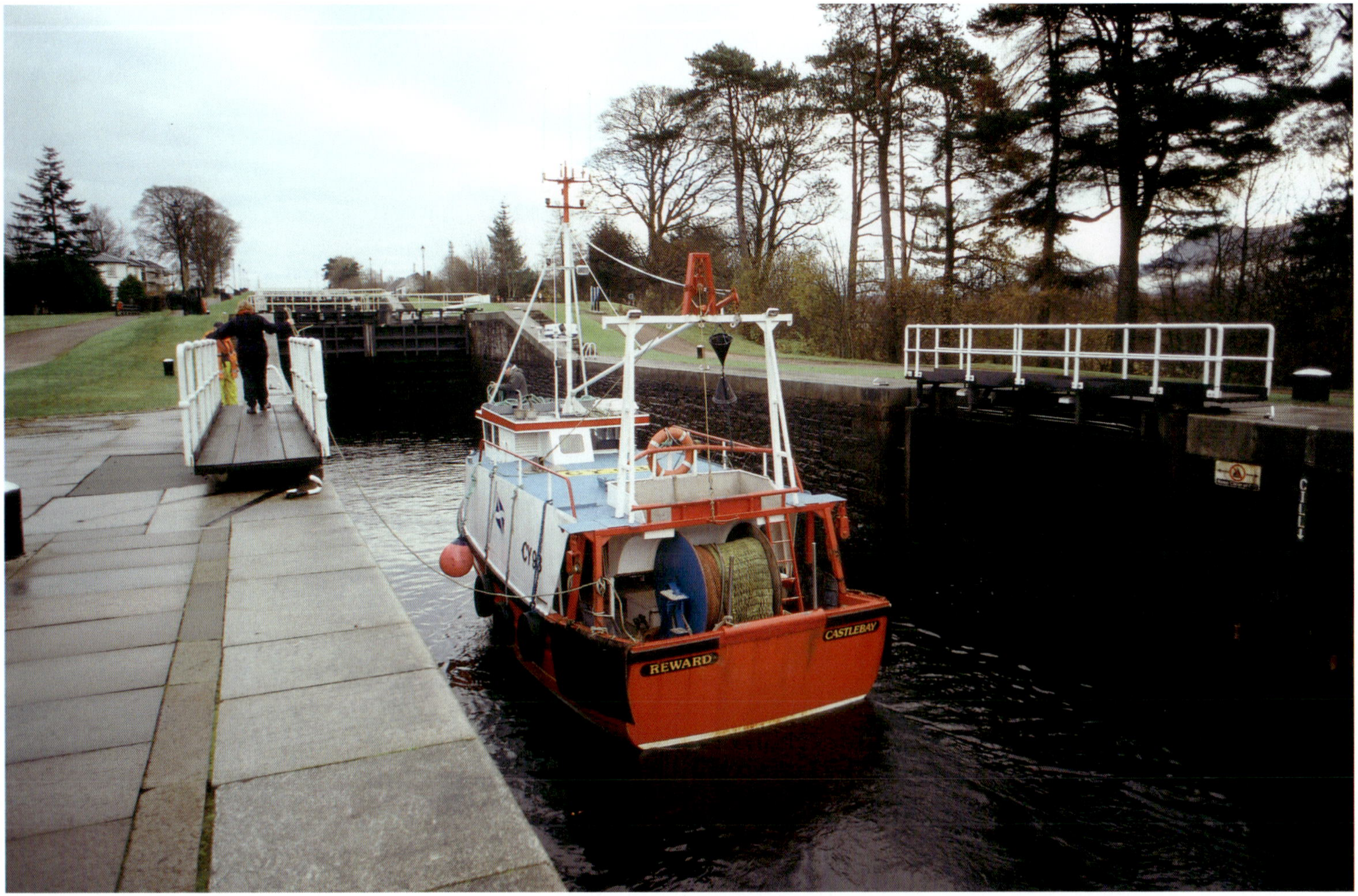

Neptune's Staircase.

A fishing boat makes its slow way through the first of a set of eight locks known as Neptune's Staircase on the Caledonian Canal at Banavie near Fort William. Neptune's Staircase, designed by Thomas Telford and completed in 1822, takes the canal up 64ft/19.5m from sea level into the Great Glen.

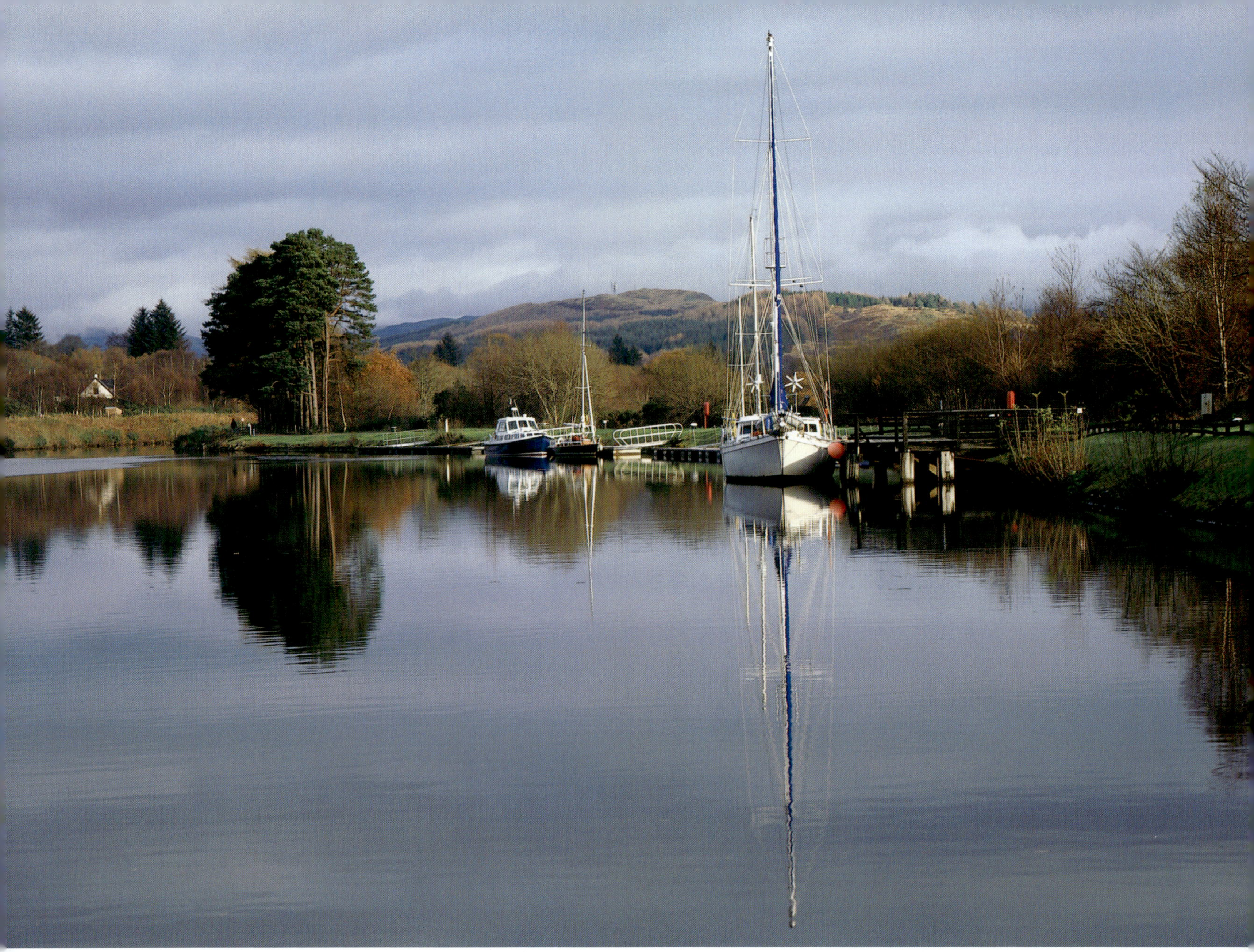

Idyllic mooring.

Boats reflected in the canal basin at the top of Neptune's Staircase, a great place for an overnight stop. The Caledonian Canal follows a natural geological fault stretching along the Great Glen and links Loch Linnhe, in the west, to the Moray Firth in the east via Lochs Lochy, Oich and Ness.

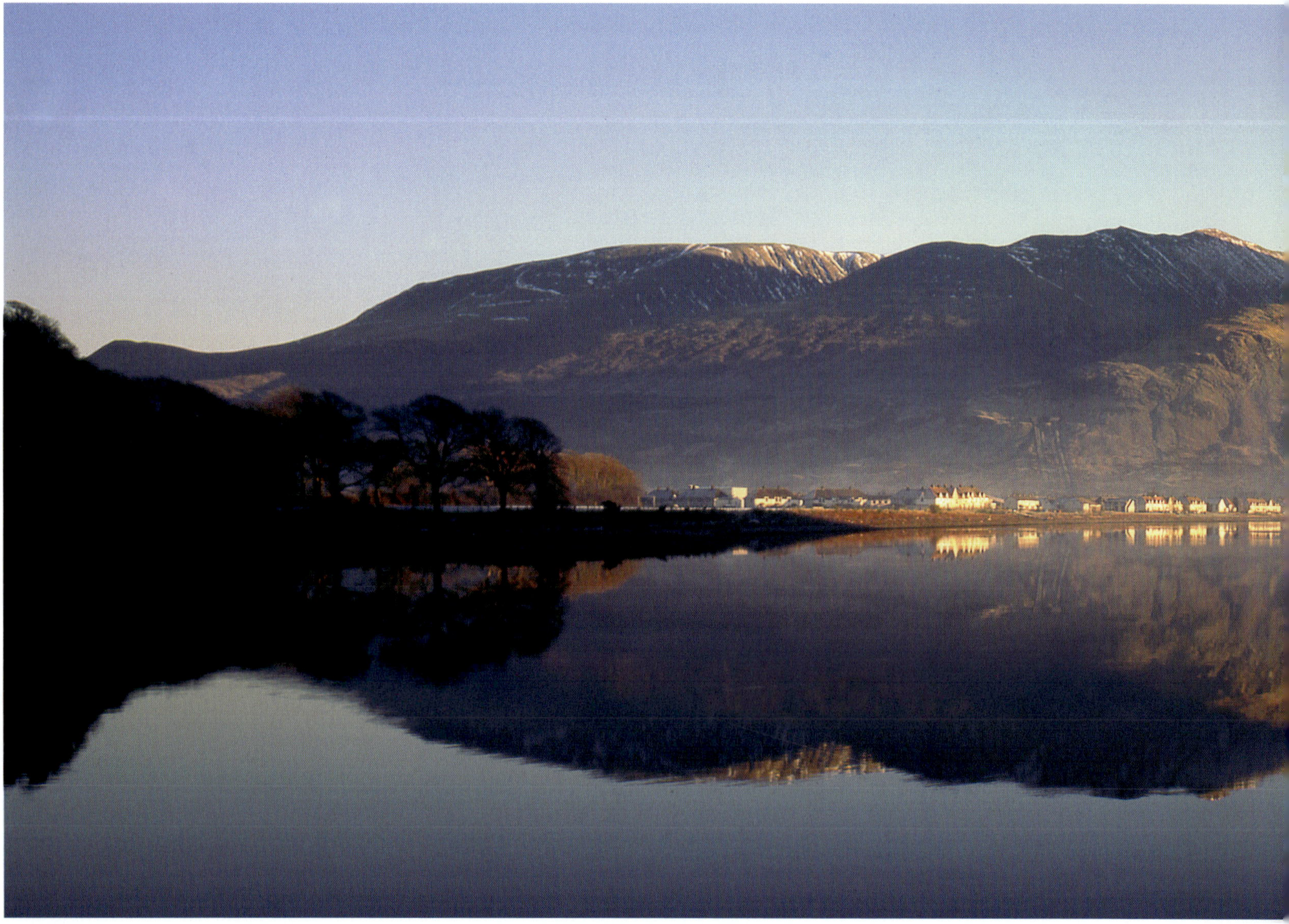

Tranquillity.
The uncommonly still waters of Loch Linnhe provide the perfect reflection of Ben Nevis and the Aonach range in its early winter colours.

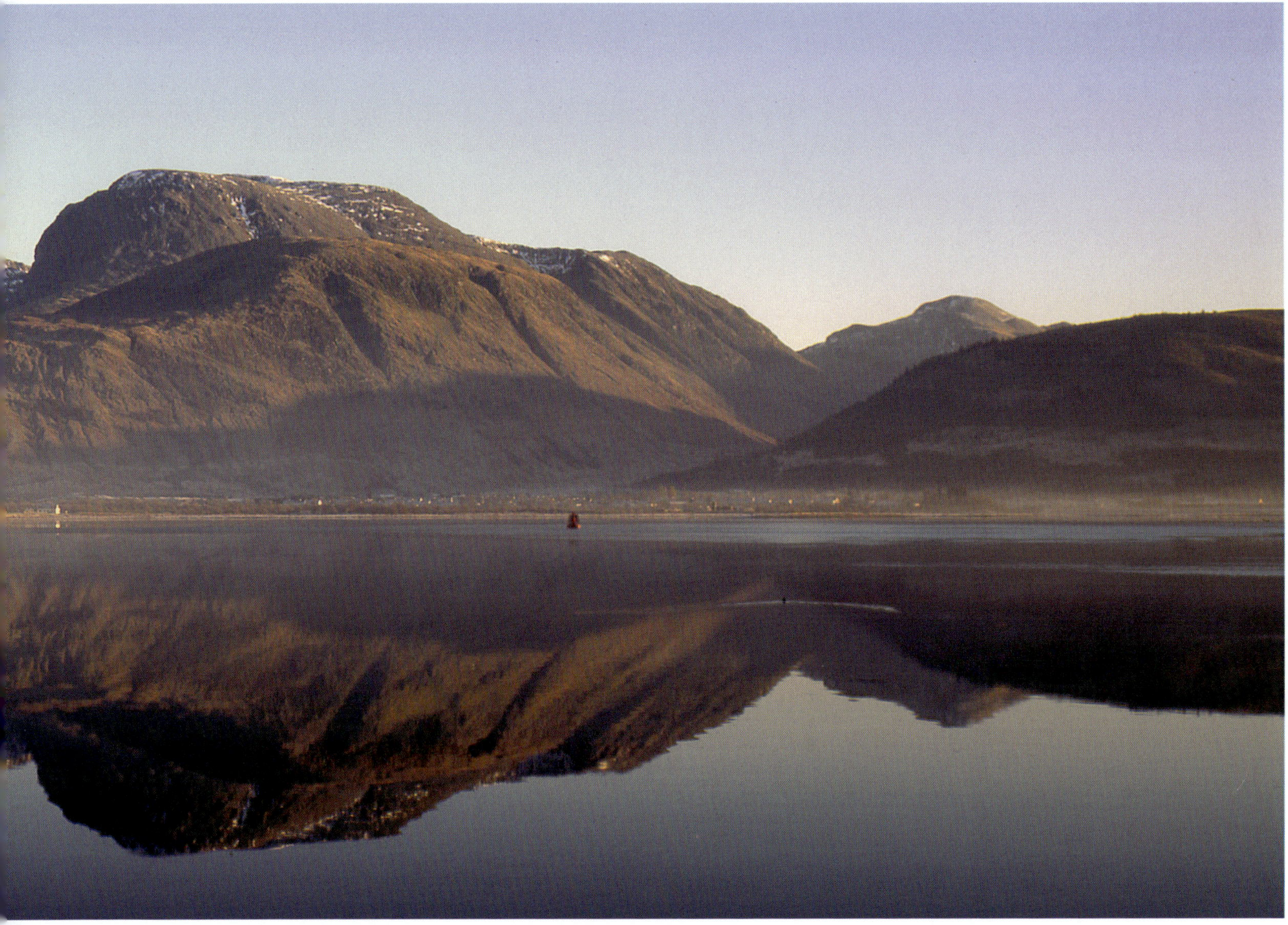

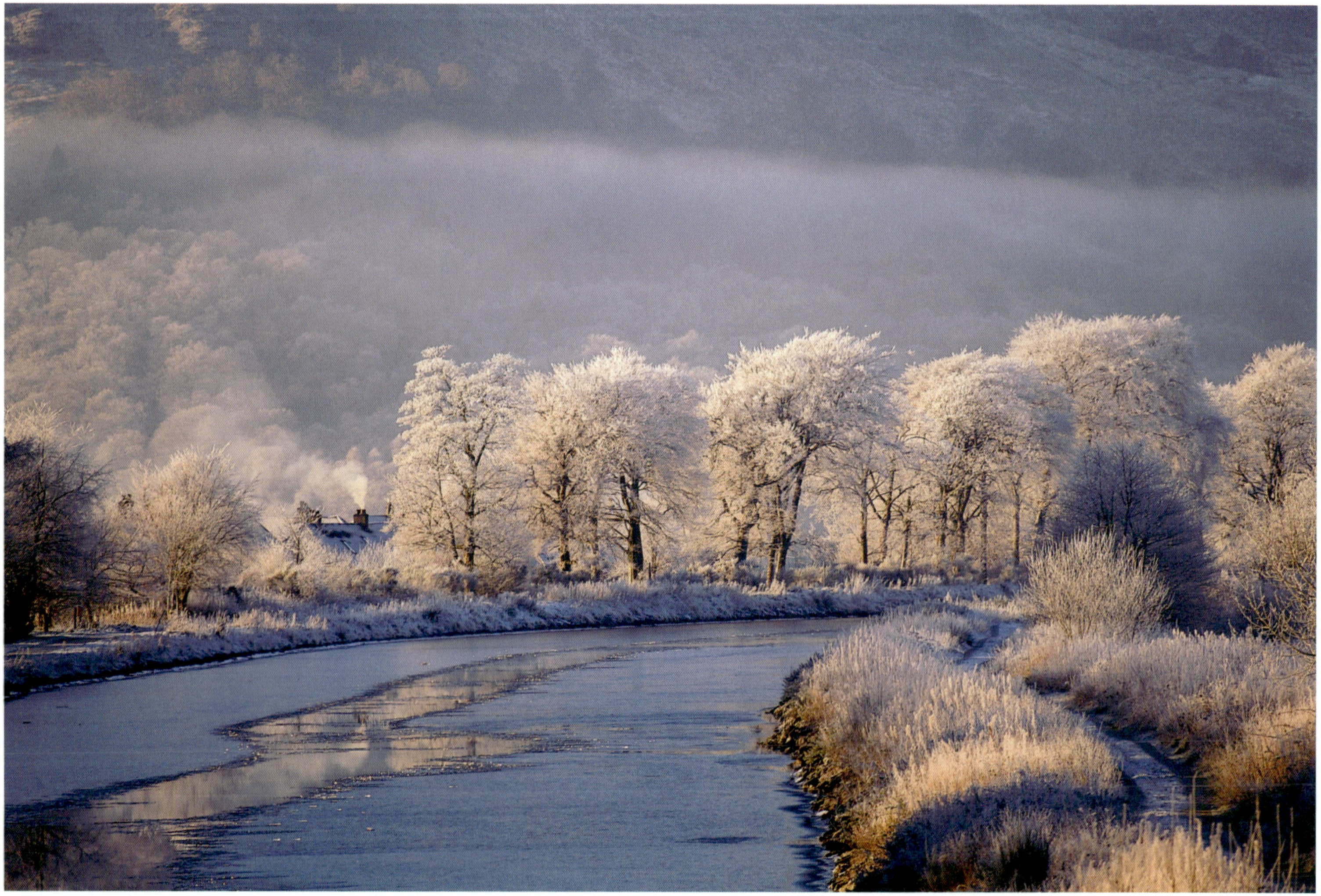

Hoar frost.
A frosty morning on the Caledonian Canal near Fort William.

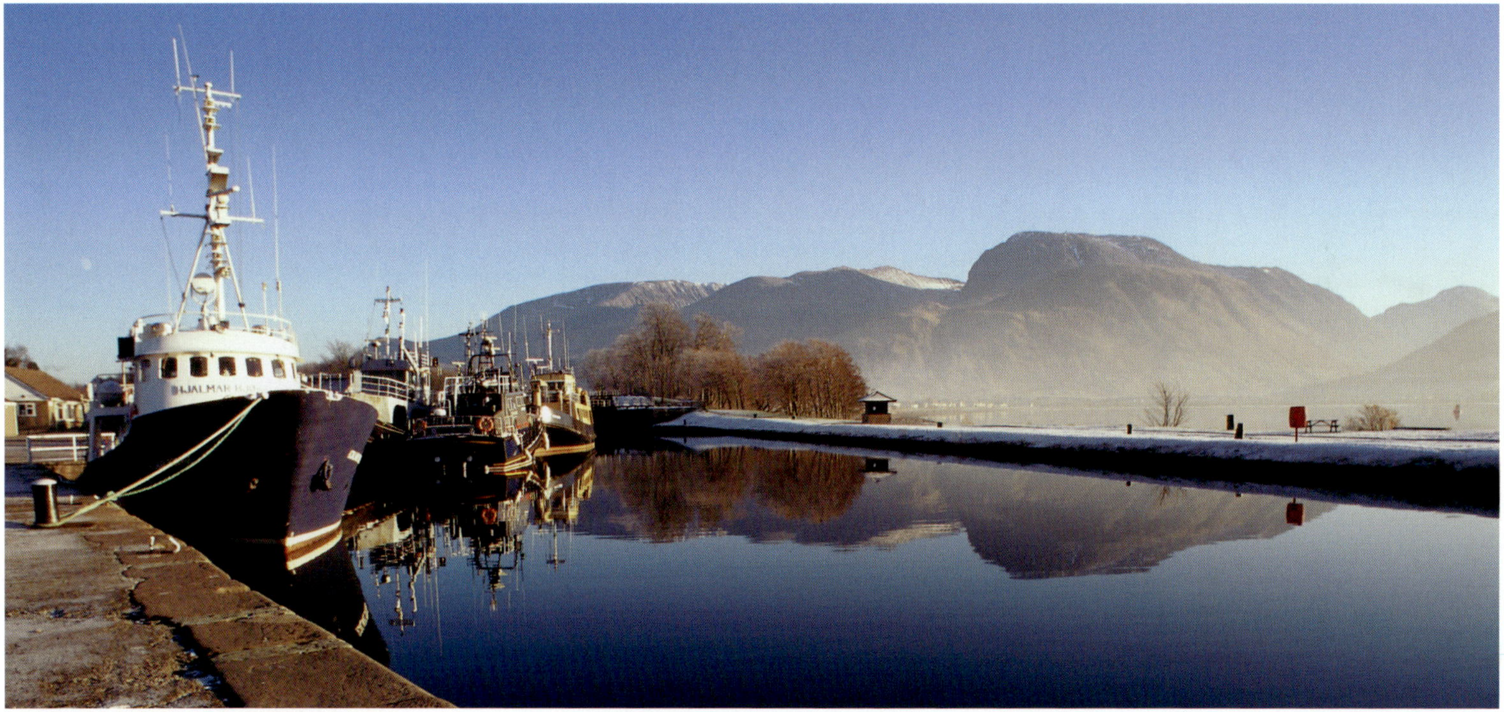

Canal basin.
Ben Nevis reflected in the Caledonian Canal basin at Corpach near Fort William on a beautiful calm winter's morning.

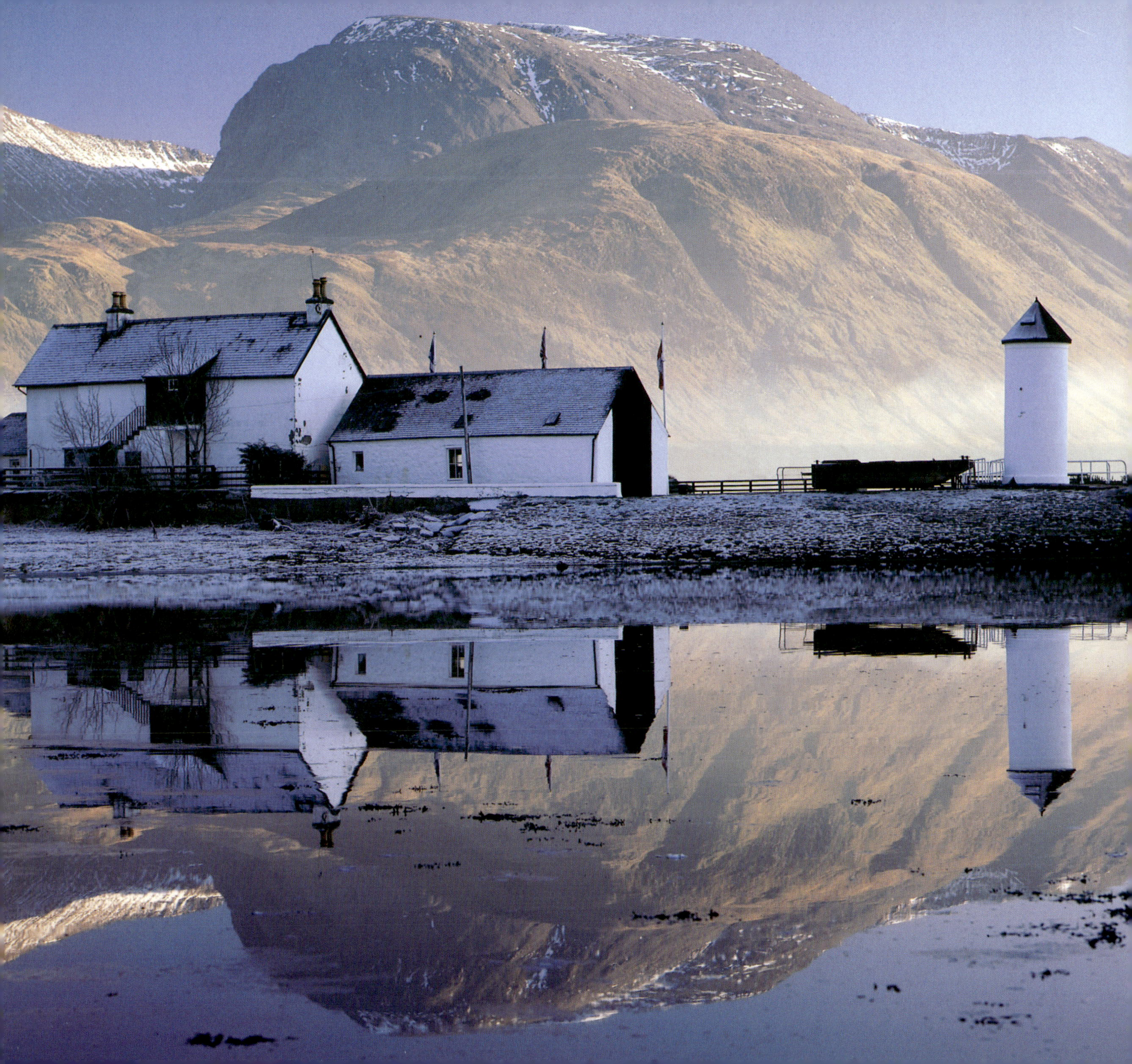

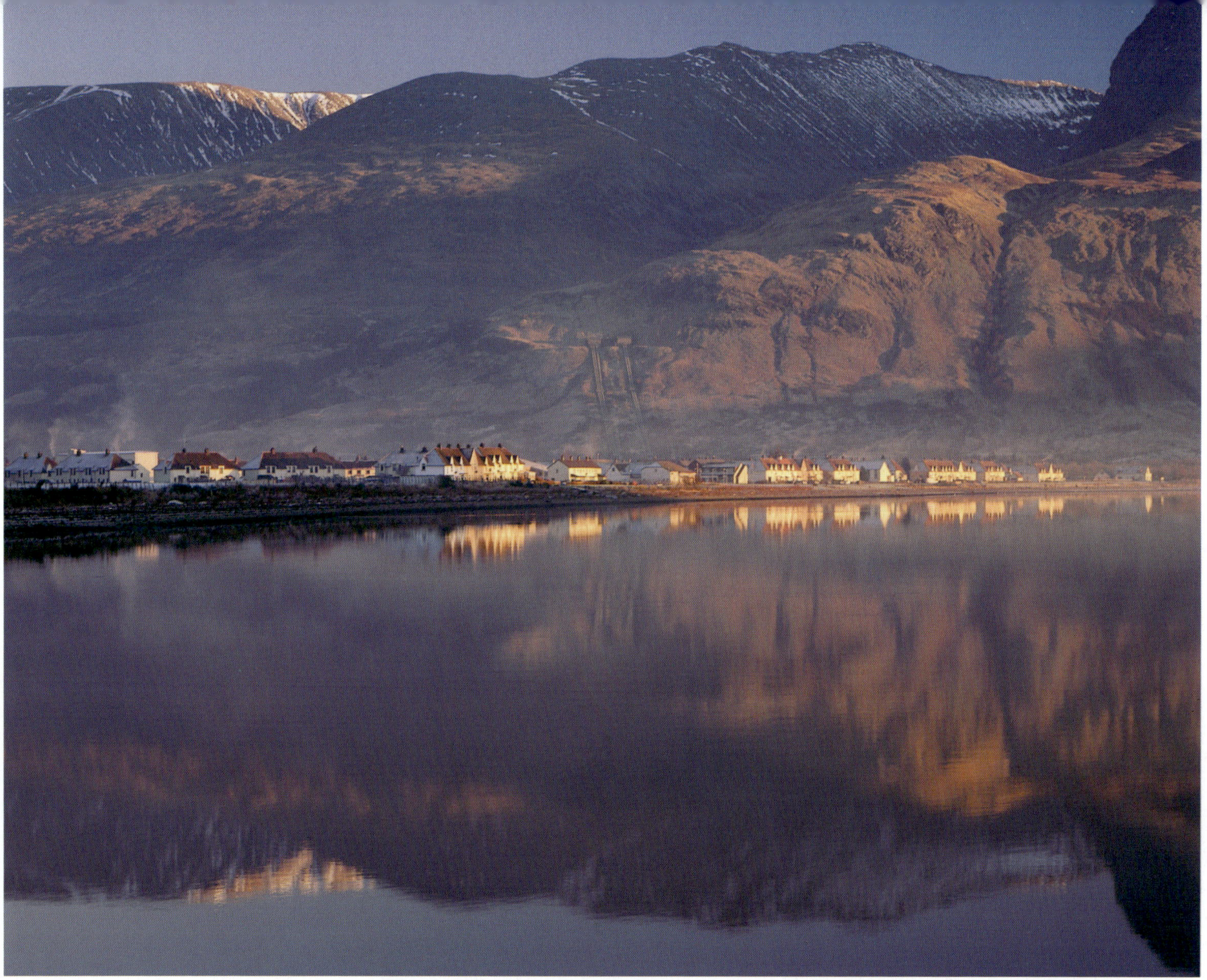

Last light of day.
Weak winter sunshine highlights the houses at Caol, Fort William backed by Carn Mor Dearg and the glen of the Allt a'Mhuilinn.

Opposite: Corpach Pier.
The pier and buildings at Corpach at the southern end of the Caledonian Canal make a lovely foreground to this view of Ben Nevis.

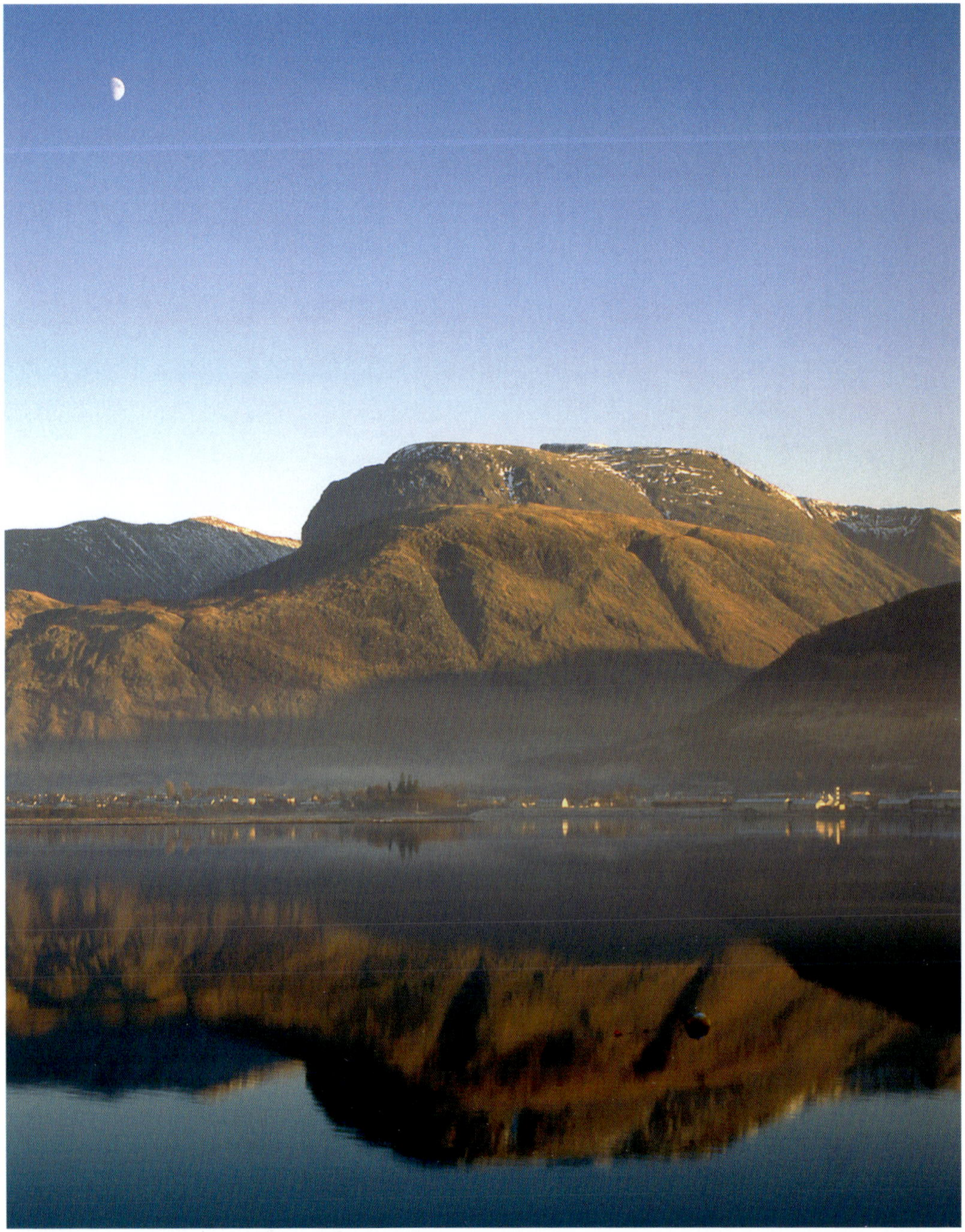

Moonrise.
The moon rises over Fort William and Ben Nevis. The round-shouldered bulk of the famous mountain is really a façade which protects the north-east facing cliffs and high corries above the Allt a'Mhuilinn.

Opposite: Brooding atmosphere.
The mist-shrouded cliffs of the north-east face of Ben Nevis overlook the glen of the Allt a'Mhuilinn, hemmed in on the left by Carn Mor Dearg (*big red hill*). Ben Nevis, affectionately known as the Ben, has few completely mist-free days.

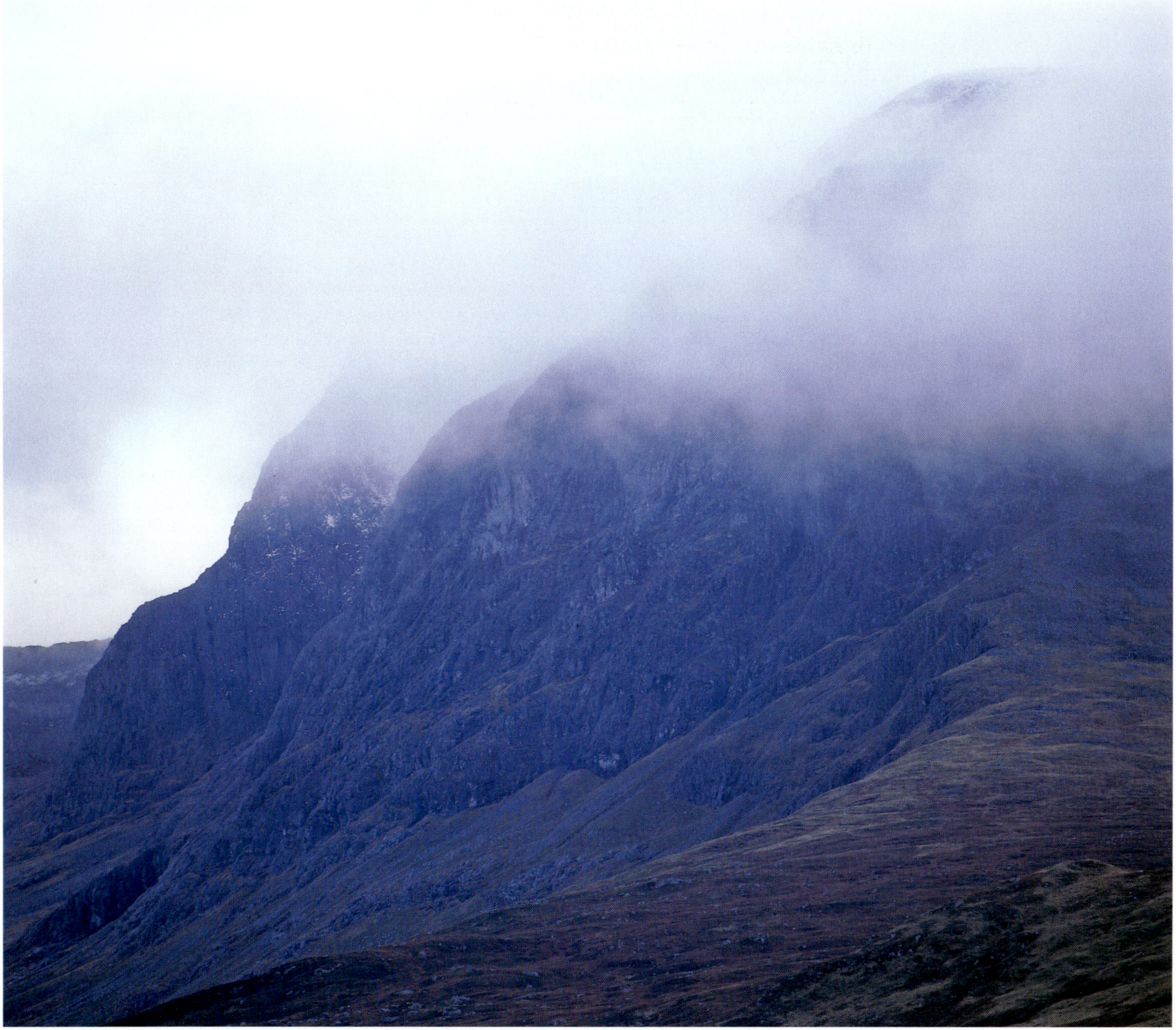

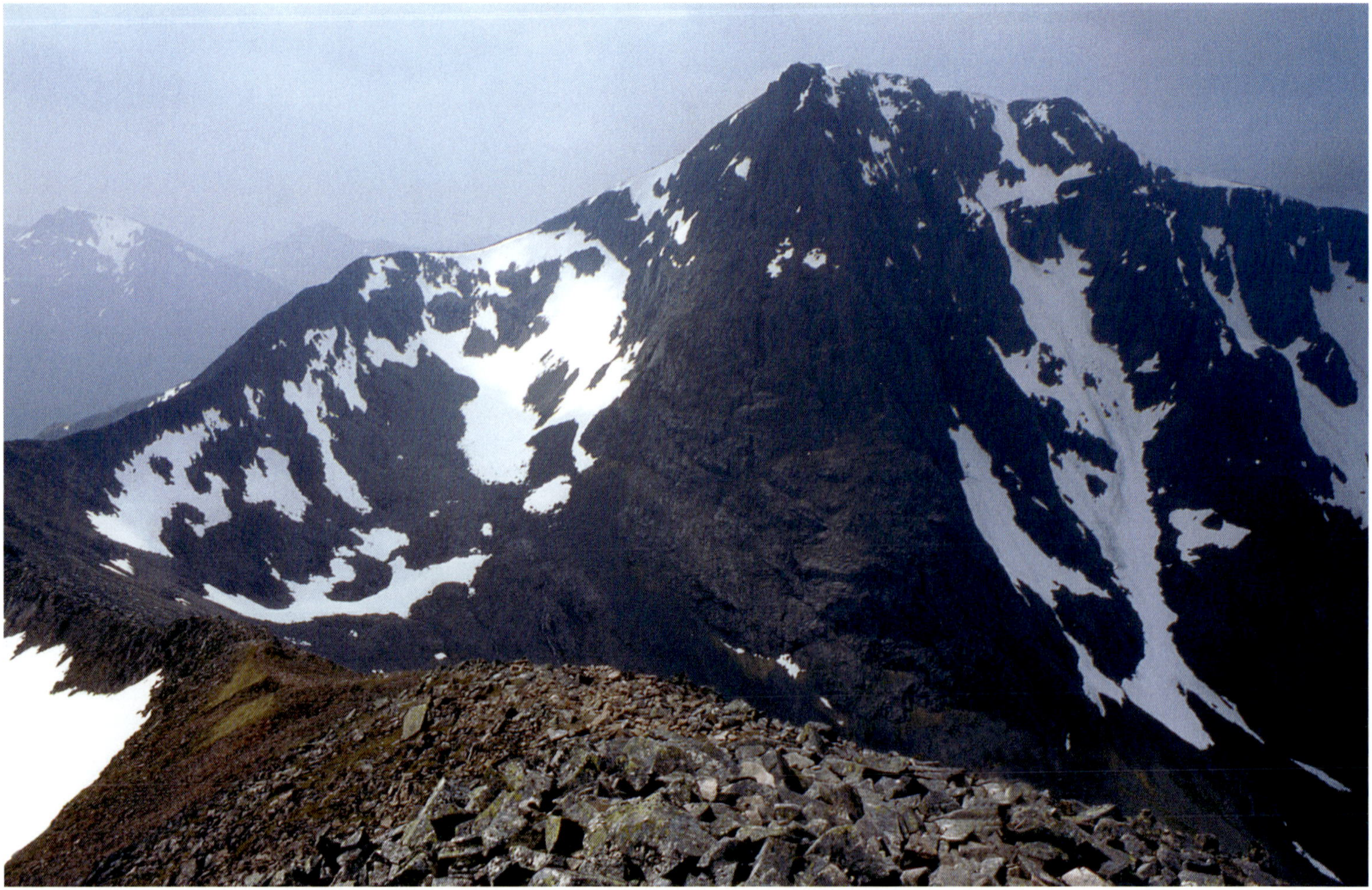

Late snow.

The north-east face of Ben Nevis usually retains snow well into late spring. Its ascent, combined with a crossing of the sweeping narrow ridge of Carn Mor Dearg arête, which connects with the south-east ridge of Ben Nevis, provides walkers with a magnificent outing around the head of the glen of the Allt a'Mhuilinn.

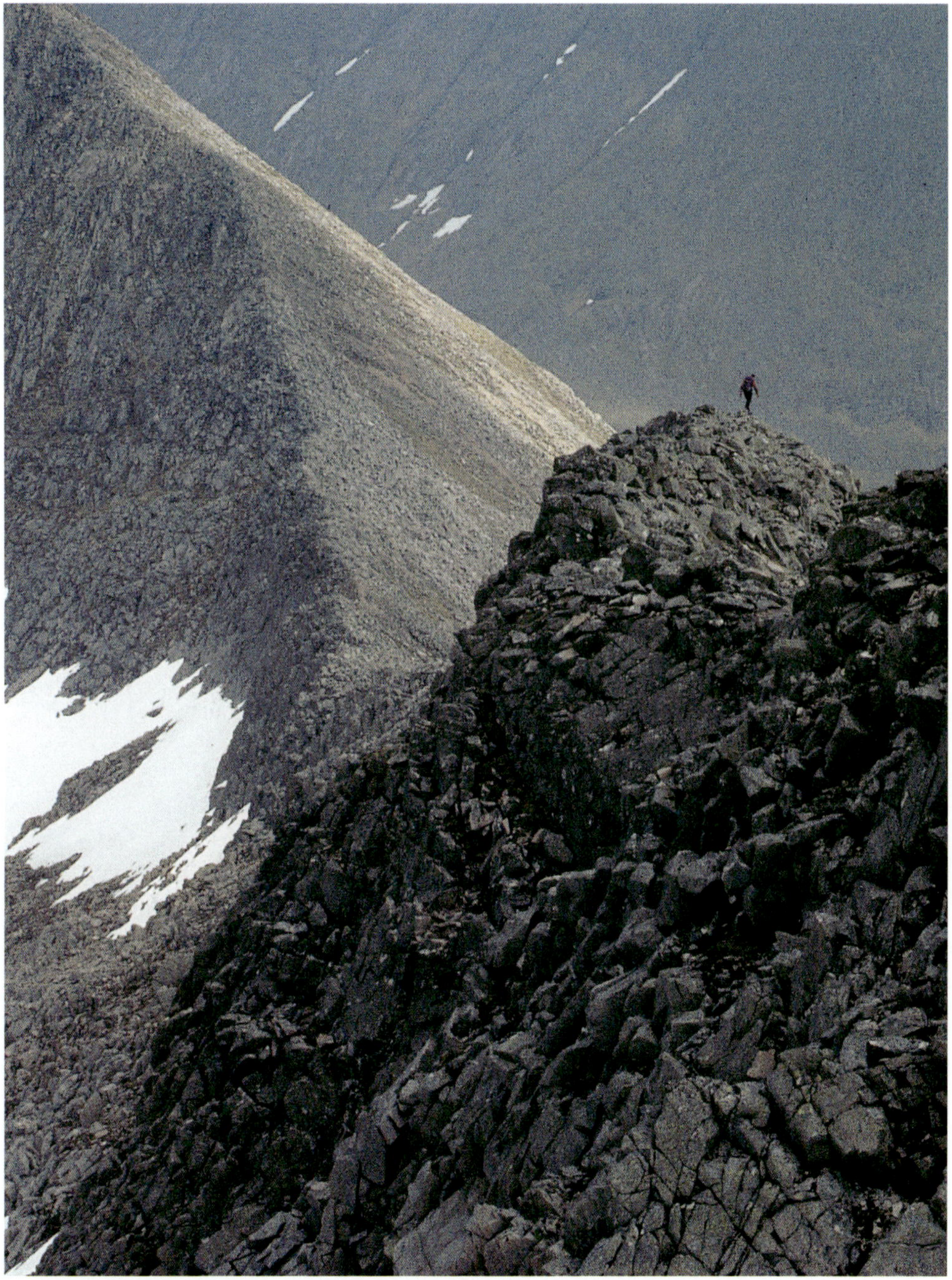

Dizzy heights.
A crossing of the crest of the high-level tightrope-like arête linking Ben Nevis with Carn Mor Dearg requires a steady head.

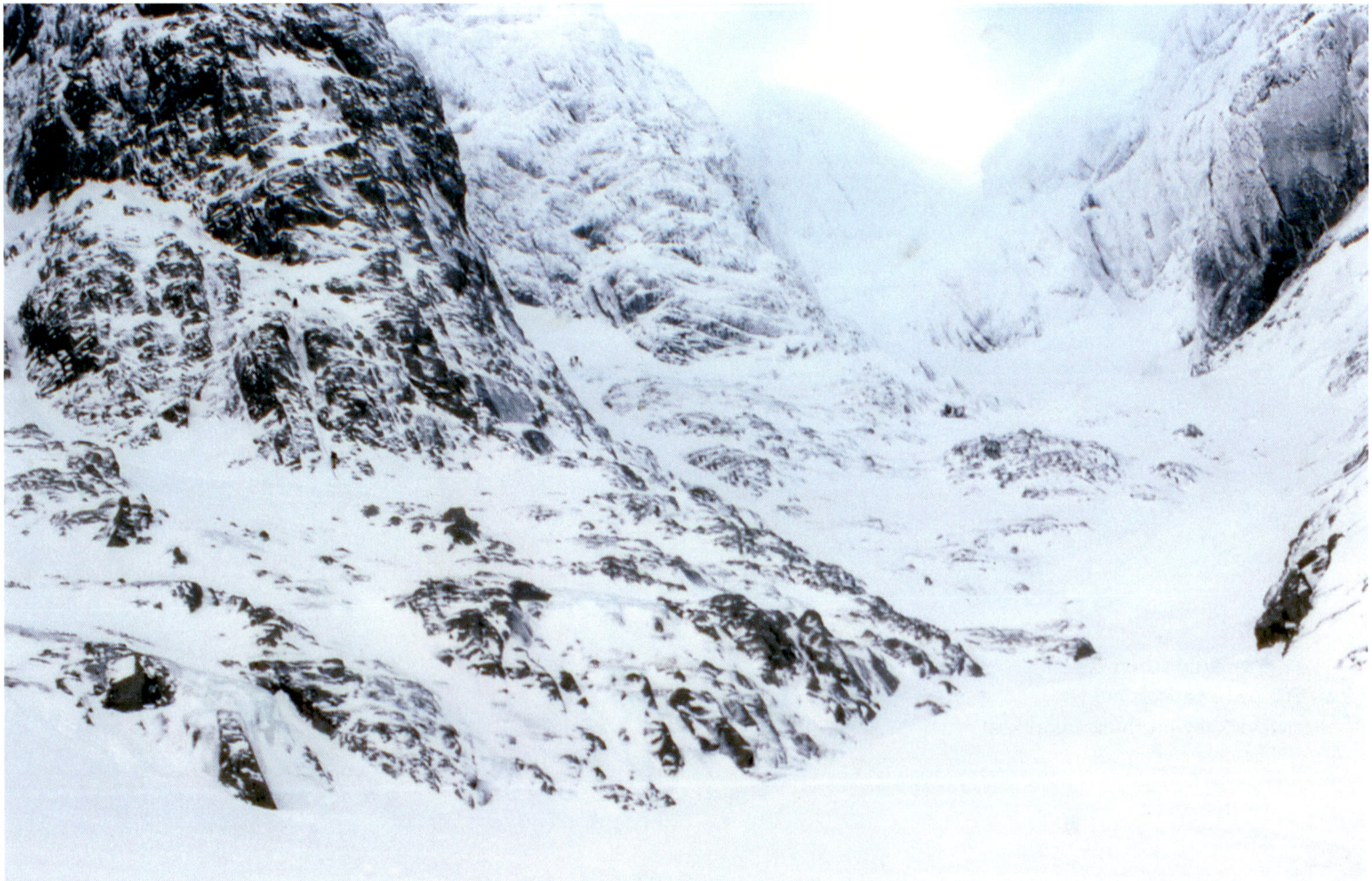

Winter paradise.
The snow- and ice-plastered cliffs of Ben Nevis are a Mecca for winter mountaineers. In winter the gullies and faces can be alpine in character and some of the climbs are formidable undertakings.

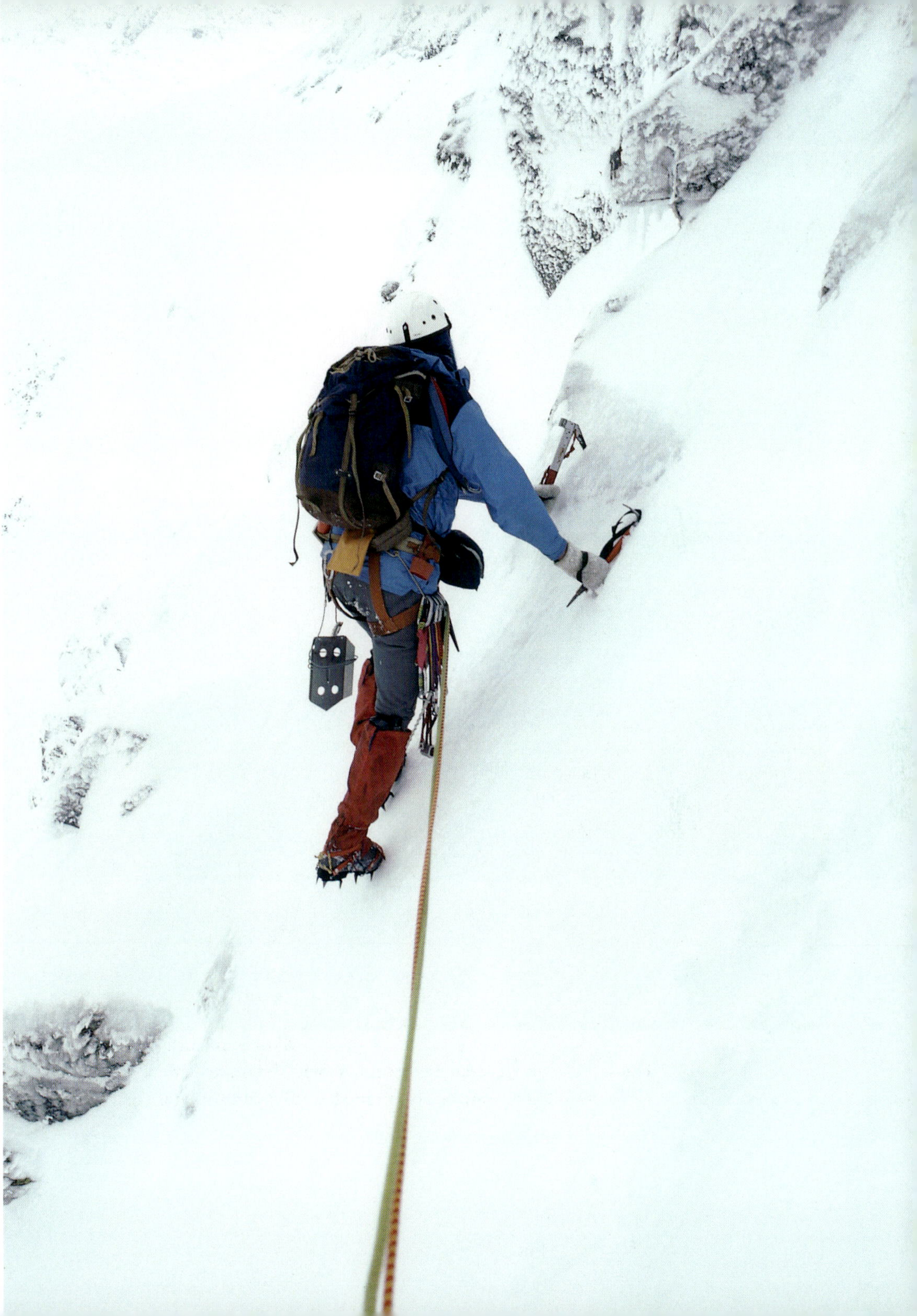

Steady progress.
A climber makes his way up
Ben Nevis's icy north-east buttress.

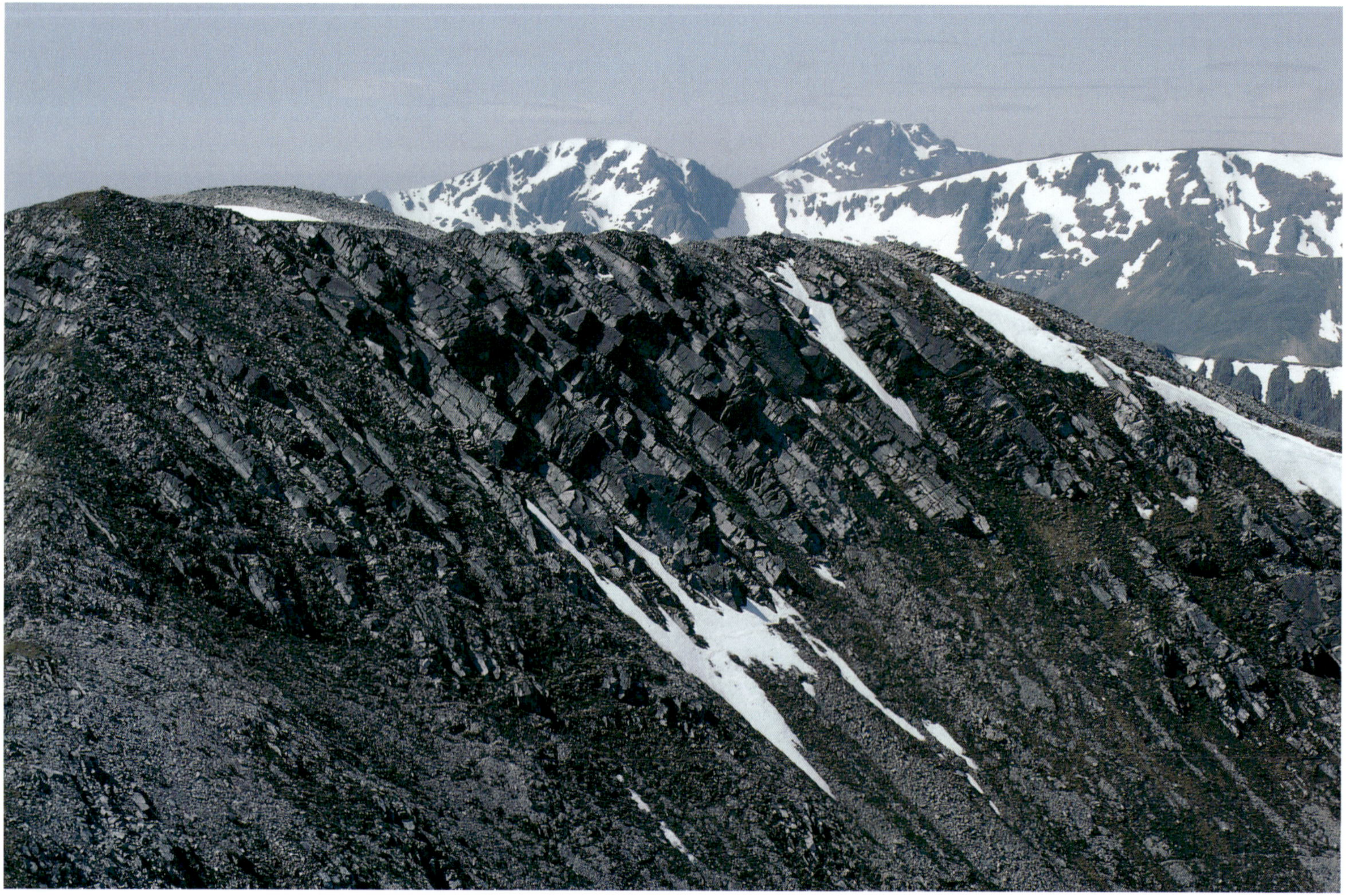

Peeping giants.
Ben Nevis, Aonach Beag (*little hill*) and Aonach Mor (*big hill*) emerge from behind the Grey Corries.

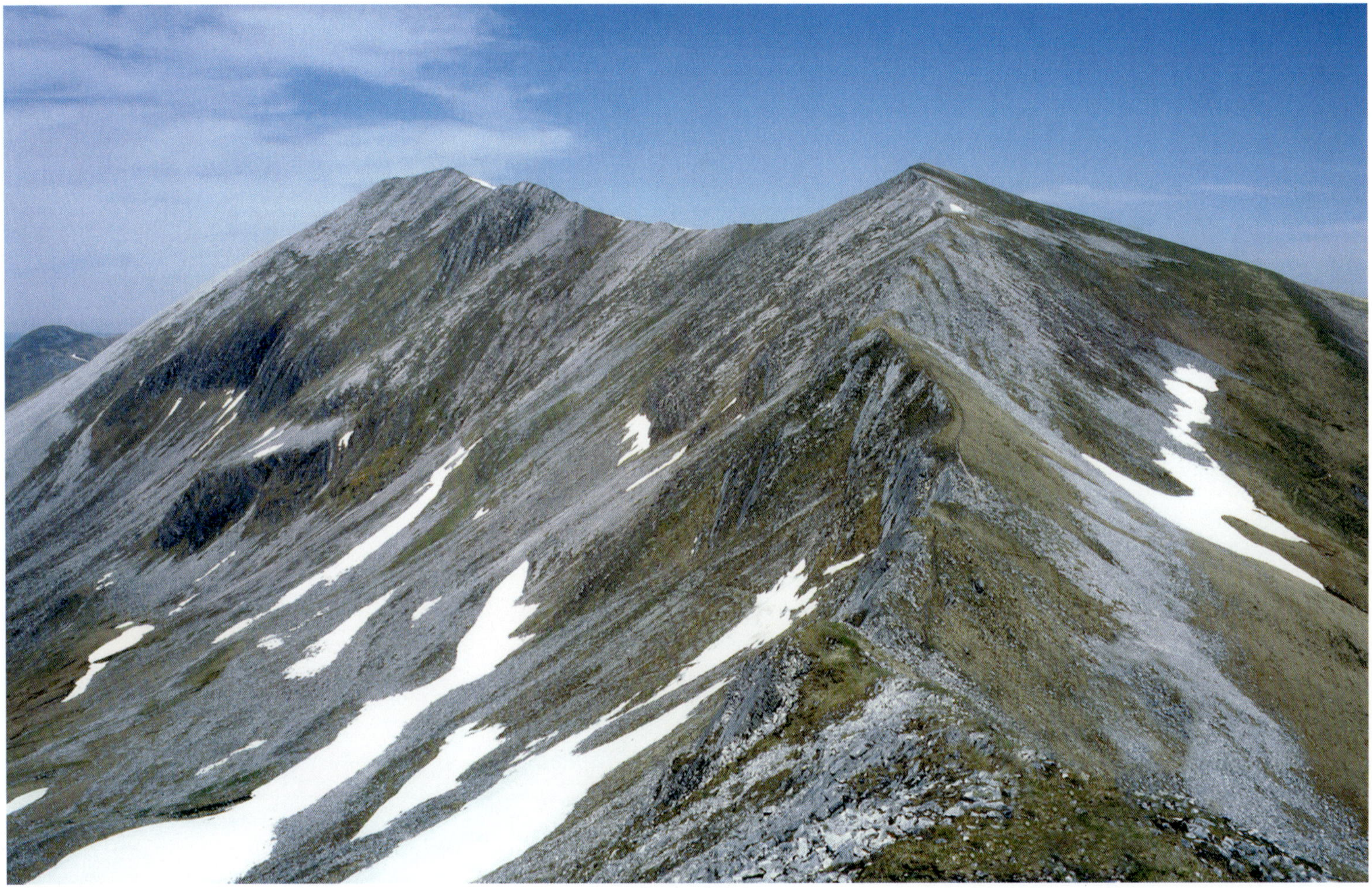

A grey ridge.

The ridge of the aptly named Grey Corries is part of a long chain of mountains stretching east from Ben Nevis over Aonach Beag.

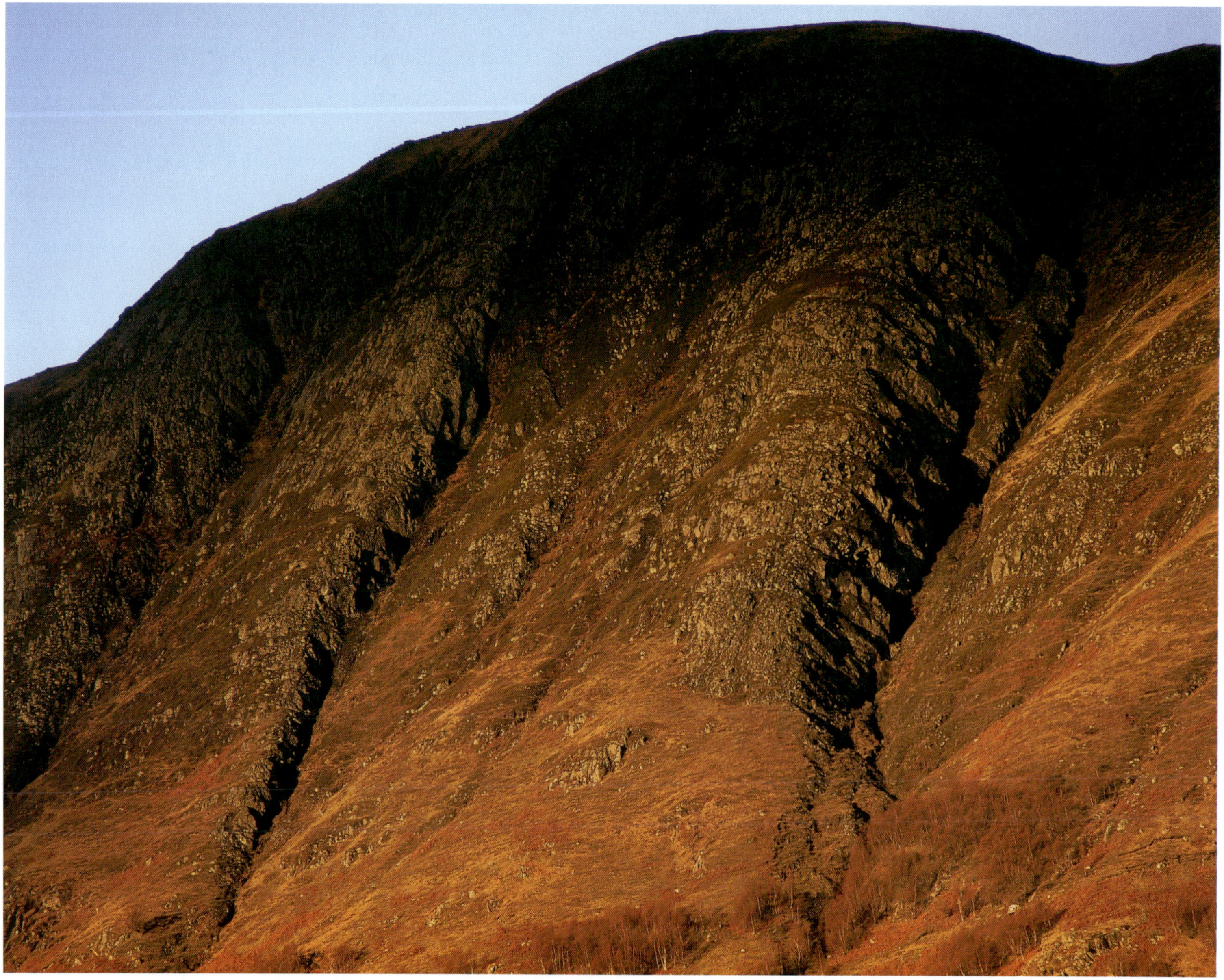

Autumn shadows.

The soft play of evening autumn light casts an orange glow across Meall an t-Suidhe in Glen Nevis. The 'tourist path' up Ben Nevis from Achintree in Glen Nevis crosses the lower slopes of the face.

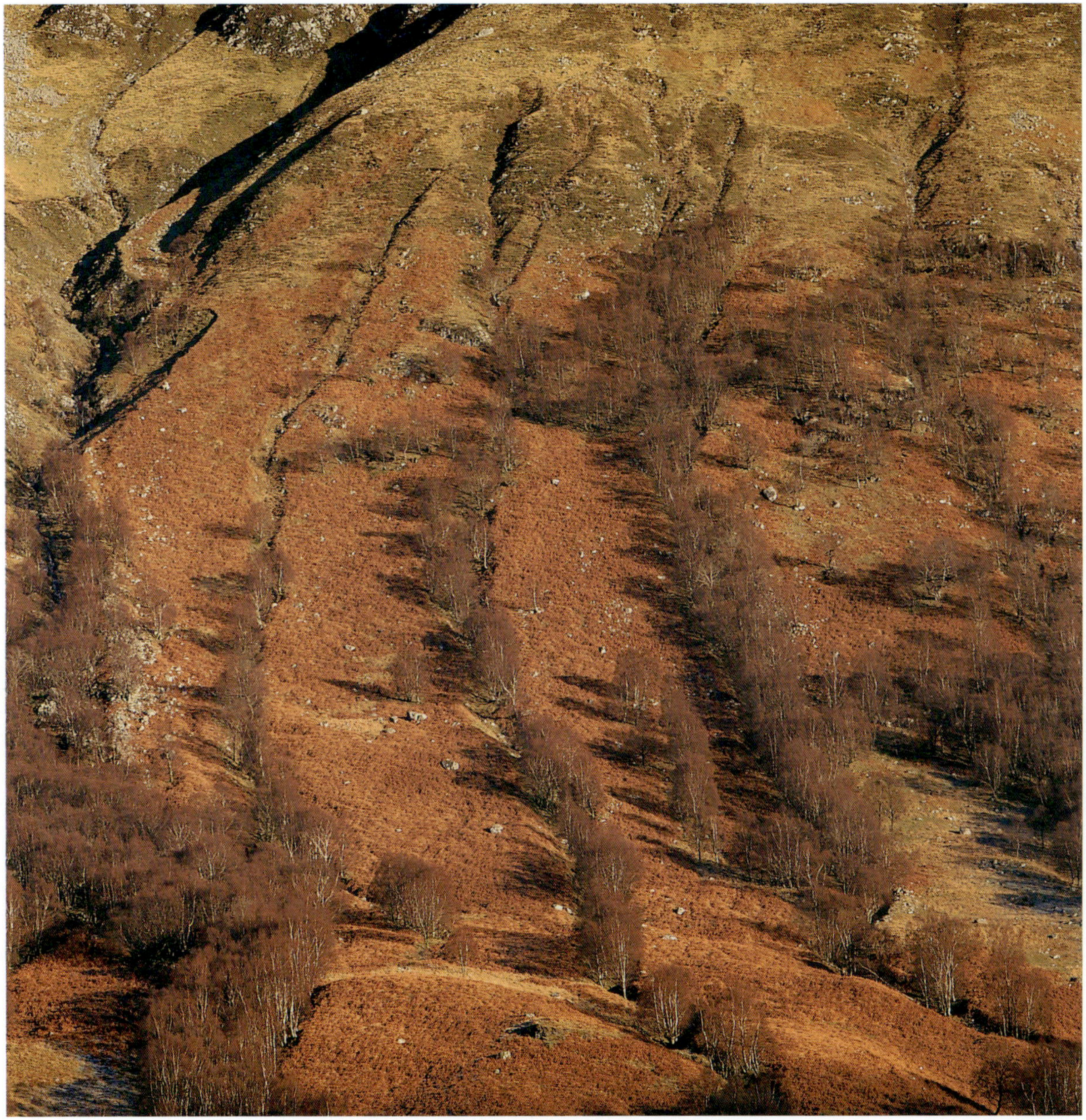

Tree patterns.
Rows of trees on the eastern slopes of Ben Nevis create pleasing patterns.

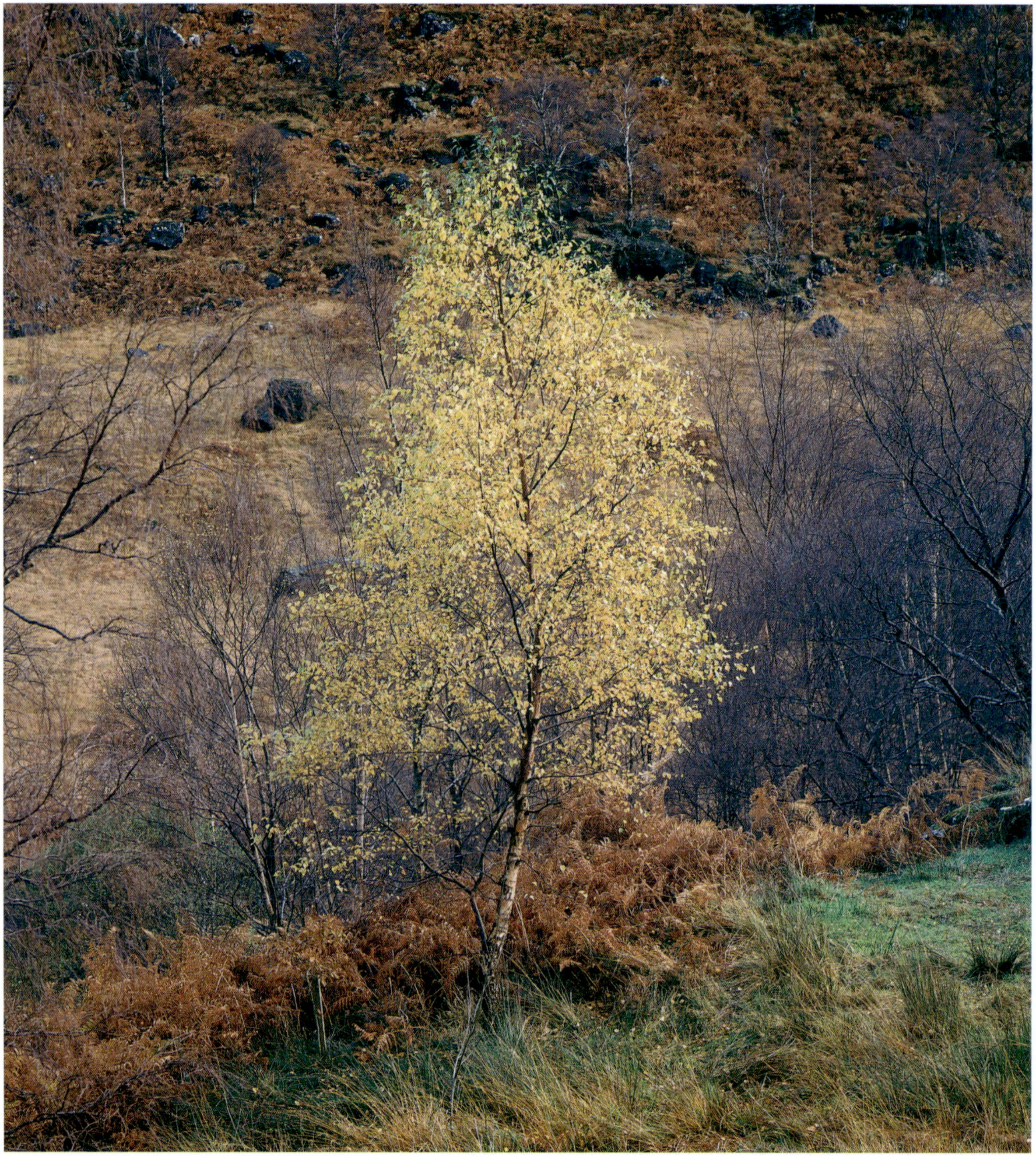

Golden leaves.
A Glen Nevis silver birch in its autumnal colours. Starting at Fort William, the deeply-cut Glen Nevis is one of the best known glens in Scotland and is a beautiful place to explore.

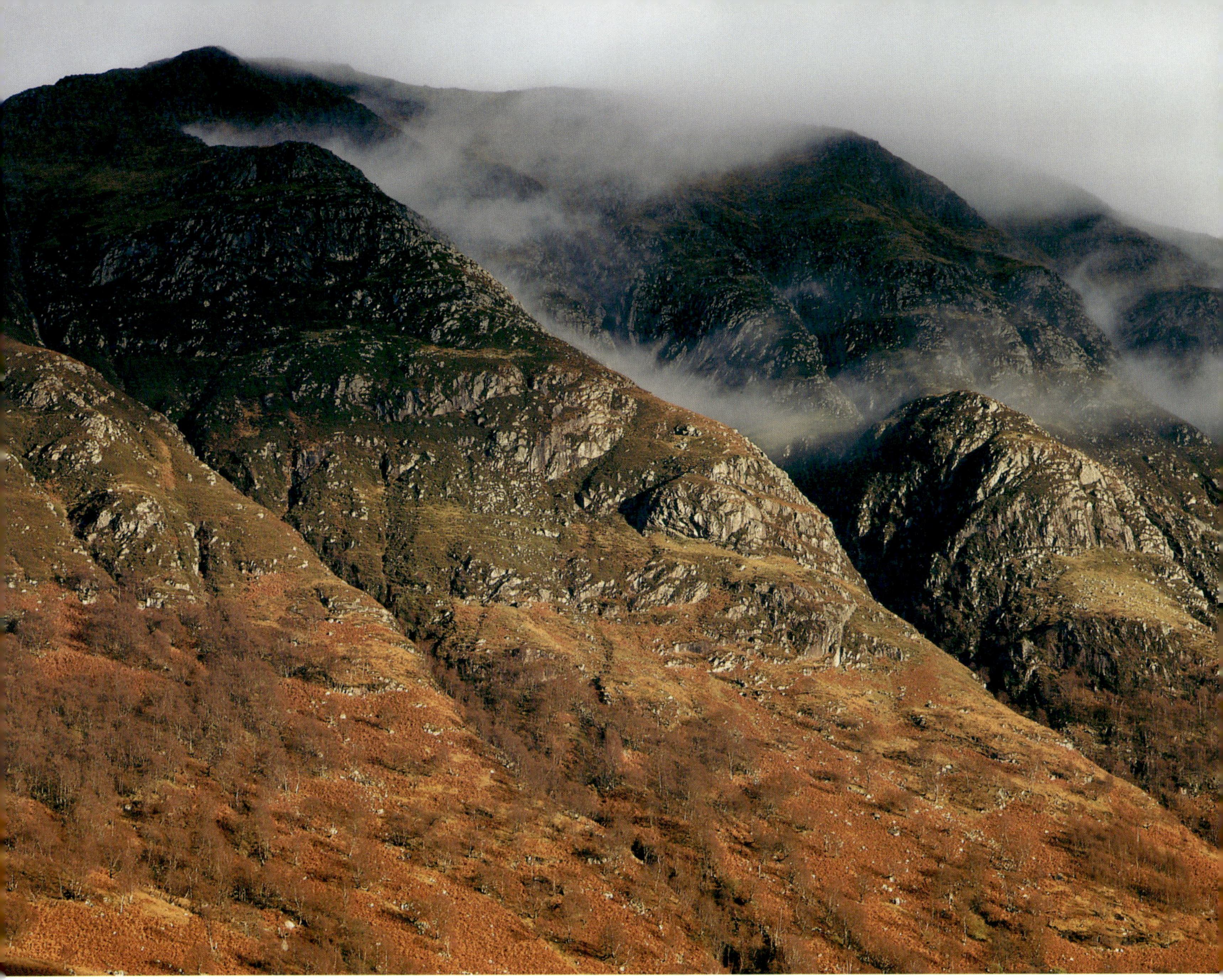

Swirling mist.
Autumn light picks out a series of deep gullies which split the lower slopes of Ben Nevis overlooking Glen Nevis.

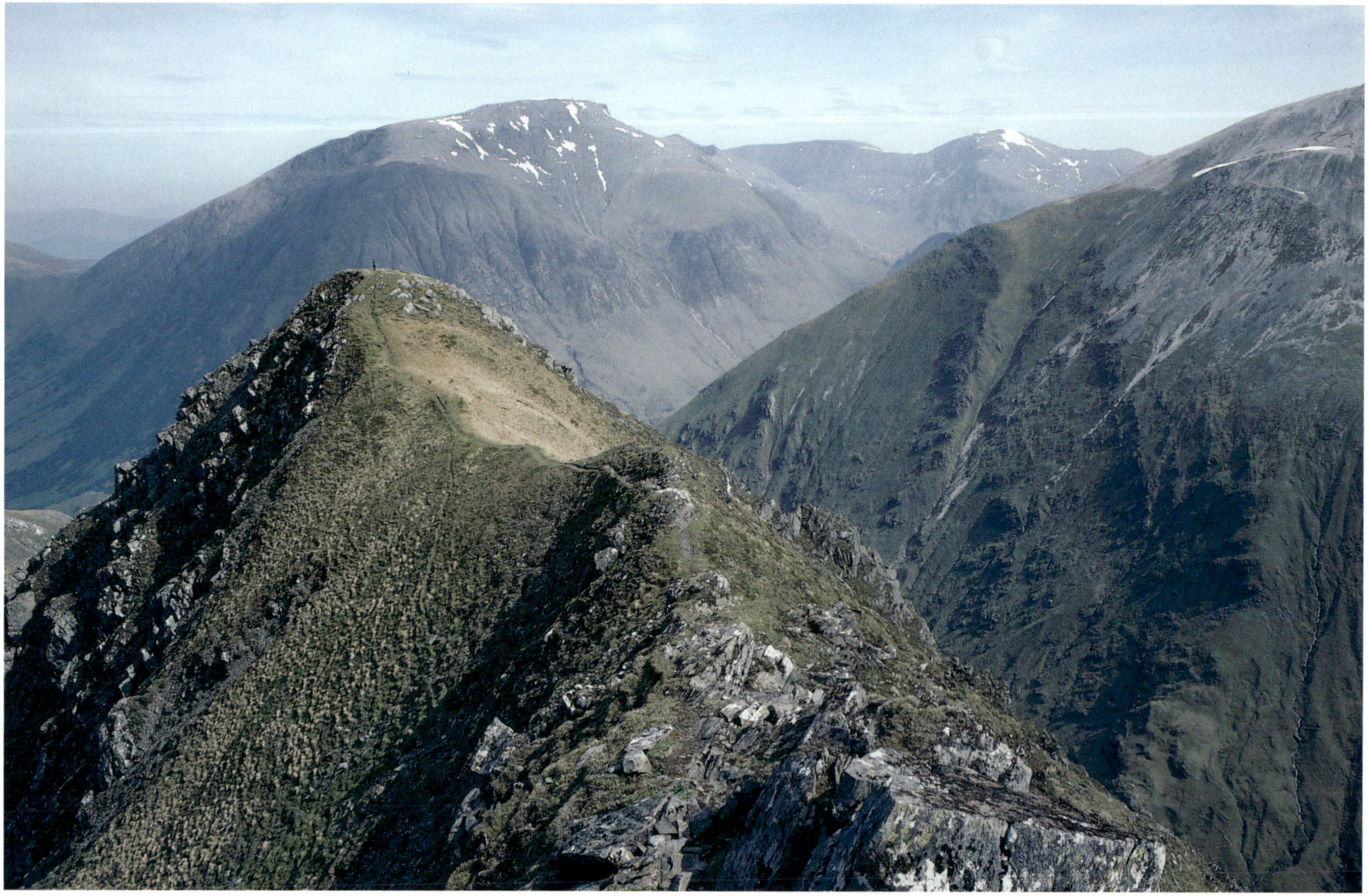

Across the valley.
Looking across Glen Nevis from An Garbhanach to Ben Nevis, whose conspicuous Coire Ghaimhnean usually retains snow into early summer.

Opposite: Snow showers.
Late autumn snow showers sweep across Coire Ghaimhnean high on the western slopes of Ben Nevis.

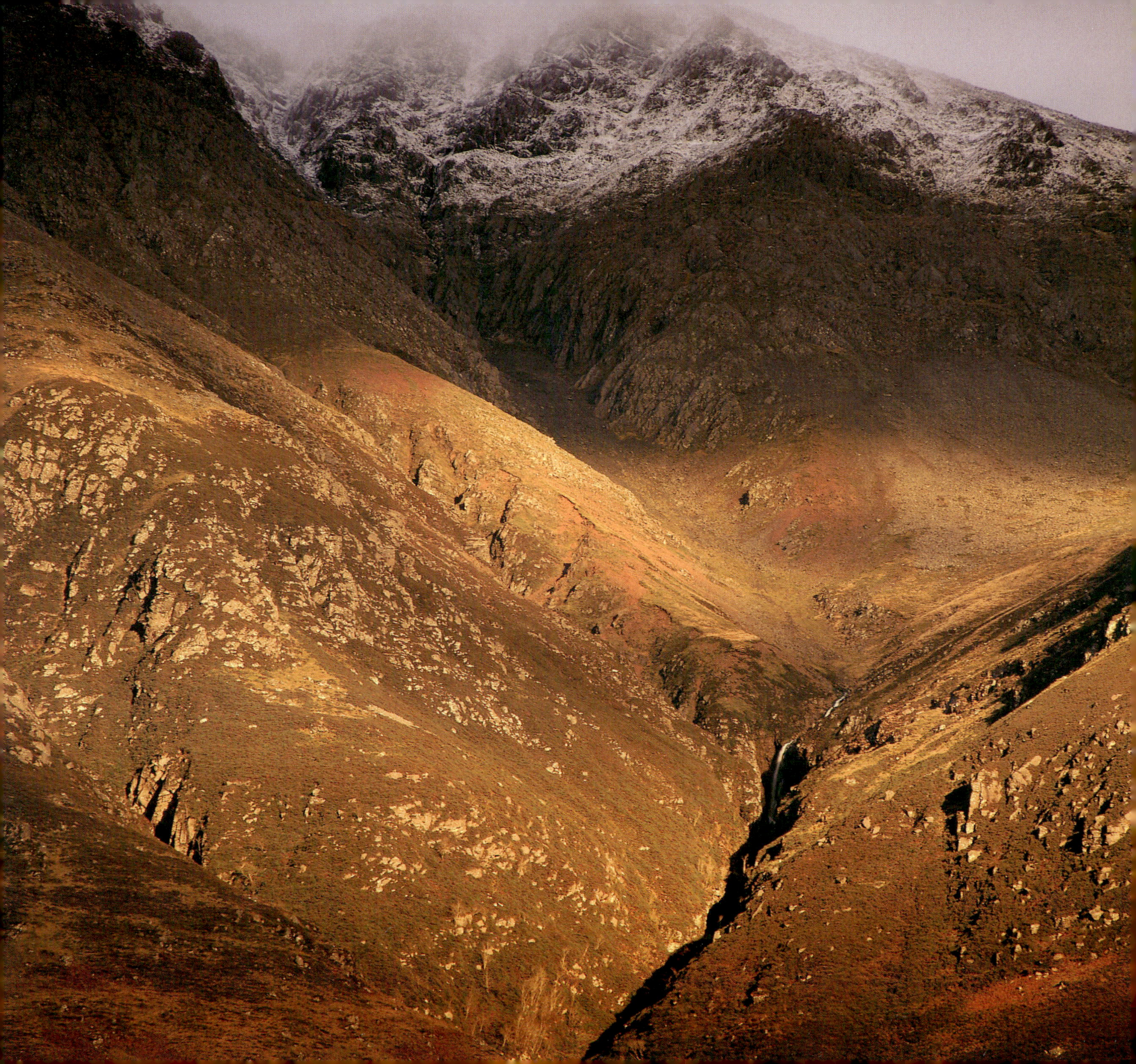

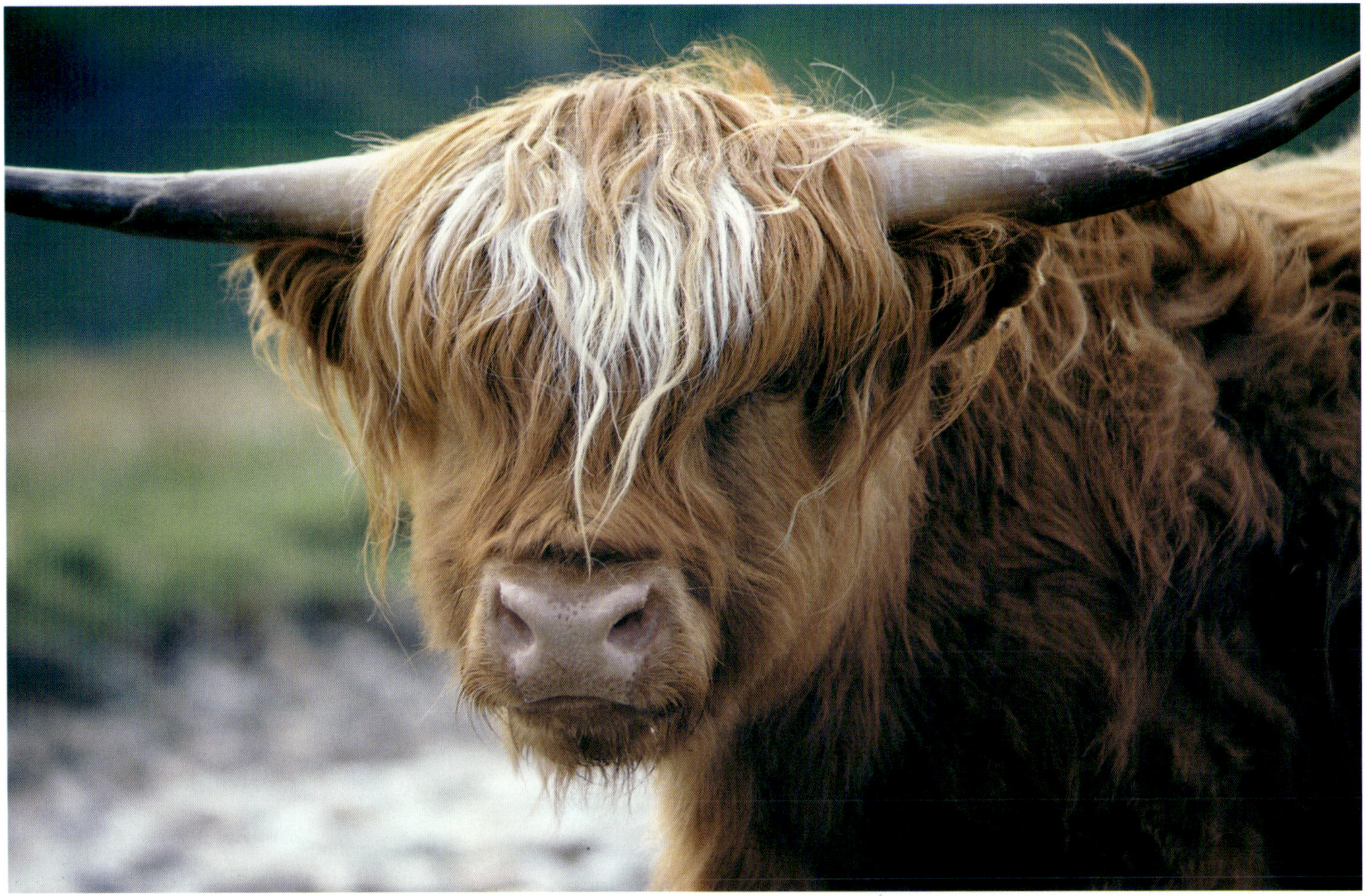

Highland cattle.
Highland cattle regularly wander along the road through the upper reaches of Glen Nevis.

Opposite: Rushing river.
The River Nevis dashes below the scattered Polldubh Crags on the southern flanks of Carn Dearg in upper Glen Nevis.

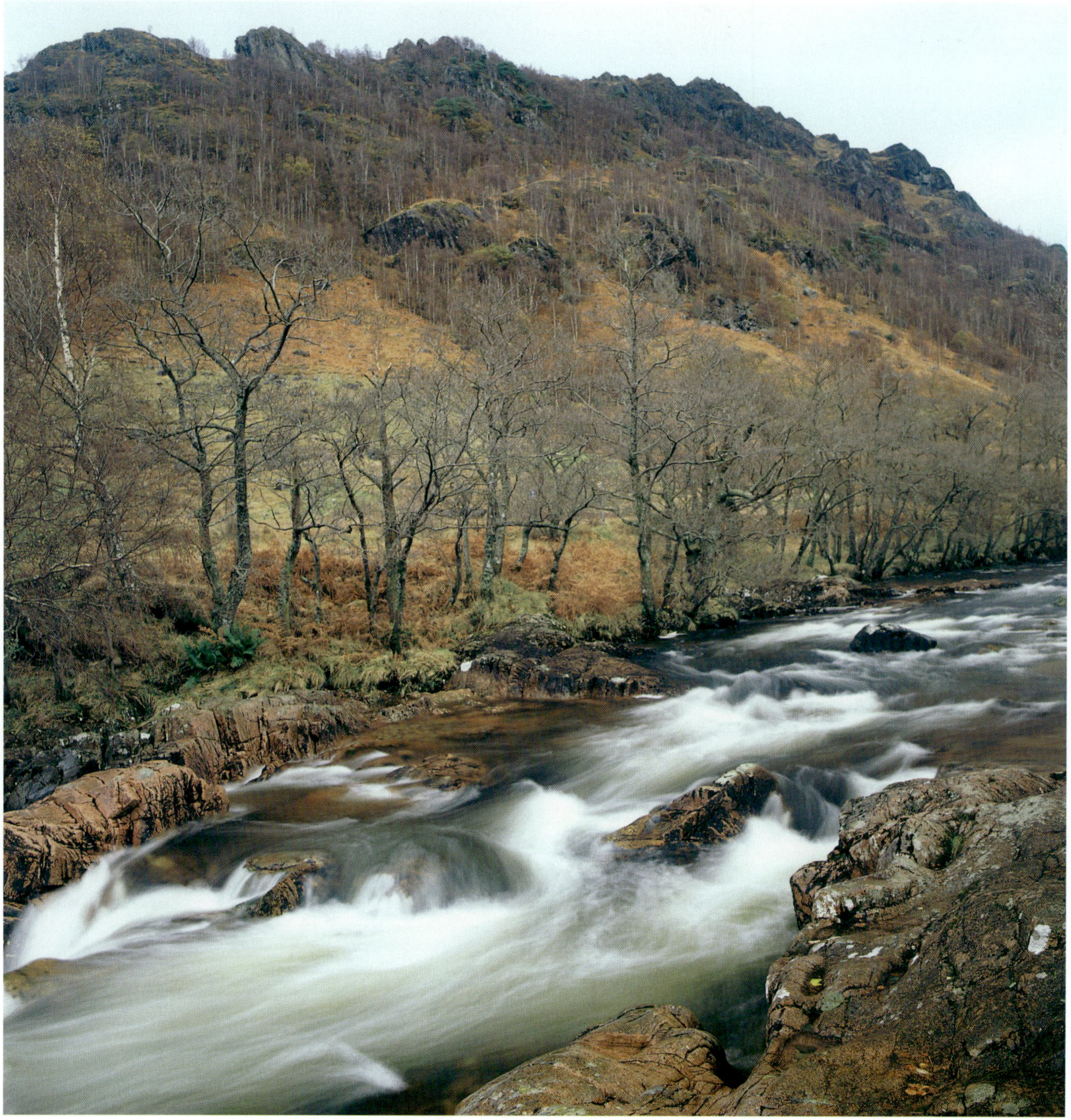

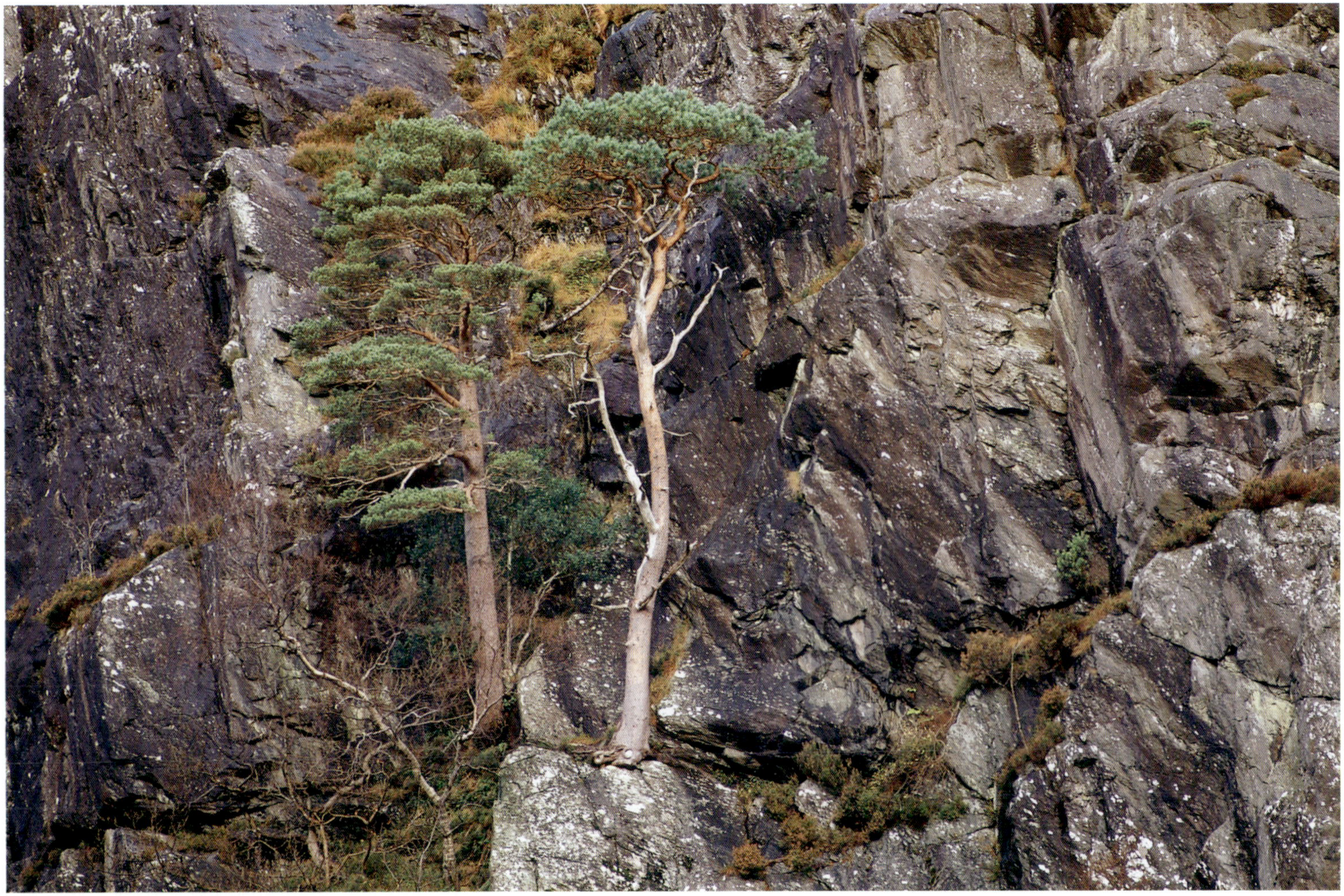

Survival.
Scots Pines have a tenuous hold on a rocky ledge on one of the Polldubh Crags in upper Glen Nevis.

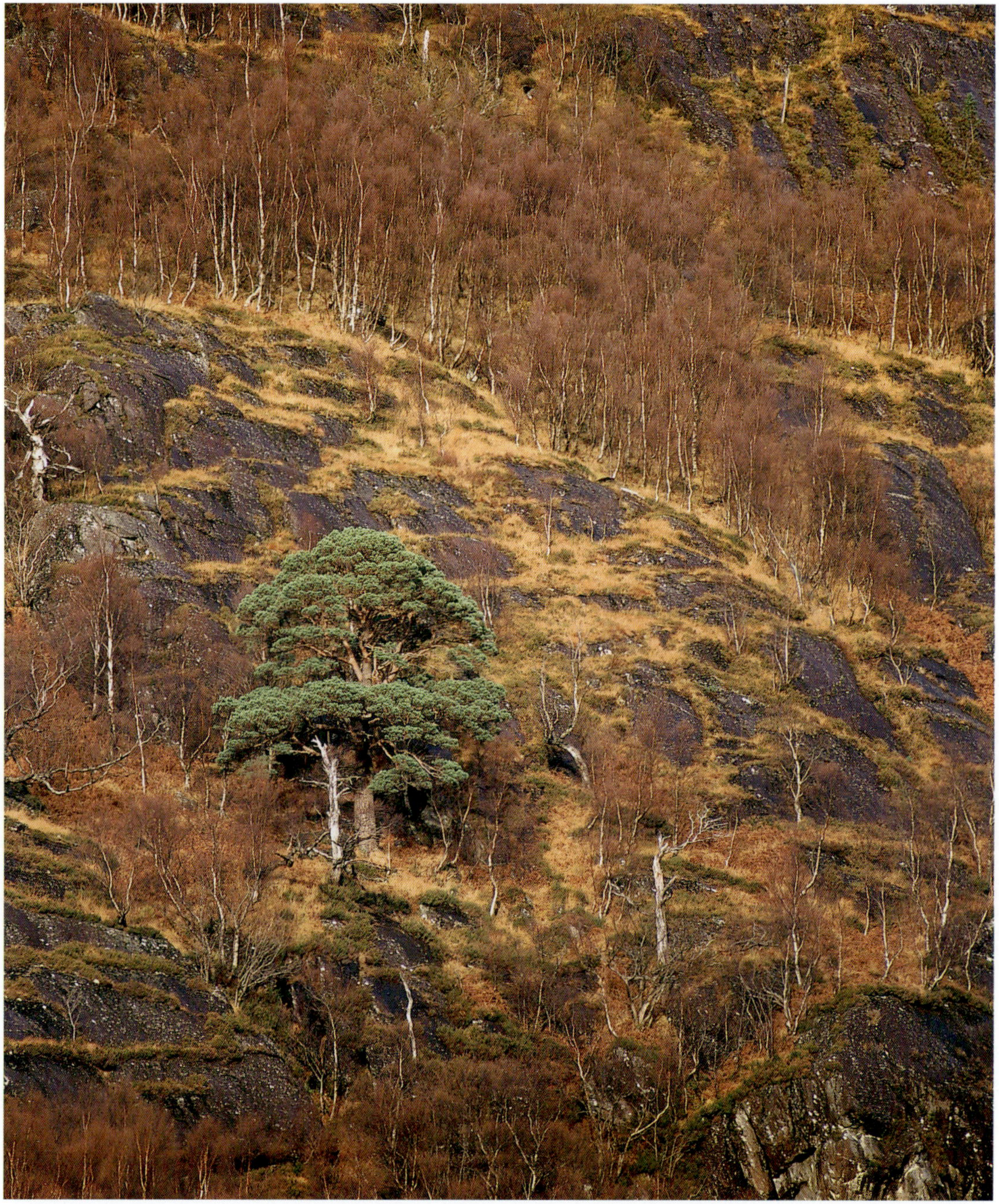

Lone tree.
Sunshine picks out a lone pine tree on the slopes above Polldubh Crags in upper Glen Nevis.

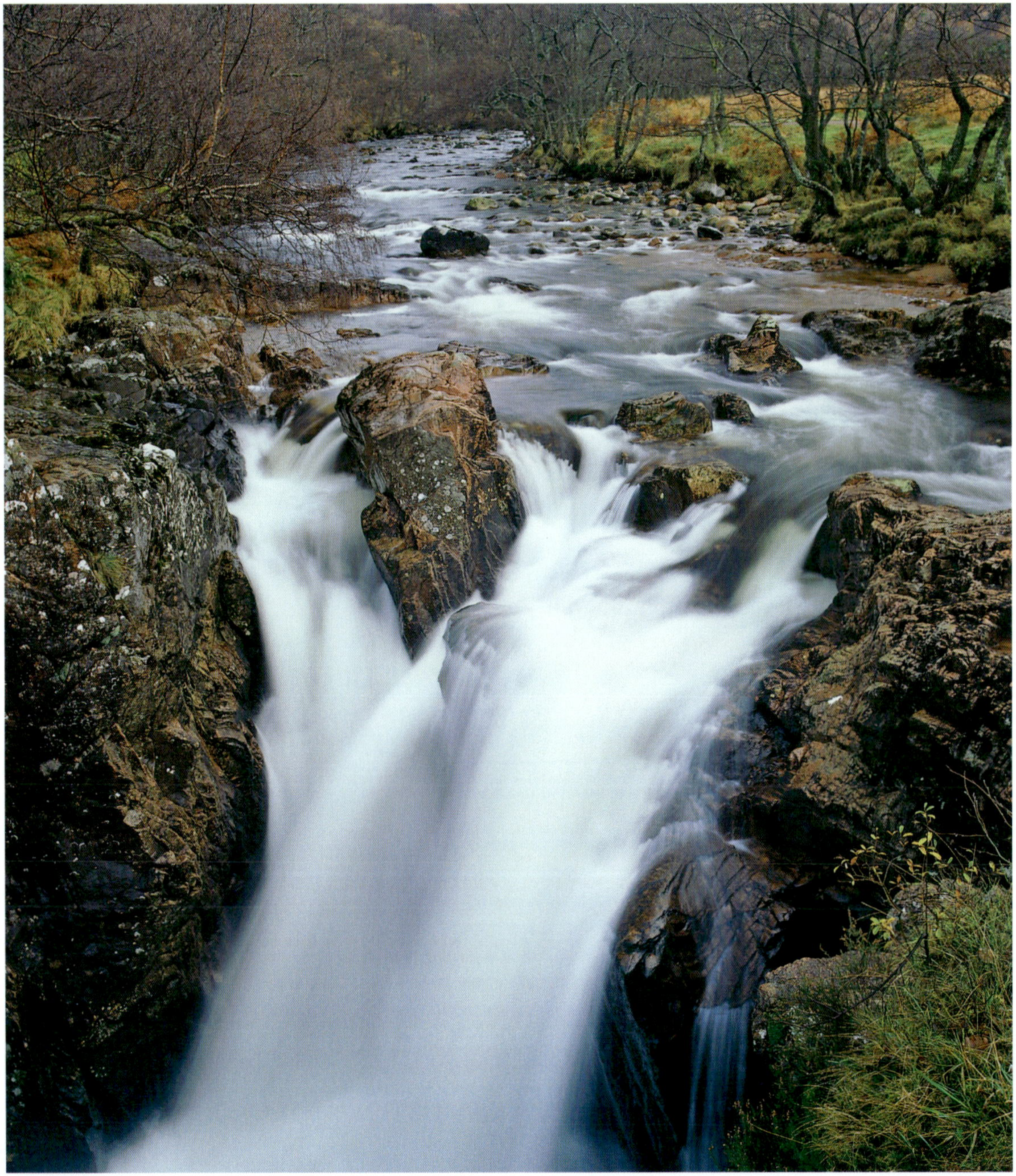

Crashing water.
The lower falls of Glen Nevis tumble some 40ft/12m down a rocky section of the glen. A nearby car park makes the falls very accessible.

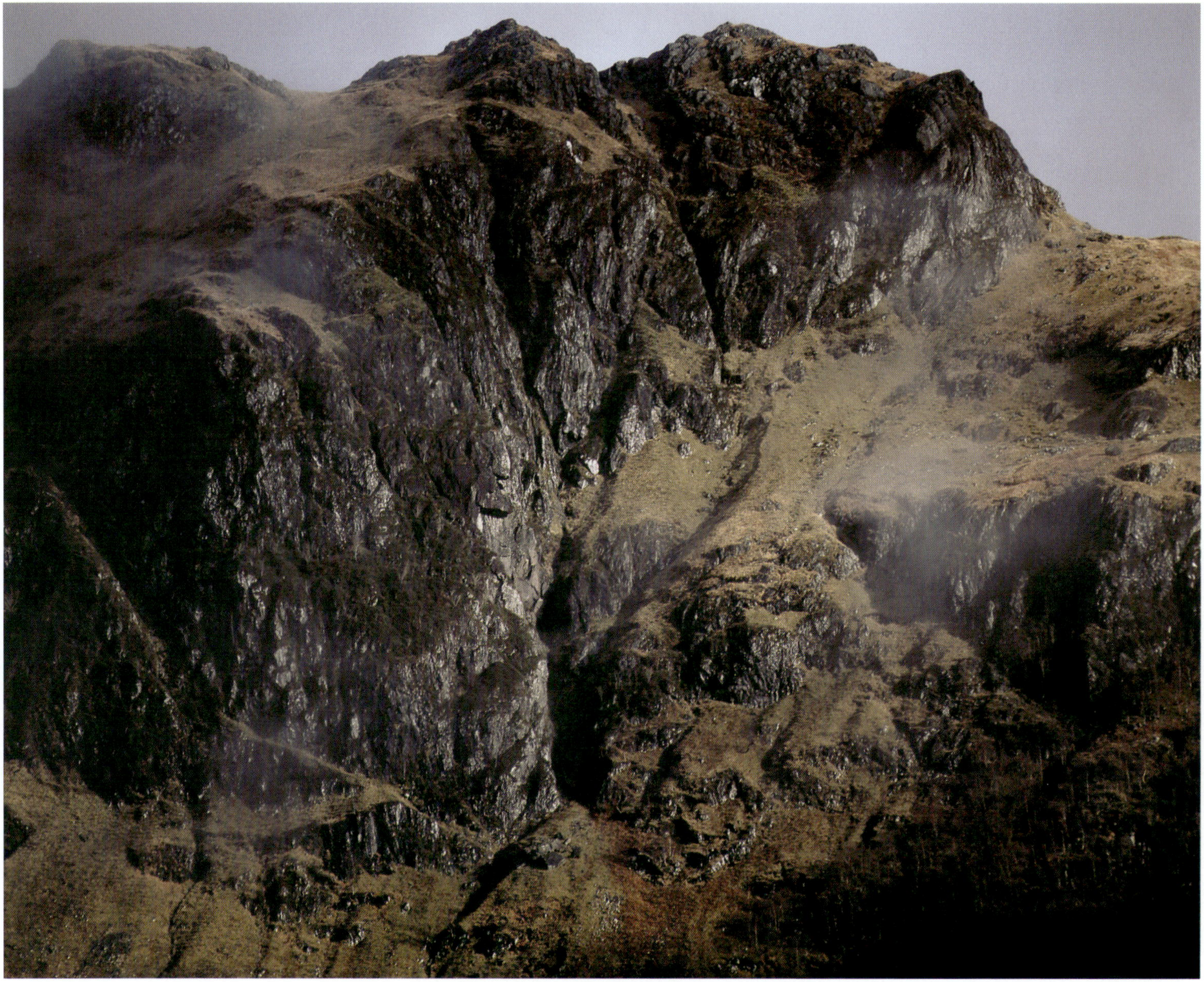

A craggy outlook.
The buttresses of Meall Cumhann dominate the head of Glen Nevis

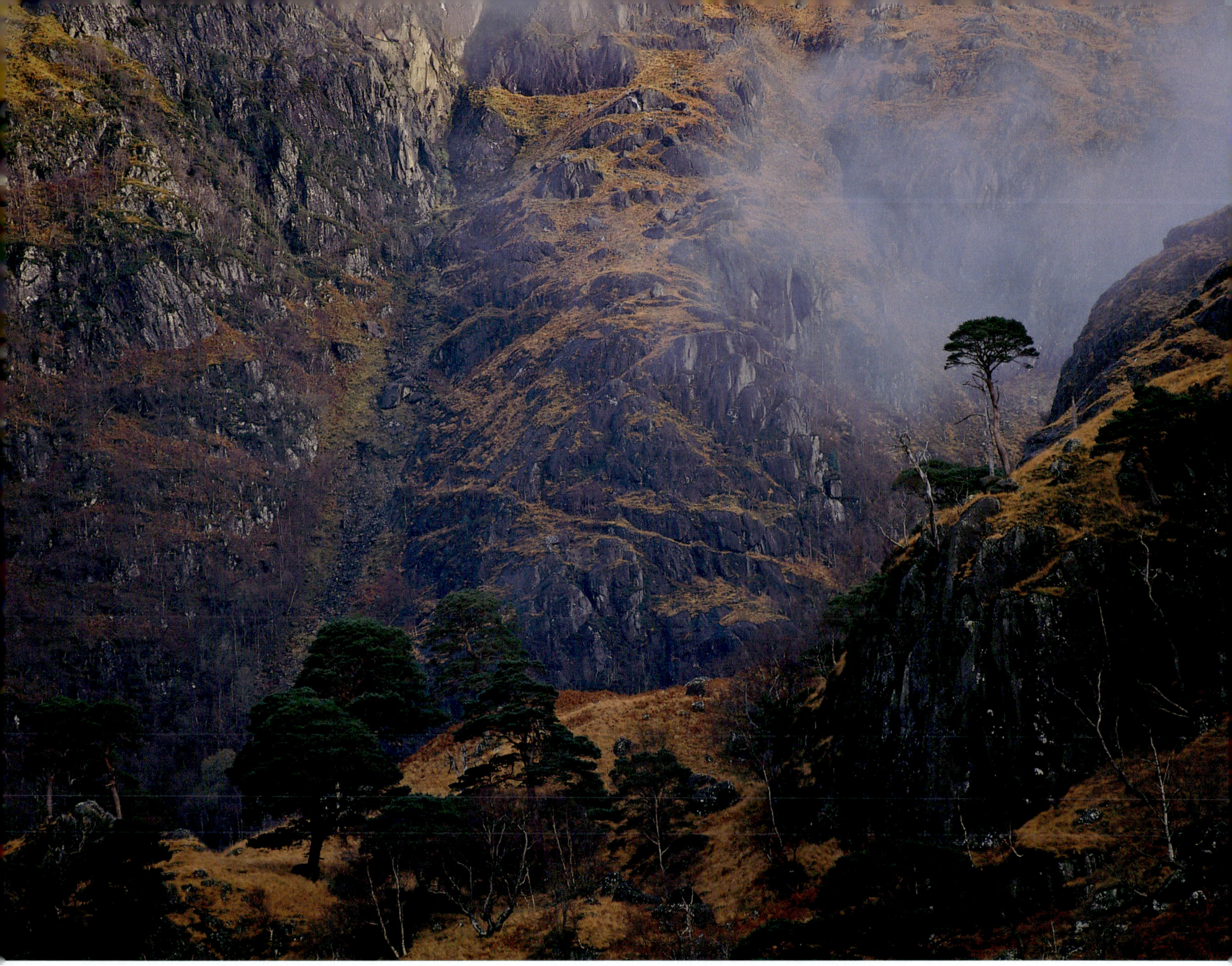

Misty gorge.
The dramatic entrance to the wild and wooded Nevis Gorge at the head of Glen Nevis looks quite atmospheric when mist swirls across the rocky bluffs. The view is often described as looking almost Himalayan in character.

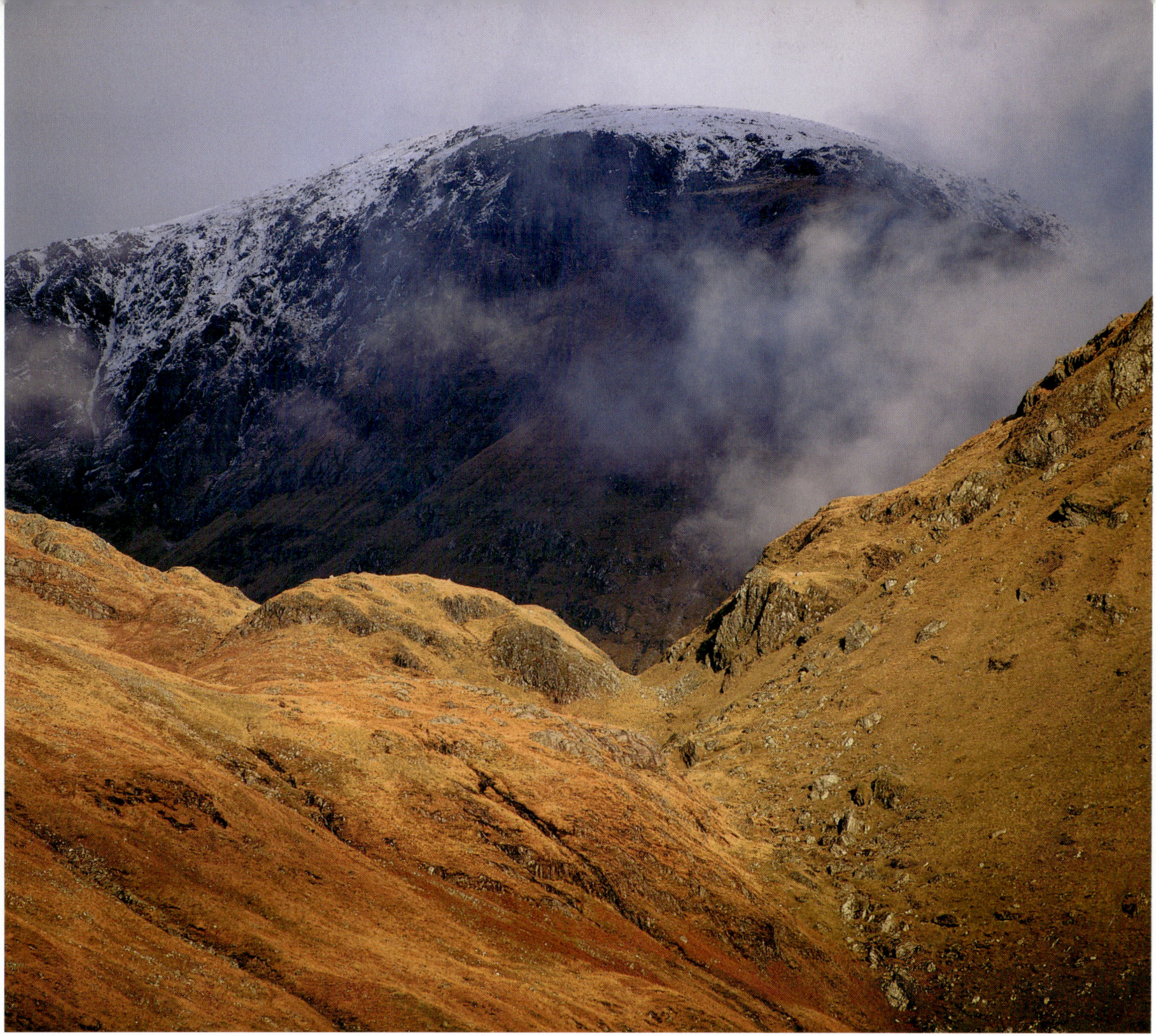

Passing snow shower.
A break during a snow shower allows the late afternoon autumn sunshine to highlight the head of Glen Nevis backed by the craggy slopes of Aonach Beag.

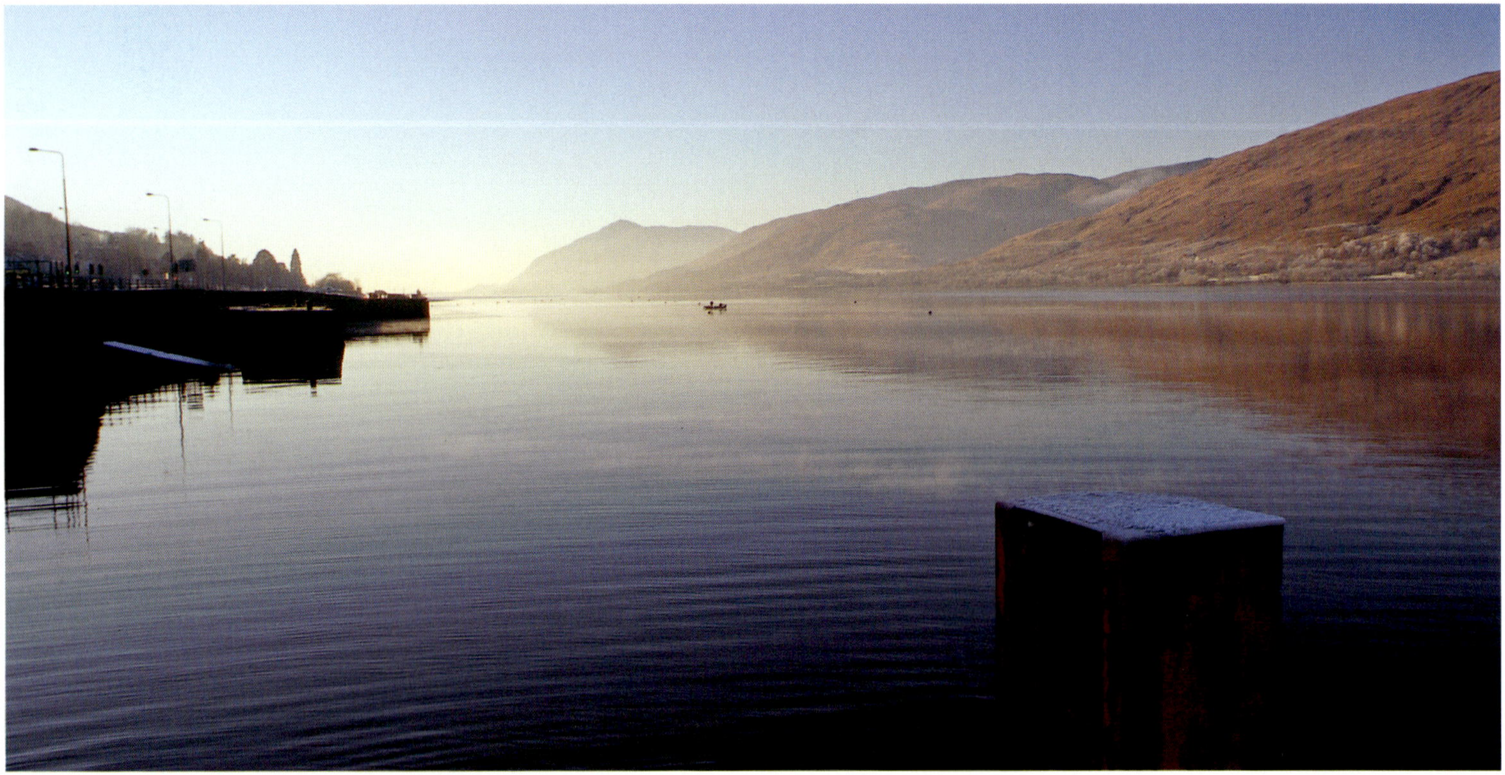

Misty morning.
Early morning sunshine evaporates the mist from Loch Linnhe in this view from the foreshore of Fort William.

Opposite: West to the Isles.
A summer view across Loch Airlort. For any visitor to Fort William, the road trip, or steam train journey to Mallaig aboard 'The Jacobite', should not be missed. It is one of the great train journeys of the world and passes through a dramatic landscape of mountain, loch and sea including Glenfinnan, Loch Airlort, Arisaig and Morar.

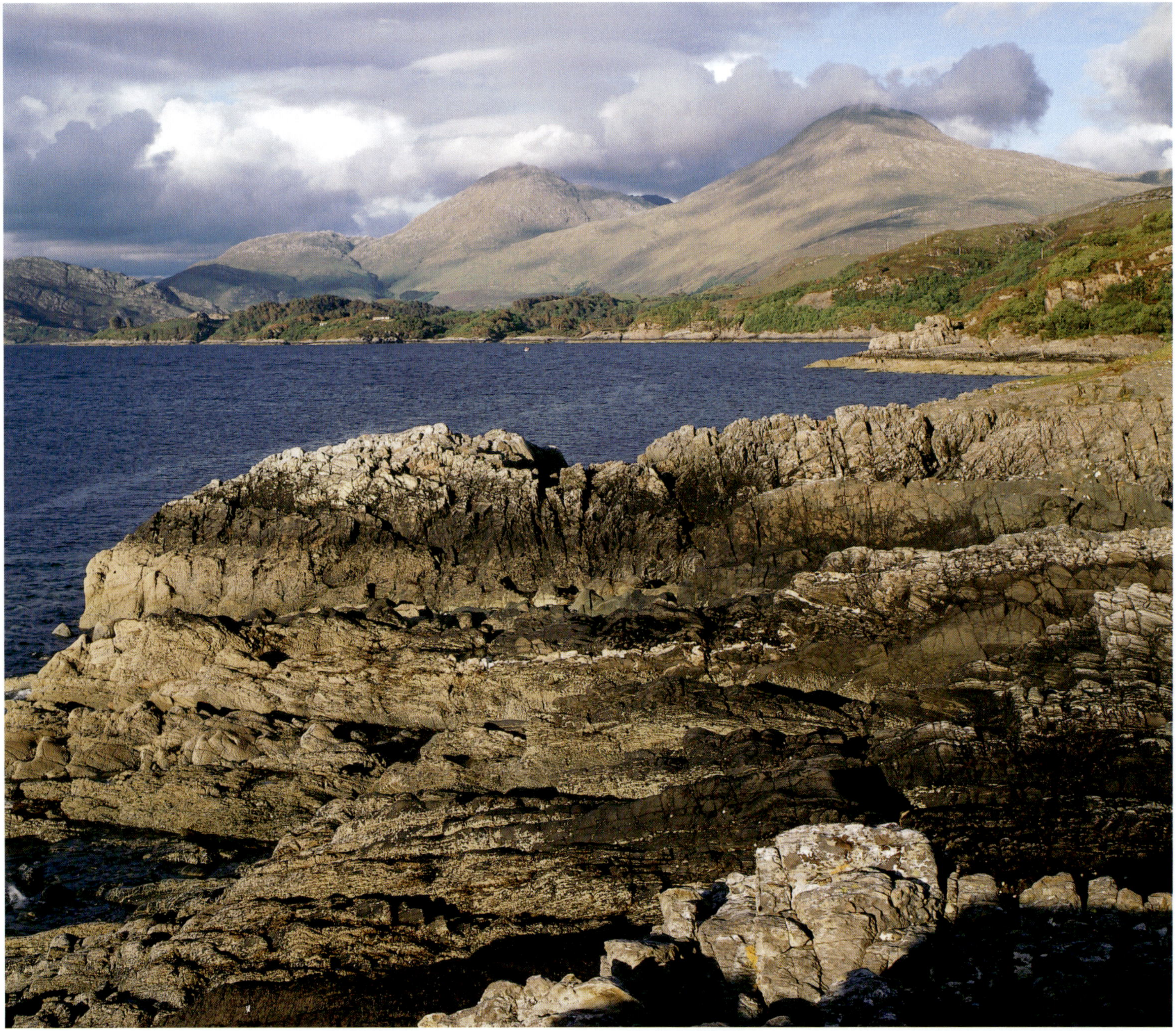

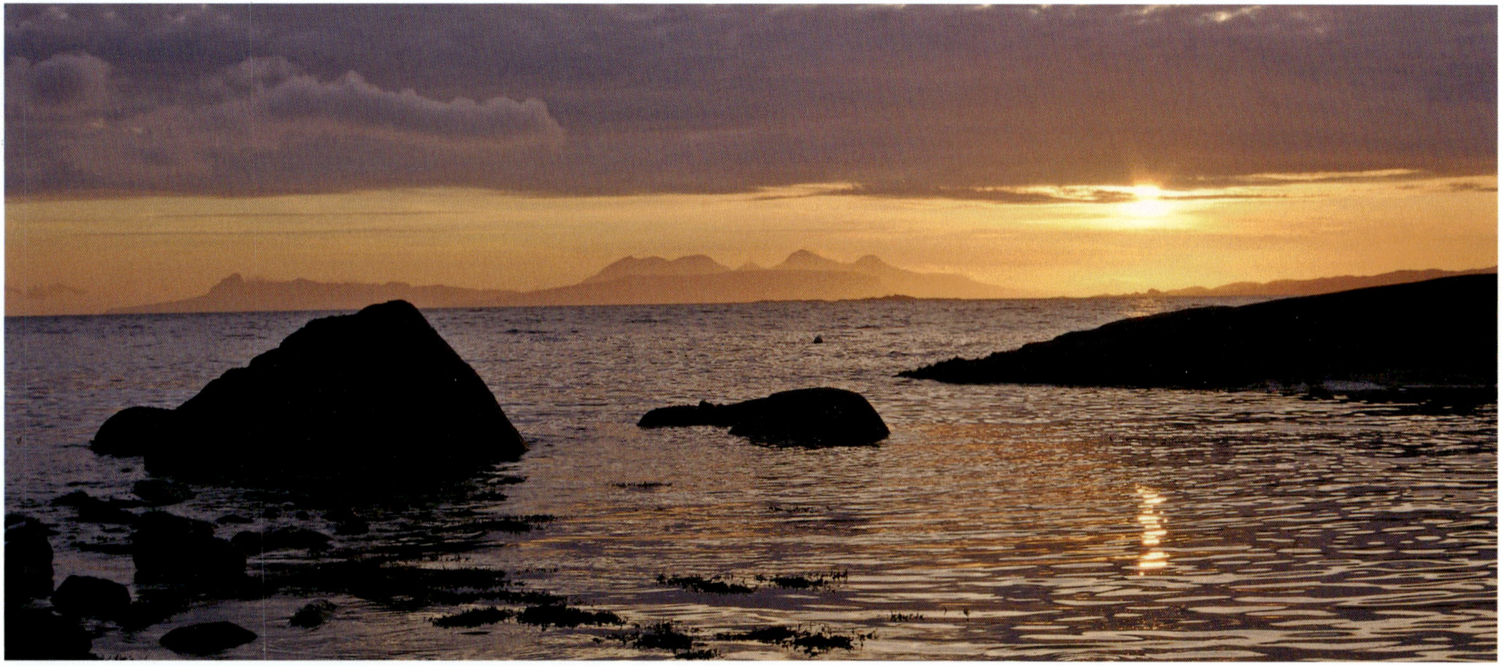

Sunset over Arisaig.
The sun sets beyond the islands of Rum and Eigg across the Sound of Arisaig.
This view is one of the visual delights on the journey from Fort William to Mallaig.